Helpful Hints

- Don't turn off your computer without giving Windows 95 fair warning. First, click on the Start button and then choose Shut Down from the menu. When Windows 95 asks if you're sure that you want to shut down, click on Yes. When Windows 95 says it's okay to turn off your computer, go ahead and turn it off.

- Don't know what a certain button does in a program? Rest your mouse pointer over the button for a few seconds; a helpful box often pops up to explain the button's purpose.

- If you're baffled, try pressing F1, that "function key" in the upper-left corner of your keyboard. A "help" window appears, bringing hints about your current program.

- To quickly organize the windows on the desktop, click on the taskbar's clock with your *right* mouse button. When a menu appears, click on one of the tile options, and all your open windows neatly tile across your screen.

- To keep icons organized in neat rows across your desktop or in windows, click on the icon's background. When the menu pops up, choose Auto Arrange from the Arrange Icons menu.

Click on these words to see helpful menus

Click here for a helpful menu

Click here to shrink the window

Click here to enlarge the window

Click here to close the window

Click here to move up the page

Click here to move down the page

Click on the arrows to move up or down a single line

Point here, hold down the mouse button, and move the mouse to change the window's size

Helpful Hints Dept. - Notepad

File Edit Search Help

```
Push the mouse across your desk,
and the mouse's arrow will move
across your screen.

Push the mouse's left button with
your finger to "click" the mouse.
Push the button twice in rapid
succession to "double-click."

By pointing to different parts of
the window and either "clicking"
or "double-clicking," you can
perform different chores.
```

Windows® 95 For Dummies, 2nd Edition

Cheat Sheet

Handling Files within a Program

To Do This . . .	Do This . . .
Start a new file	Press Alt, F, N.
Open an existing file	Press Alt, F, O.
Save a file	Press Alt, F, S.
Save a file under a new name	Press Alt, F, A.
Print a file	Press Alt, F, P.

Organizing a Pile of Windows

To Do This . . .	Do This . . .
See a list of all windows	Look at the names open on the taskbar.
Move from one window to another window	Press Alt+Tab+Tab or click on the window's name on the taskbar.
Tile the windows across the screen	Click on the taskbar's clock with the *right* mouse button and then click on Tile Horizontally or Tile Vertically.
Cascade the windows across the screen	Click on the taskbar's clock with the *right* mouse button and then click on Cascade.
Shrink a window into an icon	Click on the window, press Alt+spacebar, and press N.
Make a window fill the screen	Click on the window, press Alt+spacebar, and press X.

DOS Window Stuff

To Do This . . .	Do This . . .
Toggle DOS program from a full-screen display to a window-sized display	Press Alt+Enter.
Change a DOS program from a taskbar button to a full screen	Click on the program's icon on the taskbar.
Close a DOS window	Use that program's normal exit command and then click on the X in the window's upper-right corner.

Windows Explorer and My Computer Programs

To Do This . . .	Do This . . .
Copy a file to another location on the *same* disk drive	Hold down Ctrl and drag it there.
Copy a file to a *different* disk drive	Hold down Shift and drag it there.
Remember how to copy or move files	Hold down the *right* mouse button while dragging and then choose Copy or Move from the menu.
Select several files	Hold down Ctrl and click on the filenames.
Look at a different directory	Double-click on that directory's icon.

Cut and Paste Stuff

To Do This . . .	Press These Keys . . .
Copy highlighted stuff to the Clipboard	Ctrl+C or Ctrl+Insert
Cut highlighted stuff to the Clipboard	Ctrl+X or Shift+Delete
Paste stuff from the Clipboard to the current window	Ctrl+V or Shift+Insert
Copy an entire screen to the Clipboard	PrintScreen (Shift+PrintScreen on some keyboards)
Copy the current window to the Clipboard	Alt+PrintScreen

...For Dummies: #1 Computer Book Series for Beginners

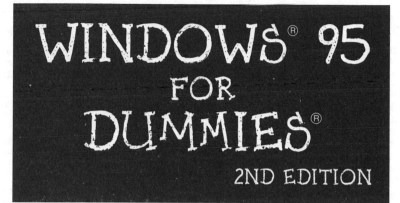

WINDOWS® 95 FOR DUMMIES®

2ND EDITION

by Andy Rathbone

IDG Books Worldwide, Inc.
An International Data Group Company

Foster City, CA ♦ Chicago, IL ♦ Indianapolis, IN ♦ Southlake, TX

Windows® 95 For Dummies®, 2nd Edition

Published by
IDG Books Worldwide, Inc.
An International Data Group Company
919 E. Hillsdale Blvd.
Suite 400
Foster City, CA 94404
http://www.idgbooks.com (IDG Books Worldwide Web site)
http://www.dummies.com (Dummies Press Web site)

Library of Congress Catalog Card No.: 96-80286

ISBN: 0-7645-0180-1

Printed in the United States of America

10 9 8 7 6 5 4 3 2 1

2B/SY/QS/ZX/IN

Distributed in the United States by IDG Books Worldwide, Inc.

Distributed by Macmillan Canada for Canada; by Transworld Publishers Limited in the United Kingdom and Europe; by WoodsLane Pty. Ltd. for Australia; by WoodsLane Enterprises Ltd. for New Zealand; by Longman Singapore Publishers Ltd. for Singapore, Malaysia, Thailand, and Indonesia; by Simron Pty. Ltd. for South Africa; by Toppan Company Ltd. for Japan; by Distribuidora Cuspide for Argentina; by Livraria Cultura for Brazil; by Ediciencia S.A. for Ecuador; by Addison-Wesley Publishing Company for Korea; by Ediciones ZETA S.C.R. Ltda. for Peru; by WS Computer Publishing Company, Inc., for the Philippines; by Unalis Corporation for Taiwan; by Contemporanea de Ediciones for Venezuela. Authorized Sales Agent: Anthony Rudkin Associates for the Middle East and North Africa.

For general information on IDG Books Worldwide's books in the U.S., please call our Consumer Customer Service department at 800-762-2974. For reseller information, including discounts and premium sales, please call our Reseller Customer Service department at 800-434-3422.

For information on where to purchase IDG Books Worldwide's books outside the U.S., please contact our International Sales department at 415-655-3023 or fax 415-655-3299.

For information on foreign language translations, please contact our Foreign & Subsidiary Rights department at 415-655-3021 or fax 415-655-3281.

For sales inquiries and special prices for bulk quantities, please contact our Sales department at 415-655-3200 or write to the address above.

For information on using IDG Books Worldwide's books in the classroom or for ordering examination copies, please contact our Educational Sales department at 800-434-2086 or fax 817-251-8174.

For press review copies, author interviews, or other publicity information, please contact our Public Relations department at 415-655-3000 or fax 415-655-3299.

For authorization to photocopy items for corporate, personal, or educational use, please contact Copyright Clearance Center, 222 Rosewood Drive, Danvers, MA 01923, or fax 508-750-4470.

is a trademark under exclusive
license to IDG Books Worldwide, Inc.,
from International Data Group, Inc.

About the Author

Andy Rathbone started geeking around with computers in 1985 when he bought a boxy CP/ M Kaypro 2X with lime-green letters. Like other budding nerds, he soon began playing with null-modem adaptors, dialing up computer bulletin boards, and working part-time at Radio Shack.

In between playing computer games, he served as editor of the *Daily Aztec* newspaper at San Diego State University. After graduating with a comparative literature degree, he went to work for a bizarre underground coffee-table magazine that sort of disappeared.

Andy began combining his two interests, words and computers, by selling articles to a local computer magazine. During the next few years, Andy started ghostwriting computer books for more famous computer authors, as well as writing several hundred articles about computers for technoid publications like *Supercomputing Review, CompuServe Magazine, ID Systems, DataPro,* and *Shareware.*

In 1992, Andy and *DOS For Dummies* author/legend Dan Gookin teamed up to write *PCs For Dummies,* which was runner-up in the Computer Press Association's 1993 awards. Andy subsequently wrote the first edition of *Windows For Dummies* plus *OS/2 For Dummies, Upgrading & Fixing PCs For Dummies, Multimedia & CD-ROMs For Dummies,* and *MORE Windows For Dummies.*

Andy lives with his most-excellent wife, Tina, and their cat in San Diego, California. When not writing, he fiddles with his MIDI synthesizer and tries to keep the cat off both keyboards.

ABOUT IDG BOOKS WORLDWIDE

Welcome to the world of IDG Books Worldwide.

IDG Books Worldwide, Inc., is a subsidiary of International Data Group, the world's largest publisher of computer-related information and the leading global provider of information services on information technology. IDG was founded more than 25 years ago and now employs more than 8,500 people worldwide. IDG publishes more than 275 computer publications in over 75 countries (see listing below). More than 60 million people read one or more IDG publications each month.

Launched in 1990, IDG Books Worldwide is today the #1 publisher of best-selling computer books in the United States. We are proud to have received eight awards from the Computer Press Association in recognition of editorial excellence and three from *Computer Currents'* First Annual Readers' Choice Awards. Our best-selling *...For Dummies®* series has more than 30 million copies in print with translations in 30 languages. IDG Books Worldwide, through a joint venture with IDG's Hi-Tech Beijing, became the first U.S. publisher to publish a computer book in the People's Republic of China. In record time, IDG Books Worldwide has become the first choice for millions of readers around the world who want to learn how to better manage their businesses.

Our mission is simple: Every one of our books is designed to bring extra value and skill-building instructions to the reader. Our books are written by experts who understand and care about our readers. The knowledge base of our editorial staff comes from years of experience in publishing, education, and journalism — experience we use to produce books for the '90s. In short, we care about books, so we attract the best people. We devote special attention to details such as audience, interior design, use of icons, and illustrations. And because we use an efficient process of authoring, editing, and desktop publishing our books electronically, we can spend more time ensuring superior content and spend less time on the technicalities of making books.

You can count on our commitment to deliver high-quality books at competitive prices on topics you want to read about. At IDG Books Worldwide, we continue in the IDG tradition of delivering quality for more than 25 years. You'll find no better book on a subject than one from IDG Books Worldwide.

John J. Kilcullen

John Kilcullen
CEO
IDG Books Worldwide, Inc.

Eighth Annual Computer Press Awards ≥1992

Ninth Annual Computer Press Awards ≥1993

Tenth Annual Computer Press Awards ≥1994

Eleventh Annual Computer Press Awards ≥1995

Dedication

To my wife, parents, sister, and cat.

Author's Acknowledgments

Thanks to Dan Gookin and his wife Sandy, Matt Wagner, Sandy Blackthorn, Jennifer Ehrlich, Terrie and David Solomon, the Kleskes, and the Tragesers.

Publisher's Acknowledgments

We're proud of this book; please send us your comments about it by using the Reader Response Card at the back of the book or by e-mailing us at feedback/dummies@idgbooks.com. Some of the people who helped bring this book to market include the following:

Acquisitions, Development, and Editorial

Project Editor: Jennifer Ehrlich

Acquisitions Editor: Michael Kelly, Quality Control Manager

Associate Permissions Editor: Heather H. Dismore

Editors: Tamara S. Castleman, Susan Diane Smith, Robert H. Wallace

Technical Editor: Jim McCarter

Editorial Manager: Kristin A. Cocks

Editorial Assistants: Constance Carlisle, Chris H. Collins, Michael D. Sullivan

Production

Project Coordinator: Valery Bourke

Layout and Graphics: Brett Black, Dominique Defelice, Angela F. Hunckler, Todd Klemme, Michael A. Sullivan

Proofreaders: Henry Lazarek, Nancy Reinhardt, Joel Draper, Rachel Garvey, Nancy Price, Karen York

Indexer: Sherry Massey

General and Administrative

IDG Books Worldwide, Inc.: John Kilcullen, CEO; Steven Berkowitz, President and Publisher

IDG Books Technology Publishing: Brenda McLaughlin, Senior Vice President and Group Publisher

Dummies Technology Press and Dummies Editorial: Diane Graves Steele, Vice President and Associate Publisher; Judith A. Taylor, Brand Manager; Kristin A. Cocks, Editorial Director

Dummies Trade Press: Kathleen A. Welton, Vice President and Publisher; Stacy S. Collins, Brand Manager

IDG Books Production for Dummies Press: Beth Jenkins, Production Director; Cindy L. Phipps, Supervisor of Project Coordination, Production Proofreading, and Indexing; Kathie S. Schutte, Supervisor of Page Layout; Shelley Lea, Supervisor of Graphics and Design; Debbie J. Gates, Production Systems Specialist; Tony Augsburger, Supervisor of Reprints and Bluelines; Leslie Popplewell, Media Archive Coordinator

Dummies Packaging and Book Design: Patti Sandez, Packaging Specialist; Lance Kayser, Packaging Assistant; Kavish+Kavish, Cover Design

♦

The publisher would like to give special thanks to Patrick J. McGovern, without whom this book would not have been possible.

♦

Contents at a Glance

Cartoons at a Glance

By Rich Tennant • Fax: 508-546-7747 • E-mail: the5wave@tiac.net

Table of Contents

Introduction

. . . .

Welcome to *Windows 95 For Dummies,* 2nd Edition!

The basic premise of the book boils down to this: Some people want to be Windows wizards. They love interacting with dialog boxes. In their free moments, they randomly press keys on their keyboards, hoping to stumble onto a hidden, undocumented feature. They memorize long strings of computer commands while they're rinsing dishes to go in the dishwasher.

And you? Well, you're no dummy, that's for sure. In fact, you're light-years ahead of most computer nerds. You can make casual conversation with a neighbor without mumbling about ordering pizzas over the Internet, for example. But when it comes to Windows and computers, the fascination just isn't there. You just want to get your work done, go home, fill the cat's water dish, and relax for a while. You have no intention of changing, and there's nothing wrong with that.

That's why this book will come in handy. It won't try to turn you into a Windows wizard, but you'll pick up a few chunks of useful computing information while reading it. Instead of becoming a Windows 95 expert, you'll know enough to get by quickly, cleanly, and with a minimum of pain so that you can move on to the more pleasant things in life.

About This Book

Don't try to read this book at one sitting; there's no need to. Instead, treat this book like a dictionary or an encyclopedia. Turn to the page with the information you need and say, "Ah, so that's what they're talking about." Then put down the book and move on.

Don't bother trying to remember all the Windows 95 buzzwords, such as "Select the menu item from the drop-down list box." Leave that stuff for the computer gurus. In fact, if anything technical comes up in a chapter, a road sign warns you well in advance. That way you can either slow down to read it or speed on around it.

You won't find any fancy computer jargon in this book. Instead, you'll find subjects like these, discussed in plain old English:

✔ Preparing your computer to run Windows 95

✔ Running favorite DOS and Windows programs under Windows 95

✔ Performing chores in Windows 95 that you used to do in older versions of Windows

✔ Finding the file you saved yesterday

✔ Starting programs by clicking on an icon

✔ Figuring out if you need one of those new, fun-looking Windows palmtop computers

There's nothing to memorize and nothing to learn. Just turn to the right page, read the brief explanation, and get back to work. Unlike other books, this one enables you to bypass any technical hoopla and still get your work done.

How to Use This Book

Something in Windows 95 will eventually leave you scratching your head. No other program brings so many buttons, bars, or babble to the screen. When something in Windows 95 has you stumped, use this book as a reference. Look for the troublesome topic in this book's table of contents or index. The table of contents lists chapter and section titles and page numbers. The index lists topics and page numbers. Page through the table of contents or index to the spot that deals with that particular bit of computer obscurity, read only what you have to, close the book, and apply what you've read.

There's no learning involved. There's no remembering, either, unless you want to remember something so that you don't have to grab the book the next time the same situation comes up.

If you're feeling spunky and want to learn something, read a little further. You can find a few completely voluntary extra details or some cross-references to check out. There's no pressure, though. You won't be forced to learn anything that you don't want to or that you simply don't have time for.

If you have to type something into the computer, you'll see easy-to-follow text like this:

```
C:\> TYPE THESE LETTERS
```

In the preceding example, you type **TYPE THESE LETTERS** after the C:\> and then press the keyboard's Enter key. Typing words into a computer can be confusing, so a description of what you're supposed to type usually follows. That way, you can type the words exactly as they're supposed to be typed. You won't, for example, accidentally type **"TYPE THESE LETTERS"** — complete with quotation marks — as many users do after seeing text like *At the DOS prompt, type "TYPE THESE LETTERS"* in other computer manuals.

Whenever I describe a message or information that you see on-screen, I present it as follows:

```
This is a message on-screen.
```

This book doesn't wimp out by saying, "For further information, consult your manual." No need to pull on your wading boots. This book covers everything you need to know to use Windows 95. The only thing you won't find is general information about using DOS or other software packages. Yep — even though Windows 95 doesn't use DOS, it comes with a copy of DOS for running DOS programs. The best crowbar for DOS is this book's grandfather, *DOS For Dummies,* published by IDG Books Worldwide, Inc. Other *...For Dummies* books mercifully explain other popular software packages, as well.

Note that if you need to know something about DOS to use Windows 95, that part of DOS is covered here in enough detail for you to get the job done. You also find help for some of the more popular Windows programs.

Finally, keep in mind that this book is a *reference*. It's not designed to teach you how to use Windows 95. Instead, this book dishes out enough bite-sized chunks of information so that you don't *have* to learn Windows. If you prefer a complete tutorial that gently takes you by the hand and teaches you how to use Windows 95, please pick up one of my other books, *Dummies 101: Windows 95,* 2nd Edition, published by IDG Books Worldwide, Inc.

Please Don't Read This!

Computers thrive on technical stuff. Luckily, you're warned in advance when you're heading for something even vaguely obtuse. Chances are it's just more minute details concerning something you've already read about. Feel free to skip any section labeled Technical Stuff. Those niblets of information aren't what this book's about. But, if you're feeling particularly ornery, keep reading and you may learn something. (Just don't let anybody see you do it.)

And What about You?

Well, chances are that you have a computer. You have Windows 95, or are thinking about picking up a copy. You know what *you* want to do with your computer. The problem is with making the *computer* do what you want it to do. You've gotten by one way or another, hopefully with the help of a computer guru — either a friend at the office or somebody down the street. Unfortunately, though, that computer guru isn't always around. This book can be a substitute for the computer guru during your times of need. Keep a Jack-in-the-Box Jumbo Jack gift certificate nearby, however, just in case you need a quick bribe.

How This Book Is Organized

The information in this book has been well sifted. This book contains six parts, and each part is divided into chapters related to the part's theme. Each chapter is divided into short sections to help you navigate the stormy seas of Windows 95. Sometimes you may find what you're looking for in a small, boxed tip. Other times you may need to cruise through an entire section or chapter. It's up to you and the particular task at hand.

Here are the categories (the envelope, please):

Part I: Bare-Bones Windows 95 Stuff (Start Here)

This book starts out with the basics. You find out how to turn on your computer, and you examine all your computer's parts and what Windows 95 does to them. This part walks you through the steps for installing Windows 95 and explains all the Windows 95 stuff that everybody thinks you already know. It explains the new features in Windows 95, separating the wheat from the chaff while leaving out any thick, technical oatmeal. You discover whether your computer has enough oomph to run Windows 95. And you end this part (with great relief) by turning off your computer.

Part II: Making Windows 95 Do Something

The biggest problem with using Windows 95 isn't opening programs or moving windows around on-screen. It's making Windows 95 do something *useful*. Here, you find ways to overcome the frustratingly playful tendencies of Windows 95 and force it to shovel the walkway or blow leaves off the driveway.

Part III: Using Windows 95 Applications (And Running DOS, Should the Mood Strike)

Windows 95 comes with a whole bunch of free programs. In this part, you find practical information about your new word processor and automatic phone dialer, as well as ways to start surfing that World Wide Web thing you've heard everyone mumbling about suspiciously.

But there's more. See, for years, Windows was simply fancy clothing over an ugly DOS belly — curly hairs and all. If you ever left Windows, you'd fall into the ugly DOS navel underneath. Windows 95 doesn't need DOS anymore, thank goodness; Windows 95 is finally robust enough to run by itself. That's not to say that DOS has disappeared, however. Windows 95 keeps a copy of DOS around for any old DOS programs you may have in the closet. This part offers tips to keep you from falling into the DOS navel — especially if you still cling to a few DOS programs under Windows.

Part IV: Been There, Done That: Quick References for Moving to Windows 95

Millions of people bought Windows 3.1, the precursor to Windows 95. This means that millions of Windows 3.1 users are muttering, "How do I make Windows 95 work like my *old* version?" This part of the book offers quick tips, work-arounds, and quick-reference charts to help translate your work from the Windows 3.1 language to the snappy new Windows 95 dialect.

Part V: Help!

Are your windows stuck? Broken? Do you need new screens? Although glass doesn't shatter when Windows 95 crashes, it can still hurt. In this part, you find some soothing salves for the most painful and irritating maladies. Plus, you find ways to unleash the Troubleshooting Wizards in Windows 95. Imagine: A computer that can grab a wrench and fix itself!

Part VI: The Part of Tens

Everybody loves lists (unless they're published by boring government agencies). This part contains lists of Windows-related trivia — ten aggravating things about Windows 95 (and how to fix them), ten DOS commands you shouldn't run under Windows, ten weird Windows 95 icons and what they mean, ten expensive things that make Windows 95 easier, ten mystifying acronyms, and other solutions to tense problems.

Icons Used in This Book

Already seen Windows 95? Then you've probably noticed its *icons,* which are little pictures for starting various programs. The icons in this book fit right in. They're even a little easier to figure out:

 Watch out! This signpost warns you that pointless technical information is coming around the bend. Swerve away from this icon, and you'll be safe from the awful technical drivel.

 This icon alerts you about juicy information that makes computing easier. For example, take your new Windows CE palmtop out of your back pants pocket *before* you sit down at the bar.

 Don't forget to remember these important points. (Or at least dog-ear the pages so that you can look them up again a few days later.)

 The computer won't explode while you're performing the delicate operations associated with this icon. Still, wearing gloves and proceeding with caution is a good idea when this icon is near.

 Already familiar with Windows 3.1, the predecessor to Windows 95? This icon marks information that can ease the transition from the two systems.

Where to Go from Here

Now you're ready for action. Give the pages a quick flip and maybe scan through a few sections that you know you'll need later. Oh, and this is *your* book — your weapon against the computer criminals who've inflicted this whole complicated computer concept on you. So pretend that you're Xena, the Warrior Princess, and personalize your sword: Circle the paragraphs you find useful, highlight key concepts, cover up the technical drivel with sticky notes, and draw gothic gargoyles in the margins next to the complicated stuff. The more you mark up the book, the easier it will be for you to find all the good stuff again.

Part I
Bare-Bones
Windows 95 Stuff
(Start Here)

The 5th Wave — By Rich Tennant

IN A DISPLAY OF PERVERSE BRILLIANCE, CARL THE REPAIRMAN MISTAKES A ROOM HUMIDIFIER FOR A MID-RANGE COMPUTER BUT MANAGES TO TIE IT INTO THE NETWORK ANYWAY.

In this part . . .

Windows 95 is an exciting, modern way to use the computer. That means it's as confusing as a new car's dashboard. Even the most wizened old computer buffs stumble in this strange new land of boxes, bars, and bizarre oddities like Dynamic Link Libraries.

Never used a computer before but bought Windows 95 because it's "easy to use"? Well, Windows 95 can be intuitive, but that doesn't mean it's as easy to figure out as a steak knife.

In fact, most people are dragged into Windows 95 without a choice. Your new computer probably came with a version of Windows 95 already installed. Or maybe you had installed Windows 95 at the office, where everyone has to learn it except for Jerry, who moved over to the Art Department and got his own Macintosh. Or perhaps the latest version of your favorite program, like Microsoft Word, requires Windows 95, so you've had to learn to live with the darn thing.

No matter how you were introduced, you can adjust to Windows 95, just like you eventually learned to live comfortably with that funky college roommate who kept leaving hair clogs in the shower.

Whatever your situation, this part keeps things safe and sane, with the water flowing smoothly. If you're new to computers, the first chapter answers the question you've been afraid to ask around the lunch room: "Just what is this Windows 95 thing, anyway?"

Chapter 1

What Is Windows 95?

*O*ne way or another, you've probably already heard about Windows and Windows 95. Windows posters line the walls of computer stores. While you're stuck in traffic, the Microsoft roadside billboards cheerfully ask "Where do you want to go today?" Everybody who's anybody talks breezily about Windows and the World Wide Web. Weird code words, like www.vw.com, stare out cryptically from magazine, newspaper, and television advertisements.

To help you play catch up in the world of Windows, this chapter fills you in on the basics of the latest version of Windows, called Windows 95. The chapter explains what Windows 95 is and what it can do. You also examine how Windows 95 and DOS (the system used by *really* old computers) work together, letting you run programs from either camp. (Oh, and when you're ready to take a virtual test-drive of a hot, new Volkswagen Eurovan, Chapter 15 shows how to get to www.vw.com.)

What Are Windows and Windows 95?

Windows is just another computer program, like the zillions of others lining the store shelves. But it's not a program in the normal sense — something that enables you to write letters or play Bozark the Destroyer over the phone lines against your nephew in Los Angeles. Rather, Windows changes the way you work with your computer.

For years, computer programs have made computers cling to the typewriter look. Just as on a typewriter, people type letters and numbers into the computer. The computer listens and then places letters and numbers onto the screen. This time-tested system works well. But it takes a long time to learn, and it's as boring as reading the ingredients on a jar of reduced-fat mayonnaise.

The method is boring because computer engineers designed computers for other computer engineers many moons ago. They thought that computers would be forever isolated in narrow hallways where somber youngsters with crewcuts, clipboards, and white lab coats jotted down notes while the big reels whirled. Nobody expected normal people to use computers — especially not in their offices, their dens, or, heaven help us, their kitchens.

✔ Windows software dumps the typewriter analogy and updates the *look* of computers. Windows replaces the words and numbers with pictures and buttons. It's splashy and modern, like an expensive new coffeemaker.

✔ Because Windows software looks and acts differently from traditional computer programs, understanding it can take a few days. After all, you probably couldn't make perfect coffee the first day, either.

✔ Windows 95 is the latest version of Windows software. It's the version that updates Windows 3.1, just like Windows 3.1 replaced Windows 3.0, which replaced, well, you get the idea.

✔ Okay, I lied. *Windows NT* is the latest version of Windows. However, Microsoft created Windows NT mostly for large networks. It works a lot like Windows 95, but because it has all that logging in/logging off stuff built-in, it gets its own book, *Windows NT 4 For Dummies* (written by me and Sharon Crawford and published by IDG Books Worldwide, Inc.).

What Does Windows Do?

Like the mother with the whistle in the lunch court, Windows controls all the parts of your computer. You turn on your computer, start Windows, and start running programs. Each program runs in its own little *window* on-screen. Yet Windows keeps things safe, even if the programs start throwing food at each other.

While it's keeping order, Windows makes computing a little easier. Windows purges an ugly, old computing custom called the *DOS command line.* The command line lives next to a confusing little symbol, *the DOS prompt,* which looks something like this:

```
C:\>
```

With DOS, people boss around their computers by typing a command at the prompt. To start the WhipIt program, for example, they type the program's name and then press Enter, like this:

```
C:\> WHIPIT
```

That is, they type **whipit** at the prompt and then press Enter. The computer dutifully loads the WhipIt program and brings it to the screen. DOS is tense, shoulder-tightening stuff. You must memorize the names of all your programs because DOS doesn't offer any clues — not even a quick spelling tip. (For more information on DOS, see the section "What Is DOS, and Do I Still Need It?")

Windows, in contrast, replaces that dreary DOS prompt with little pictures. To start your WhipIt program in Windows, for example, you look for the picture representing your WhipIt program. It may look something like the picture in the margin.

By selecting the picture of the whip, Windows users can start the WhipIt program even if they can't spell. Figures 1-1 and 1-2 compare the way Windows 95 and DOS look.

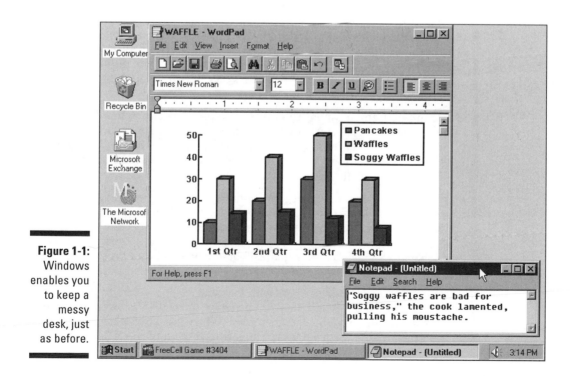

Figure 1-1: Windows enables you to keep a messy desk, just as before.

```
C:\>
```

Windows fills the screen with lots of fun little boxes and pictures; DOS is for no-nonsense minimalists who never put bumper stickers on their cars. Luckily for Windows 95 users, Windows 95 can run both Windows programs and DOS programs, as you see in the next section. (You can guess which programs are more fun to use, though.)

- ✔ Some people say that colorful pictures make Windows easier to use; others say that Windows is a little too arty. To write a letter in Windows, for example, do you select the picture of the notepad, the quill, or the clipboard? And what do you do with the icon of the little man juggling?

- ✔ A computer environment that uses little pictures and symbols is called a *graphical user interface*, or *GUI*. (It's pronounced *gooey*, believe it or not.) Pictures require more computing horsepower than letters and numbers, so Windows 95 requires a relatively powerful computer. (You can find a list of its requirements in Chapter 2.)

- ✔ Windows gets its name from all the cute little windows on-screen. Each window shows some information: a picture, perhaps, or a program you're running. You can put several windows on-screen at the same time and jump from window to window, visiting different programs. (Actually, the windows look like little squares, but who would buy a program called *Squares*?)

- ✔ When the word *Windows* starts with a capital letter, it refers to the Windows program. When the word *windows* starts with a lowercase letter, it refers to windows you see on-screen. When the word *Windows* ends with the number *95*, it refers to the latest version of the Windows software, Windows 95.

Because Windows uses graphics, it's much easier to use than to describe. To tell someone how to move through a document in a DOS-based program, you simply say, "Press the PgDn key." In Windows, you say, "Click in the vertical scroll bar beneath the scroll box." Those directions sound awfully weird, but after you've done it, you'll say, "Oh, is that all? Golly!" (Plus, you can still press the PgDn key in Windows. You don't have to "click in the vertical scroll bar beneath the scroll box" if you don't want to.)

What Is DOS, and Do I Still Need It?

MS-DOS is as boring as the words it stands for: Microsoft Disk Operating System. An age-old method of working with computers, DOS handles the chores required to make the computer do its traditional computer stuff: shuffle information to and from various parts of your computer and put it on your screen for you to labor over.

When you turn on a computer that uses DOS, DOS wakes up, takes control, and starts making things happen. It handles all the dreadful, background computing mechanics so that you can concentrate on what's happening on-screen.

DOS protects you from that internal computer stuff, but DOS is kind of technical itself. That's why Microsoft invented Windows. For years, Windows would ride on top of DOS, insulating you from your computer's technical side. When you told Windows to do something, it would turn around and tell DOS to do something. Until recently, Windows was just a translator, converting languages and collecting cash for its services.

Windows 95 no longer needs DOS. It has pretty much outgrown it, although Windows 95 comes with a version of DOS in case you need to run an old DOS program.

After all, Microsoft wrote both DOS and Windows, so it's no big deal for them to toss in an old DOS version for long-time computer users who still have piles of old DOS software.

✔ With Windows 95, Windows and DOS are no longer two separate programs. Instead, Windows 95 has absorbed the code that made DOS work. That way, Windows 95 can run DOS programs in a window on-screen, or a DOS program can grab the entire screen — whichever looks best. Either way, you don't have to buy a separate copy of DOS anymore; Windows 95 can run your DOS programs as if they were Windows programs.

> ✔ Windows 95 can even bring up a C:\> thing in a window for people who want to use the "DOS command line." Instead of using a mouse to start programs, these people type the name of the program at the command line and press Enter.
>
> ✔ DOS is too boring to be discussed in detail this early. If you're into it, turn to Chapter 14.

DOS rhymes with boss. Don't pronounce it as *dose* unless you're pretending you're a novice at the software store to see whether the salesperson will try to rip you off.

Should I Bother Using Windows 95?

Windows 3.1 users are elbowing each other nervously by the watercooler and whispering the Big Question: Why bother buying Windows 95, going through the hassle of installing it, and learning all its new programs? Windows 95 offers improvements over Windows 3.1.

First, Windows 95 is a little easier for beginners to figure out. A lot less pointing and clicking is involved when finding files and starting programs. For example, Windows 95 automatically keeps track of the past 15 files or programs you've used and stores their names in a special spot. Do you want to load the file again? Just click on the file's name from the pop-up list — no wading through menus or opening programs. White-gloved Windows 95 opens the car door and lets you start moving immediately.

Boring technical glop

Many computer nerds spend their idle hours arguing about whether Windows 95 is a full-fledged operating system or a shell.

An *operating system* controls a computer's innards at a bare-bones, blood-pumping level. DOS is an operating system because it handles all the raw, messy mechanics of computing. When you tell DOS to copy something to a floppy disk, DOS wakes up the floppy drives and tells the computer to find the appropriate information and move it, one morsel at a time, to the floppy disk. All you do is type the COPY command; DOS jumps in there and does the rest.

A *shell*, on the other hand, rides on top of DOS, making DOS easier to use. (Sure, the DOS COPY command is easy enough, but *try* remembering other commands, like MODE LPT1:=COM2:.) Shells always have DOS in the background, just as Windows used to. Now, Microsoft says that Windows 95 has replaced DOS — it has absorbed the DOS code. Other people say that Windows 95 still relies on parts of DOS, so it's not a full-fledged operating system. The debate rages. Luckily, computer nerds tend to mumble, so you don't have to listen.

You see lots more little buttons with pictures on them — *icons* — used in Windows 95 programs. You don't know what the icon with the little policeman picture is supposed to do? Then just rest your mouse pointer over the icon; after a few seconds, a window often pops up on-screen, explaining the policeman button's role on the streets of Windows. The most helpful messages appear when you rest the pointer over the unlabeled buttons that hang out along the tops of programs, like word processors and spreadsheets — in their toolbar areas.

Windows 95 finally allows longer filenames. After 15 years of frustration, IBM-PC users can call their files something more descriptive than RPT_45.TXT. In fact, it offers you 255 characters to describe your computer creations.

Ready to upgrade your computer? Windows 95 can give you a hand with its upgraded "Plug and Play" concept. A new Windows 95 "Wizard" keeps better track of the parts inside your computer and can alert you when internal brawls start. Better yet, it prevents many brawls from even starting by making sure that two computer parts aren't assigned the same areas of your computer's memory.

✔ Windows 95 automates many computing chores. To install a program, for example, just push the floppy (or compact disc) into the drive and click the Control Panel's Add/Remove Programs button (which I cover in Chapter 10, by the way). Windows searches all your drives for the installation program and runs it automatically. Windows 95 can automatically search for any new hardware you've installed as well, recognizing quite a few of the most popular upgrades.

✔ Are you tired of twiddling your thumbs while Windows formats a floppy? Windows 95 can handle floppy chores in the background so that you can continue playing your card game. (And boy, the new card game, FreeCell, is an incredibly delicious time-waster.)

✔ Dare I say the word, *Macintosh?* Windows looks more and more like the age-old Mac every year. That means that Windows 95 will make Macintosh users feel more at home than ever.

Bracing Yourself (and Your Computer) for Windows 95

DOS, for all its faults, at least *looks* simple because the programs run one at a time. They take their time on the center stage and then exit politely, letting another program hit the spotlight.

With Windows, however, everything happens at the same time. Its many different parts run around like hamsters with an open cage door. Programs cover each other up on-screen. They overlap corners, hiding each other's important parts. Occasionally, they simply disappear.

Be prepared for a bit of frustration when things don't behave properly. You may be tempted to stand up, bellow, and toss a nearby stapler across the room. After that, calmly pick up this book, find the trouble spot listed in the index, and turn to the page with the answer.

(And don't forget to pick up the stapler. Jerry Schuster from Anaheim reports that his stapler jammed in the janitor's vacuum cleaner, and the guy stopped emptying the trash cans in the whole department.)

✔ Windows software may be accommodating, but that can cause problems, too. For example, Windows 95 often offers more than three different ways for you to perform the same computing task. Don't bother memorizing each command. Just choose one method that works for you and stick with it. For example, Andrew and Deirdre Kleske use scissors to cut their freshly delivered pizza into slices. It stupefies most of their house guests, but it gets the job done.

✔ Windows 95 runs best on a powerful computer with the key words *Pentium, Pentium Pro,* or *testosterone* somewhere in the description. Look for lots of *RAM* (random-access memory), too, as well as a huge hard disk. You can find the detailed rundown of Windows 95's finicky computer requirements in the very next chapter.

Chapter 2

Ignore This Chapter on Computer Parts (Because You'll Probably Come Back to It Later)

• •

In This Chapter

▶ Finding out the names for the gizmos and gadgets on the computer

▶ Understanding what all those things do

▶ Finding out what your computer needs in order to use Windows 95

• •

*T*his chapter introduces computer gizmos and gadgets. Go ahead and ignore it. Who cares about what all your PC gadgetry is called? Unless your PC's beeping at you like a car alarm (or not beeping when it's supposed to beep), don't bother messing with it. Just dog-ear the top of this page, say, "So, that's where all that stuff is explained," and keep going.

In Windows 95, you just press the buttons. Windows 95 does the dirty work, scooting over to the right part of your computer and kick-starting the action. In case Windows 95 stubs a toe, this chapter explains where you might need to put the bandages. And, as always, the foulest-smelling technical chunks are clearly marked; just hold your nose while stepping over them gingerly.

The Computer

The computer is that beige box with all the cables. It probably answers to one of three names: IBM (called *True Blue* when people try to dump their old ones in the classifieds); an *IBM compatible* or *clone;* or a plain old PC.

Most people just call their computers *PCs* because that's what IBM called its first *personal computer* back in 1981. In fact, the first IBM PC started this whole personal computing craze, although some people lay the blame on video games.

The concept of a small computer that could be pecked on in an office or den caught on well with the average Joe, and IBM made gobs of money. So much money, in fact, that other companies immediately ripped off the IBM design. They *cloned,* or copied, IBM's handiwork to make a computer that worked just like it. These clone computers by companies like Dell and Gateway are *compatible* with IBM's own PC; they can all use the same software as an IBM PC without spitting up.

Clones generally have an obscure brand name and a lower price on their invoice, but they work just as well (or better) than IBM's own line of computers. In fact, more people own clones than personal computers from IBM's own line. (Just look at the recent IBM quarterly earnings statements for proof.)

✔ People used to say that *IBM-compatible* computers were made by big corporations, such as COMPAQ and Toshiba. A *clone,* on the other hand, was thrown together by a kid in a back room. The distinction has waned through the years. If it's not an IBM computer, it's a clone.

✔ Windows 95 runs equally well on IBM-compatible computers and on IBM's own computers; the key word is *IBM.* Computers from other planets, like the Macintosh, don't run Windows 95, but their owners don't care. They just stifle their giggles when you try to figure out how to create a Windows 95 "file association."

✔ Some muscular people heft their desktop PCs onto one side and put them in a special stand. Other computers are designed to work sideways. These upright PCs are called *tower PCs.* The tilt doesn't affect their performance, but it makes them look really cool — especially when they use the Windows 95 "Storm" color scheme. (The color-loving crowd can check out Chapter 10 for decorating tips.)

✔ As other companies built *compatible* computers, they strayed a bit from the IBM design. Tandy, for example, added sound. A few years ago, IBM itself strayed from its classic design by launching a new *PS series* of computers. Some of these design quirks can befuddle Windows 95 — especially when you first install it. After you tell Windows 95 what brand of computer it's dealing with, however, any hard feelings are soothed. All this stuff is covered in Chapter 3.

✔ Laptop and notebook computers can run Windows 95 with no problems. Airplane-bound laptoppers should check out this chapter's mouse section for a mouse substitute. Owners of the shiny new Windows CE palmtops can check out the book's appendix for tips on playing with their new toy.

When laptopping on an airplane, drop a few smoked almonds on your neighboring passenger's thigh. If he doesn't wake up, you can use his kneecap as a makeshift mousepad for a few double-clicks.

Microprocessor

The computer's brain is a small chip of silicon buried deep inside the computer's case. Resembling a Girl Scout's Thin Mint with square corners, this flat little wafer is the *microprocessor,* but nerds tend to call it a *central processing unit,* or *CPU.* (You may have seen flashy microprocessor TV commercials that say, "Intel Inside." Intel is a leading CPU developer.)

The computer's microprocessor determines how fast and powerful the computer can toss information around. Refer to Table 2-1 for a look at the power of your particular computer.

Table 2-1	Microprocessor Power Ratings
Computer	**Comments**
XT, AT, 386SX, 386DX	Nearly obsolete, these chips just can't handle Windows 95. The computers make great gifts to friends and charities.
486SX, 486DX	Will run Windows 95, but slowly. (The 486DX runs a tad faster, if any anxious owners want to know.)
Pentium (sometimes called 586)	A Pentium runs Windows 95 much faster than a 486, meaning less thumb-twiddling while opening programs and files. (Computer games play *much* smoother, too.)
Pentium Pro	Here's a surprise: This chip doesn't run Windows 95 much faster than a top-of-the-line Pentium, which often costs much less. Why? Because the Pentium Pro was designed for Windows NT, the more advanced version of Windows used primarily in large networks.

 ✔ A microprocessor is the current evolution of the gadget that powered those little 1970s pocket calculators. It performs all the computer's background calculations, from juggling spreadsheets to swapping dirty jokes through office e-mail.

 ✔ Microprocessors are described by two numbers: the chip's class (8088, 286, 386, 486, Pentium or 586, and so on) and the chip's processing speed, measured in *megahertz,* or *MHz.* The bigger the numbers, the faster Windows performs. For example, a 133 MHz Pentium microprocessor is faster than a 90 MHz Pentium. (And both of them are faster than *any* 486.)

Don't bother with all the number stuff: Windows 95 works best on a Pentium with a big number, such as 133 MHz or 200 MHz. Don't bother trying to run Windows 95 on an XT, 286, or an age-old original IBM PC. It chokes. And skip the Pentium Pros, too, unless you're lusting to build a computer network and eventually upgrade to Windows NT 4.0.

Disks and Disk Drives

The computer's disk drive, that thin slot in its front side, is like the drawer at the bank's drive-up teller window. That disk drive enables you to send and retrieve information from the computer. Instead of making you drop information into a cashier's drawer, the computer makes you send and receive your information from disks. I cover the three main types — the floppy disk, the hard disk, and the compact disc — in the next three sections.

Floppy disks

You can push anything that's flat into a disk drive, but the computer recognizes only one thing: *floppy disks*. Things get a little weird here, so hang on tight. See, by some bizarre bit of mechanical wizardry, computers store information on a floppy disk as a stream of magnetic impulses.

A disk drive spits those little magnetic impulses onto the floppy disk for safe storage. The drive can slurp the information back up, too. You just push the disk into the disk drive and tell Windows whether to spit or slurp information. That's known as *copy to* or *copy from* in computer parlance. (The procedure is covered in the very front of Chapter 17.)

Floppy disks come in two main sizes: a sturdy $3^1/_2$-inch disk, and its ancestor, the rather flimsy $5^1/_4$-inch disk. Both are called floppy disks, but only one of them flops around when you dangle it by one corner. Hardly any software comes on the older, $5^1/_4$-inch disks anymore (Windows 95 included). Windows 95 comes on either an armful of $3^1/_2$-inch disks, or, much more common, a compact disc. (I cover compact discs later in this section.)

> ✔ A disk drive automatically grabs the $3^1/_2$-inch disk when you push it in far enough. You hear it *clunk,* and the disk sinks down into the drive. If it doesn't, you're putting it in the wrong way. (The disk's silver edge goes in first, with the little round silver thing in the middle facing down.) To retrieve the disk, push the button protruding from around the drive's slot and then grab the disk when the drive kicks it out.

- Computer stores sell blank floppy disks so that you can copy your work onto them and put them in a safe place. Unless your new box of blank disks has the word *preformatted,* you can't use them straight out of the box. They must be *formatted* first. This merry little chore is covered in Chapter 12.

- Computers love to *copy* things. When you're copying a file from one disk to another, you aren't *moving* the file. You're just placing a copy of that file onto that other disk.

Hard disks

Hard disks are thick little Frisbees inside the computer that can hold thousands of times more information than floppy disks. Hard disks are also much quicker at reading and writing information. (They're a great deal quieter, too, thank goodness.) Windows 95 insists on a hard disk because it's such a huge program.

The programs that run under Windows 95 can be pretty huge, too. The Microsoft Monster Truck Madness game grabs 200MB of hard disk space if you install all the coolest options.

- The point? Buy the largest hard disk you can afford. If you're shopping for a computer, make sure that it has room to add a second hard disk. You'll eventually need the room. Windows 95 itself can gobble up 150MB of space, if you're the type who likes to install all the bells and whistles.

- If a program has a lot of *multimedia* — sound, graphics, or movies — you need a huge hard disk. That type of information eats up a lot of space on a hard disk.

Windows 95 comes with "DriveSpace" that claims to compress your computer's hard disk so that you can fit twice as many files on it. Don't bother — installing it can do more harm than good. Save disk compression for people who *like* to play with their computer's ailing innards. Hard disks are relatively cheap these days, so just buy a big one.

Compact discs (CD-ROM drive stuff)

Most people think that compact discs contain music. Nope. Compact discs contain numbers. That's all the information they can handle. The CD factory translates music into numbers, and the CD player translates those numbers back into music.

Computer technicians snapped up compact discs pretty quickly when they realized that they could store numbers, and now most companies sell their programs and information on compact discs. A single compact disc holds more information than hundreds of floppy disks.

To use a disc, however, your computer needs its own CD-ROM drive. The CD player with your stereo won't cut it. Luckily, most CD-ROM drives let you access programs *and* play music through your PC. Now you can sell the CD player attached to your stereo. (It's getting old anyway.)

- ✔ For years, you couldn't write information to a compact disc. Only the people at the CD factory could write to it, and that's because they had a whoppingly expensive machine. Now, some relatively cheap CD-ROM drives let you read and write information to your own discs. In fact, all the copyright attorneys are holding international conferences to make sure that nobody can create copies of their favorite Eagles albums and sell them to their friends.

- ✔ Compact disc is spelled with a *c* to confuse people accustomed to seeing disk ending with a *k*.

- ✔ Do you plan to use that new Kodak PhotoCD stuff or watch any fancy multimedia videos of Venus flytraps eating frogs? If so, you want Windows 95 to display at least 256 colors on-screen. Chapter 10 shows you how to make the Windows 95 video modes more palatable.

- ✔ Multimedia computers need a sound card as well as a CD-ROM drive; the drive alone isn't enough. This requirement is the computer industry's special way of making people spend more money.

- ✔ Windows 95 offers new technology called *Autoplay*. Just pop the CD into the CD-ROM drive, and Windows 95 automatically revs it up, whether the disc contains music, programs, or trendy videos of glass-blowers in Murano, Italy. Autoplay is one more step toward eliminating installation hassles.

What disk drives does Windows 95 like?

Microsoft, the makers of Windows 95, recommends that you have a hard disk with at least 45MB of free space, but it's keeping its fingers crossed behind its back. Depending on how much of the system you choose to install, Windows 95 can easily eat up 150MB of space. Windows 95 programs can eat up even more space. Nobody will laugh if you buy an 800MB hard disk for Windows 95 and your Windows 95 programs.

Also, Windows doesn't require a CD-ROM drive, but they're getting increasingly difficult to live without. Just about everybody puts their programs out on CDs these days, including Microsoft. (You don't have a CD-ROM drive? You can still buy the 3¹/₂-inch diskette version of Windows, but it's getting increasingly more difficult to find.)

Disks dos and doughnuts

✔ Do label your disks so that you know what's on them.

✔ Do at least make a valiant effort to peel off a disk's old label before sticking on a new one. (After a while, those stacks of old labels make the disk too fat to fit into the drive.)

✔ Do feel free to write on the label after it has been placed on the disk.

✔ Do not write on the disk's sleeve rather than the label. Disks always end up in each other's sleeves, leading to mistaken identities and faux pas.

✔ Do copy important files from your hard disk to floppy disks on a regular basis. (This routine is called *backing up* in computer lingo. You can buy special backup packages to make this chore a little easier — not much, but a little.)

✔ Do not leave disks lying in the sun.

✔ Do not place disks next to magnets. Don't place them next to magnets disguised as paper clip holders, either, or next to other common magnetized desktop items, such as older telephones.

✔ Do handle compact discs by their edges, not their surfaces. Keep the backside of the disc as clean as possible.

What does write-protected mean?

Write protection is supposed to be a helpful safety feature, but most people discover it through an abrupt bit of computer rudeness: Windows 95 stops them short with the threatening message shown in Figure 2-1 while they are trying to copy a file to a floppy disk.

Figure 2-1:
Windows 95
sends
an error
message if
a disk is
write-
protected.

A *write-protected disk* has simply been tweaked so that nobody can copy to it or delete the files it contains. Write protection is a simple procedure, surprisingly enough, requiring no government registration. You can write-protect and unwrite-protect disks in the privacy of your own home.

✔ To write-protect a 3½-inch disk, look for a tiny black sliding tab in a square hole in its corner. Slide the tab with a pencil or your thumbnail so that the hole is uncovered. The disk is now write-protected.

✔ To remove the write protection on a 3½-inch disk, slide the little black plastic thingy so that the hole is covered up.

✔ If you encounter the write-protect error shown in Figure 2-1, wait until the drive stops making noise. Remove the disk, unwrite-protect the disk, and put it back in the drive. Then repeat what you were doing before you were so rudely interrupted.

The Mouse and That Double-Click Stuff

The *mouse* is that rounded plastic thing that looks like a bar of electronic soap. Marketing people thought that the word *mouse* sounded like fun, so the name stuck. Actually, think of your mouse as your electronic finger, because you use it in Windows 95 to point at stuff on-screen.

A mouse has a little roller, or mouse ball, embedded in its belly. (Where were the animal-rights people?) When you move the mouse across your desk, the ball rubs against electronic sensor gizmos. The gizmos record the mouse's movements and send the information down the mouse's tail, which connects to the back of the computer.

As you move the mouse, you see an *arrow,* or *pointer,* move simultaneously across the computer screen. Here's where your electronic finger comes in: When the arrow points at a picture of a button on-screen, you press, or *click,* the left button on the mouse. The Windows 95 button is selected, just as if you'd pressed it with your finger. It's a cool bit of 3-D computer graphics that makes you want to click buttons again and again.

✔ You control just about everything in Windows 95 by pointing at it with the mouse and pressing and releasing the mouse button, or *clicking.* (The mouse pitches in with a helpful clicking noise when you press its button.)

✔ The plural of mouse is *mice,* just like the ones cats chew on. It's not *mouses.*

✔ Fold-down airline trays don't have enough room for a laptop, a mouse, *and* a beverage, so laptoppers often substitute trackballs for mice. A *trackball* is a small *upside-down mouse* that clips to the keyboard. You roll the mouse's ball with your thumb to move the on-screen arrow. You use your other fingers to inadvertently spill your beverage.

✔ Trackballs must be *purchased.* You can't just turn your normal mouse upside down and use masking tape. (I already tried.)

✔ Some laptops come with a *touch-pad* — a little square thing for you to slide your finger over. As you move the tip of your finger across the pad, you move the mouse across the screen. Other laptops, like the IBM suave black Thinkpads, have a *Trackpoint,* a little sausage that sticks up out of the keyboard, wedged above the b key and below the g and h. Just push the sausage in the direction you want the mouse to move, and the mouse takes off.

✔ Most mice run in two modes: Microsoft-compatible mode or some funky third-party way. Microsoft created Windows 95, so you'll have fewer problems if you run the mouse in the Microsoft-compatible mode.

✔ Mice come in two breeds: bus and serial. Windows 95 doesn't care which you have, so neither should you — unless your mouse gives you problems. Then you may need to pore through the technical trivia listed in the sidebar "The breeds of mice."

✔ If your mouse doesn't work with Windows 95 (it gets the shivers, it scurries around at random, or the arrow doesn't move), visit Chapter 18 for help.

✔ Hold the presses; Microsoft has a new mouse with "revolutionary technology" on the shelves. The new IntelliMouse has what looks like a tiny waterwheel protruding from the mouse's neck. By slowly spinning the waterwheel back or forth with your index finger, you can zoom in and out of areas on the screen. You can make fonts larger in Microsoft Word, for example, or zoom further into Sunset Cliffs Boulevard on the Microsoft Automap Streets Plus program. Unfortunately, very few programs support that little wheel thingie yet. You may want to wait and see if the technology takes off before spending your mouse money.

The breeds of mice

A serial mouse and a bus mouse look the same; both are plastic things with tails stretching toward the computer's rear. When the tails reach the back of the computer, the serial and bus mice begin to differ. A serial mouse plugs into an oblong doodad called a *serial port*. Almost all computers come with a preinstalled serial port that nerds call *COM1*.

The tail from a bus mouse doesn't head for the serial port. Instead, it creeps into a special *card* that's plugged into a slot in the computer's *expansion bus*. How did the card get there?

Well, the person who sold you the computer took off the computer's case and plugged it in.

Also, many new computers come with a mouse port already built in.

You can install a serial mouse yourself by just plugging it into the serial port. If you buy a bus mouse, however, you'd better buy a bag of Doritos, too, so that you can bribe a computer guru to pull off your computer's case and slide that card in there.

The mouse arrow changes shape, depending on what it's pointing at in Windows 95. When it changes shape, you know that it's ready to perform a new task. Table 2-2 is a handy reference for the different uniforms the mouse pointer wears for different jobs.

Table 2-2	The Various Shapes of the Mouse Pointer	
Shape	*What It Points At*	*What to Do When You See It*
⌖	Just about anything	Use this pointer for moving from place to place on-screen.
✛	A single window	Uh-oh. You've somehow selected the annoying size or move option from the Control menu. Moving the mouse or pressing the cursor-control keys now makes the current window bigger or smaller. Press Enter when you're done, or press Esc if you want to get away from this uncomfortable bit of weirdness.
↕	The top or bottom edge of a window	Hold down the mouse button and move the mouse back and forth to make the window grow taller or shorter. Let go when you like the window's new size.
↔	The left or right side of a window	Hold down the mouse button and move the mouse back and forth to make the window fatter or skinnier. Let go when you like the window's new size.
↖	The corner of a window	Hold down the mouse button and move the mouse anywhere to make the window fat, skinny, tall, or short. Let go when you're through playing.
I	A program or box that accepts text (this pointer is called an I-beam)	Put the pointer where you want words to appear, click the button, and start typing the letters or numbers.
☞	A word with a hidden meaning in the Windows help system	Click the mouse, and Windows 95 trots out some more helpful information about that particular subject.
⧖	Nothing (Windows is busy ignoring you)	Move the mouse in wild circles and watch the hourglass spin around until Windows catches up with you. This shape usually appears when you are loading files or copying stuff to a floppy disk.
⌖⧖	Anything	Keep working. This pointer means that Windows 95 is doing something in the background, so it may work a little more slowly.

Shape	What It Points At	What to Do When You See It
�?	Anything	By clicking on the little question mark found in the top-right corner of some boxes, you create this pointer. Click on confusing on-screen areas or helpful informational handouts.
⊘	Something forbidden	Let go of the mouse button and start over. (You're trying to drag something to a place where it doesn't belong.)

Don't worry about memorizing all the various shapes that the pointer takes on. The pointer changes shape automatically at the appropriate times. The shapes are described here so that you won't think that your pointer's goofing off when it changes shape.

Video Cards and Monitors

The monitor is the thing you stare at all day until you go home to watch TV. The front of the monitor, called its *screen* or *display,* is where all the Windows 95 action takes place. The screen is where you can watch the windows as they bump around, occasionally cover each other up, and generally behave like nine people eyeing a recently delivered eight-slice pizza.

Monitors have *two* cords so they won't be mistaken for a mouse. One cord plugs into the electrical outlet; the other heads for the *video card,* a special piece of electronics poking out from the computer's back. The computer tells the video card what it's doing; the card translates the events into graphics information and shoots it up the cable into the monitor, where it appears on-screen.

✔ Like herbivores and cellulose-digesting gut microorganisms, monitors and video cards come in symbiotic pairs. Neither can function without the other, and you buy them in matched sets so that they'll get along.

✔ Unlike other parts of the computer, the video card and monitor don't require any special care and feeding. Just wipe the dust off the screen every once in a while. (And at least *try* to keep the cat off the monitor.)

✔ Spray plain old glass cleaner on a rag and then wipe off the dust with the newly dampened rag. If you spray glass cleaner directly on the screen, it drips down into the monitor's casing, annoying the trolls who sleep under the bridge.

✔ Some glass cleaners contain alcohol, which can cloud the antiglare screens found on some fancy new monitors. When in doubt, check your monitor's manual to see if glass cleaner is allowed. My new Nanao monitor came with its own special rag for cleaning the glass.

- When you first install Windows 95, it interrogates the video card and monitor until they reveal their brand name and orientation. Windows 95 almost always gets the right answer from them and sets itself up automatically so that everything works fine the first time.

- Windows 95 may be dominating, but it's accommodating, too. It can handle a wide variety of monitors and cards. In fact, most monitors and cards can switch to different *modes,* putting more or fewer colors on-screen and shrinking the text so that you can cram more information onto the screen. Windows 95 enables you to play around with all sorts of different video settings if you're in that sort of mood. (If you are, check out Chapter 10.)

- For such simple gadgets, monitors and cards command a dazzling array of nerdy terms. Ignore them all. Windows 95 picks the appropriate video settings automatically and moves on to the hard stuff, like networks and third-party sound cards.

Ignore these awful graphics terms

Some people describe their monitors as "boxy" or "covered with cat hair"; others use the following strange scientific terms:

Pixel: A pixel is a fancy name for an individual dot on-screen. Everything on-screen is made up of bunches of graphic dots, or pixels. Each pixel is a different shade or color, which creates the image. (Squint up close and you may be able to make out an individual pixel.) Monochrome monitors are often called *gray-scale monitors* because their pixels can only show shades of gray.

Resolution: The resolution is the number of pixels on a screen — specifically, the number of pixels across (horizontal) and down (vertical). More pixels mean greater resolution: smaller letters and more information packed onto the same-sized screen. People with small monitors usually use 640 x 480 resolution. People with larger monitors often switch to 1024 x 768 resolution so that they can fit more windows on-screen.

Color: This term describes the number of colors the card and monitor display on-screen. The number of colors can change, however, depending on the current resolution. When the card runs at a low resolution, for example, it can use its leftover memory to display more colors. At super-duper-high 1280 x 1024 resolution, you may see only 256 colors on-screen. With a lower resolution of 640 x 480, you can probably see up to 16.7 million colors. Windows 95 runs fastest with 256 colors or less, but looks better on the screen with more colors — the traditional sacrifice of speed versus beauty: your call. *Hint:* Color settings are adjustable, as you see in Chapter 10, so use 256 colors for your routine word-processing stuff, and switch to the flashier color settings for examining potential new wallpaper files.

Mode: A predetermined combination of pixels, resolution, and colors is described as a *graphics mode.* Right out of the box, Windows 95 can handle the mode needs of most people. If the video card hails from a weird mode planet, you need a *driver* from the folks who made the card (see Chapter 18 for help).

You don't need to know any of this stuff. If you're feeling particularly modular, however, you can change the Windows 95 graphics modes after reading Chapter 10.

Keyboards

Computer keyboards look pretty much like typewriter keyboards with a few dark growths around the perimeter. In the center lie the familiar white typewriter keys. The grayish keys with obtuse code words live along the outside edges. They're described next.

Groups of keys

Obtuse code-word sorters divvy those outside-edge keys into key groups:

Function keys: These keys either sit along the top of the keyboard in one long row or clump together in two short rows along the keyboard's left side. Function keys boss around programs. For example, you can press F1 to demand help whenever you're stumped in Windows 95.

Numeric keypad: Zippy-fingered bankers like this thingy: a square, calculator-like pad of numbers along the right edge of most keyboards. (You have to press a key called Num Lock above those numbers, though, before they'll work. Otherwise, they're *cursor-control keys,* described next.)

Cursor-control keys: If you *haven't* pressed the magical Num Lock key, the keys on that square, calculator-like pad of numbers are the cursor-control keys. These keys have little arrows that show which direction the cursor moves on-screen. (The arrowless 5 key doesn't do anything except try to overcome its low self-esteem.) Some keyboards have a second set of cursor-control keys next to the numeric keypad. Both sets do the same thing. Additional cursor-control keys are Home, End, PgUp, and PgDn (or Page Up and Page Down). To move down a page in a word processing program, for example, you press the PgDn key.

The Windows Key: An overhyped waste of money. Eager to make money from selling keyboards *and* software, Microsoft came out with a bold new design: a keyboard with a special key marked "Windows." What does the key do? It opens the Start menu, which can be done at the click of a mouse, anyway. Ho hum.

More key principles

Other keyboard keys you need to be familiar with follow:

Shift: Just as on a typewriter, this key creates uppercase letters or the symbols %#@$, which make great G-rated swear words.

Alt: Watch out for this one! When you press Alt (which stands for *Alternate*), Windows moves the cursor to the little menus at the top of the current window. If you're trapped up there and can't get out, you probably pressed Alt by mistake. Press Alt again to free yourself.

Ctrl: This key (which stands for *Control*) works like the Shift key, but it's for weird computer combinations. For example, holding down the Ctrl key while pressing Esc (described next) brings up the Windows 95 taskbar that tracks down missing windows. (Check out "The Way-Cool Taskbar" section in Chapter 7.)

Esc: This key (which stands for *Escape*) was a pipe dream of the computer's creators. They added Esc as an escape hatch from malfunctioning computers. By pressing Esc, the user was supposed to be able to escape from whatever inner turmoil the computer was currently going through. Esc doesn't always work that way, but give it a try. It sometimes enables you to escape when you're trapped in a menu or a dastardly dialog box. (Those traps are described in Chapter 6.)

Scroll Lock: This one's too weird to bother with. Ignore it. (It's no relation to a *scroll bar,* either.) If a little keyboard light glows next to your Scroll Lock key, press the Scroll Lock key to turn it off. (The key's often labeled Scrl Lk or something equally obnoxious.)

Delete: Press the Delete key (sometimes labeled Del), and the unlucky character sitting to the *right* of the cursor disappears. Any highlighted information disappears as well. Poof.

Backspace: Press the Backspace key, and the unlucky character to the *left* of the cursor disappears. The Backspace key is on the top row, near the right side of the keyboard; it has a left-pointing arrow on it. Oh, and the Backspace key deletes any highlighted information, too.

If you've goofed, hold down Alt and press the Backspace key. This action undoes your last mistake in most Windows 95 programs.

Insert: Pressing Insert (sometimes labeled Ins) puts you in Insert mode. As you type, any existing words are scooted to the right, letting you add stuff. The opposite of Insert mode is Overwrite mode, where everything you type replaces any text in its way. Press Insert to toggle between these two modes.

Ugly disclaimer: Some Windows 95 programs — Notepad, for example — are always in Insert mode. There's simply no way to move to Overwrite mode, no matter how hard you pound the Insert key.

Enter: This key works pretty much like a typewriter's Return key but with a big exception. Don't press Enter at the end of each line. A word processor can sense when you're about to type off the edge of the screen. It herds your words down to the next line automatically. So just press Enter at the end of each paragraph.

You'll also want to press Enter when Windows 95 asks you to type something — the name of a file, for example, or the number of pages you want to print — into a special box.

Caps Lock: If you've mastered the Caps Lock key on a typewriter, you'll be pleased to find no surprises here. (Okay, there's one surprise: Caps Lock affects only your letters. It has no effect on punctuation symbols or the numbers along the top row.)

Tab: There are no surprises here, either, except that Tab is equal to five spaces in some word processors and eight spaces in others. Still other word processors enable you to set Tab to whatever number you want. Plus, a startling Tab Tip follows.

Press Tab to move from one box to the next when filling out a form in Windows 95. (Sometimes these forms are called *dialog boxes*.)

- ✔ A mouse works best for most Windows 95 tasks, like starting programs or choosing among various options. Sometimes the keyboard comes in handy, however. Windows 95 comes with *shortcut keys* to replace just about anything you can do with a mouse. Sometimes pressing a few keys can be quicker than wading through heaps of menus with a mouse. (The shortcut keys are described in Chapter 5 in the section on when to use the keyboard.)

- ✔ If you don't own a mouse or a trackball, you can control Windows 95 exclusively with a keyboard. But it's awkward, like when Freddy from *Nightmare on Elm Street* tries to floss his back molars.

Print Screen: The one, fun, weird code key

Windows 95 fixed something dreadfully confusing about an IBM computer's keyboard: the Print Screen key (sometimes called PrtScr, Print Scrn, or something similar). In the old days of computing, pressing the Print Screen key sent a snapshot of the screen directly to the printer. Imagine the convenience!

Unfortunately, nobody bothered to update the Print Screen key to handle graphics. If a screen showed anything other than straight text, pressing the Print Screen key sent a wild jumble of garbled symbols to the printer. And, if the printer wasn't connected, turned on, and waiting, the computer would stop cold.

Windows fixes those Print Screen woes. Pressing the Print Screen key now sends a picture of the screen to a special place in Windows 95 that is known as the *Clipboard.* When the image is on the Clipboard, you can *paste* it into your programs or save it to disk. You can even print the screen's picture if you paste the image from the Clipboard into Paint, the Windows 95 drawing program.

✔ With some older computers, you have to hold down Shift while you press Print Screen, or you get just an asterisk on-screen — not nearly as much fun.

✔ The Clipboard is described in Chapter 9.

✔ Want to peek onto your Clipboard? Use the Clipbook Viewer, a program also covered in Chapter 9. (Windows 95 doesn't normally install Clipbook Viewer onto your computer, though.) If you can't find Clipbook Viewer listed on your Start menu's Accessories page, head for Chapter 10. That chapter shows how to use Control Panel's Add/Remove Programs feature to install the Clipbook Viewer onto your own computer.

Modems and the Internet

I admit it. I used my modem the other night to order Cuban food from the place down the street. How? My wife and I dialed up "Gourmet on the Road" through the Internet, chose our items from the on-screen menu, and punched in our phone number. A few minutes later, the plantains were steaming on the dining room table.

Modems are little mechanical gadgets that translate a computer's information into squealing sounds that can be sent and received over plain, ordinary phone lines. We clicked on the checkmark next to Baked Plantain on our computer, and the chef at Andre's put our order on the stove. A modem at the credit card company tabulated the whole process, and the electric registers started ringing.

Most new computers come with modems, as well as ways to join online services like America Online; CompuServe; or, if you're hungry, the Internet and the World Wide Web. In fact, if you bought a new computer, you probably already have all the software you need to jump on the bandwagon.

✔ Chapter 15 covers the Internet and the Web, too. It doesn't say what Baked Plantain tastes like, though.

✔ The computers on both ends of the phone lines need modems in order to talk to each other. Luckily, most online services have hundreds, or even thousands, of modems connected to their call-in lines.

✔ Modems need special *communications software* to make them work. Windows 95 comes with a simple communications program called HyperTerminal. It's a mere wooden tub in a world of tile jacuzzis, and most people have abandoned this program for more glamorous Web browsers and the World Wide Web.

✔ Modems come in two breeds: *internal* and *external.* Internal modems come on special *cards* that must be buried inside the computer — a process best left to professional buriers. Luckily for you, most new computers come with their own internal modems.

✔ An external modem comes in its own little case. A cable runs from the modem's case to a *serial port,* or *COM port,* which is a special receptacle in the back of the computer. (Plugging an external modem into the port is easy, unless you have only one serial port and you've already plugged the mouse into it. Then it's time to drive back to the computer store, with your computer in the back seat, and tell the teenager to put another serial port in the computer when he's through setting a new high score.)

✔ Most people use modems to call America Online, CompuServe, and other *online services.* Online services are huge computers stuffed with information like stock prices, weather updates, news, and *message areas,* where people can swap talk about flatware, UFOs, and how much the online service is costing them. (Online services cost anywhere from $8.95 a month to more than $20 an hour, all charged to the user's credit card.) Many online services also provide access to the World Wide Web, adding to the bargain.

✔ Other people use their modems to call Internet Providers, specialized and sheared-down online services that only provide access to the Internet and World Wide Web.

✔ For more information about CompuServe, call (800) 848-8199 or (614) 718-2800. For more information about America Online, call (800) 827-6364. And, for more information about your credit rating, call those youngsters down the street.

Printers

Realizing that the paperless office still lies several years down the road, Microsoft made sure that Windows 95 can shake hands and send friendly smoke signals to more than 200 different types of printers. When you install Windows 95, you need to type in your printer's name. Windows checks its dossiers, finds your printer, and immediately begins speaking to it in its native language.

That's all there is to it. Unless, of course, your printer happens to be one of the several hundred printers *left off* the Windows 95 master list. In that case, cross your fingers that your printer's manufacturer is still in business. You have to get a *driver* from the manufacturer before your prose can hit the printed page. (For information on printers, see Chapter 10.)

> ✔ Printers must be turned on before Windows 95 can print to them. (You'd be surprised how easily you can forget this little fact in the heat of the moment.)

> ✔ Windows 95 prints in a WYSIWYG (what you see is what you get) format, which means that what you see on-screen is reasonably close to what you'll see on the printed page.

Networks

Networks connect PCs so that employees can share information. They can all send stuff to a single printer, for example, or send messages to each other asking whether Marilyn has passed out the paychecks yet.

Some networks are relatively small — less than ten computers in an office, for example. Other networks span the world; the Internet runs on a huge computer network that sprawls through nearly every country.

> ✔ You're probably on a network if you can answer "yes" to any of these questions: Can your coworkers and you share a printer, data, or messages without standing up or yelling across the room? Do you ever *log in* or *log out* on your computer? When your computer stops working, does everybody else's computer stop working, too?

> ✔ When networks are running, however, you usually don't notice them except when you first turn on Windows 95. For a description of this frivolity, see the section on networks in Chapter 4.

Sound Cards (Making Barfing Noises)

For years, PC owners looked enviously at Macintosh owners — especially when their Macs ejected a disk. The Macintosh would simultaneously eject a floppy disk from its drive and make a cute barfing sound. Macs come with sound built in; they can barf, giggle, and make *really* disgusting noises that won't be mentioned here. (Any Mac owners will be happy to play them back for you.)

But the tight shirts at IBM decided there was no place for sound on a Serious Business Machine. Windows 95 fixes that mistake, so now the accounting department's computers can barf as loudly as the ones in the art department down the hall.

- ✔ Before your computer can barf, it needs a *sound card*. A sound card looks just like a video card. In fact, all cards look alike: long, green, flat things that nestle into long flat slots inside the computer. Speakers plug into a sound card like a monitor plugs into a video card.

- ✔ Just as computers mimic IBM's original computer design, sound cards mimic the designs of the two most popular sound cards: AdLib and Sound Blaster. The AdLib card sets a standard for playing music; the Sound Blaster design is the current standard for playing music *and* for making noises. (You want the Sound Blaster AWE line of cards.)

- ✔ Windows works with a wide variety of sound cards, but you'll do best with cards that are compatible with Adlib or Sound Blaster. Windows often works with other sound cards as well, but cheaper cards cause headaches in the long run. (Chapter 18's section on installing a driver can help knock a miscreant sound card back into action.)

- ✔ Windows 95 comes with a pleasant chimes sound already included, but it doesn't have any barf noises. Most computer gurus can either find a copy for you or personally record one. In fact, most new sound cards come with a microphone, and the Windows 95 Sound Recorder program is ready to capture your own efforts. (This book's sequel, *MORE Windows 95 For Dummies,* covers sound and video recording in much more detail.)

- ✔ Just like the Macintosh, Windows enables you to assign cool sounds to various Windows 95 functions. For example, you can make your computer scream louder than you do when it crashes. For more information, refer to the section in Chapter 10 on making cool sounds with multimedia.

Parts Required by Windows 95

Table 2-3 compares what Windows 95 asks for on the side of the box with what you *really* need before it works well.

Table 2-3	What Windows 95 Requires	
Computer Requirements Politely Recommended by Microsoft	*What Your Computer Really Needs to Run Windows 95*	*Why?*
4MB of memory (RAM)	At least 8MB of memory	Windows 95 crawls across the screen with only 4MB and moves much more comfortably with 8MB. If you plan to run several large programs, however, bump that to 16MB or more. Power users may want to consider even 32MB. When buying a computer, make sure that you can upgrade its RAM inexpensively.
45MB of hard disk space	At least 150MB more than you needed to run Windows 3.1	That 45MB can hold Windows 95 but little else. Where do your programs go? Where do your files go? Some Windows programs want 10MB or 20MB of space just for themselves. Don't be afraid to buy a hard disk that's 500MB or larger.
A 386DX microprocessor	A Pentium	While at the store, compare Windows 95 running on different computers. The faster the computer, the less time you spend waiting for Windows 95 to do something exciting.
A 3$\frac{1}{2}$-inch floppy drive	At least one high-density 3$\frac{1}{2}$-inch floppy drive or CD-ROM drive	Most Windows programs come packaged on high-density, 3$\frac{1}{2}$-inch floppy disks.
Color VGA card	Accelerated color Super VGA card, VL-Bus card, or PCI bus card	Because Windows 95 tosses so many little boxes on-screen, get an accelerated high-resolution Super VGA card.
MS-DOS version 3.31 or or later; Windows 3.0 or later	MS-DOS version 3.31 or later; Windows 3.0 or later	Microsoft is selling Windows 95 as an upgrade to its older products. Not upgrading an older version of Windows? Then you'll have to buy the more expensive version of Windows 95 at the software store.
Miscellaneous	A 15-inch monitor or larger	The bigger your monitor, the bigger your desktop: Your windows won't overlap so much. Unfortunately, super-large monitors are super-expensive.

Computer Requirements Politely Recommended by Microsoft	What Your Computer Really Needs to Run Windows 95	Why?
Miscellaneous	CD-ROM drive for Windows 95	No, you don't need a CD-ROM drive. But it's a *lot* easier to install off a compact disc than an awkward handful of floppy disks. And isn't it time you joined the multimedia explosion, anyway?
Miscellaneous	Modem	You don't *need* a modem, but without one you can't dial up the online services that come packaged with Windows 95, and you can't play with Internet Explorer. (And isn't it time you joined the Internet explosion, anyway?)

Chapter 3

Out of the Box and onto the Hard Drive (Installation Chores)

• •

In This Chapter

▶ Turning on the computer

▶ Deciding whether to install Windows 95 over your old version of Windows

▶ Installing Windows 95

▶ Taking the tutorial

▶ Leaving the Setup program

▶ Turning off the computer

• •

*I*nstalling software means copying the program from the disks in the box onto the hard drive inside your PC. Unfortunately, it can also mean hours of tinkering until the newly installed software works correctly with your particular computer, printer, disk drives, and internal organs. Because of the frustration potential, installation chores should usually be left to a certified computer guru. Gurus like that sort of stuff. (They even like the smell of freshly copied floppy disks.)

Luckily, Microsoft took mercy on Windows 95 beginners. It designed Windows 95 to install itself. Just slide the first disk into the disk drive and type a magic word. After that, keep feeding disks into the computer when it asks for a new one.

Remove the first floppy disk before trying to slide in the next one, and you'll be fine. Or, if your computer has a CD-ROM drive, install the CD-ROM version of Windows 95 for an even easier time.

This chapter walks you through the installation process. You see how easy Microsoft made this chore, and you find out where else in the book you can turn if you need further information.

Turning On the Computer

The first step is to look for the computer's *power* switch. It's usually the largest switch on the computer. Sometimes it's red and important looking.

✔ Put your ear next to the computer's case: If the computer is not making any noise, it's either turned off or broken. Flip its power switch to the opposite direction, and it either jumps to life or stays broken (or stays unplugged, which is why it always works in the repair shop).

✔ When a computer is first turned on, it makes a grinding sound, several clicking noises, and a whirring sound. Then it flashes long strings of code words on-screen. You can safely ignore the words unless you're reading them to a technical support person over the telephone.

Turning the computer off and then turning it on again can send devastating jolts of electricity through the computer's tender internal organs. Turn the computer on in the morning and off when you're finished for the day. Some sensitive people even leave their computers turned on all the time to spare them that morning power jolt.

And never turn the computer off while it's running Windows 95 or any other program. Doing so can destroy data and damage your programs. If the computer is doing something weird, like freezing up solid, try the less disastrous disciplinary measures described in Chapter 18.

✔ Finally, when installing Windows 95, tell it to keep your old version of Windows hanging around, as described in Step 8 of "Installing Windows 95," later in the chapter. Windows 95 then compresses your old Windows version and hides it in a secret directory on your hard drive. Later, after you've had time to play with Windows 95, you can tell Windows 95 to purge your old version for good. (Or, if Windows 95 doesn't meet your needs, you can tell it to resurrect your old version, removing itself in the process.)

Removing the Wrapper from the Box

Pick up the box that contains the Windows 95 software and look for where the plastic bunches up in the corners. With your incisors, bite into that little chunk of bunched-up plastic and give it a good tug. Repeat this procedure a few times until you've created a finger-sized hole. Then peel back the plastic until the box is free.

Should you install Windows 95 over your old version of Windows?

Should you copy this new version of Windows 95 over your older, faithful version of Windows 3.1 — a version that serves you so well except when it crashes?

Yeah, go ahead. The new version won't wipe out the important parts of the old version. The desktop will have the same programs as before. In fact, if you don't install Windows 95 over your old version of Windows, you must reinstall all your old programs by hand.

To be on the safe side, copy your important data files to floppy disks before you begin. You've probably been backing up your work anyway, so copying the files shouldn't take long.

✔ If you *haven't* been copying your important files to floppy disks for safekeeping, head to the store and ask for a tape backup unit that's compatible with Windows 95.

✔ If you're the extra-cautious sort, you can install the new version of Windows 95 into a separate directory and try it out for a while. I did. After 15 minutes or so, I deleted the old version because it was just cluttering up my hard drive.

✔ Finally, Windows 95 lets you keep your old version of Windows around until it has proved itself. When you're ready to delete the old version and free up some space, head for the Control Panel's Add/Remove Programs icon.

Installing Windows 95

Forget those awkward experiences setting up metal Christmas trees or listening to your car make funny noises. Windows 95 caters to beginners with an installation program that checks under your PC's hood and sets itself up automatically, adjusting the fluid levels as needed.

Here's how to pull into the full-service lane:

First, make sure that your computer is turned on; then make sure that anything plugged into your computer is turned on, as well. That includes modems, printers, compact disc drives, yogurt makers, and other goodies. Plug in your joysticks, too; Windows 95 finally recognizes them. Hurrah!

If you are using DOS 5.0 or an earlier version, make sure that you've made a *boot disk* that contains a copy of the SYS.COM file. You'll need this in case you ever want to uninstall Windows 95, as described in the appendix at the back of this book.

What's this I hear about a *newer* version of Windows 95?

Microsoft has now complicated matters even further by selling three almost identical versions of Windows 95, and they're all called the same thing.

The first version of Windows 95 came out in 1995. With 40 million copies sold, it's most likely the version running on your computer. The second version started hitting the shelves in late 1996. It looks and acts just like the older version. What's the only significant difference? Microsoft tossed in an extra CD containing Internet Explorer, which they used to make you purchase separately.

If you bought a new computer in 1997, however, you probably have the third and *newest* version of Windows 95. Not sold in stores, it only comes preinstalled on new PCs. You aren't missing much, though. The new version merely handles files a tad faster and comes with the Internet Explorer program built-in.

What's the moral? Don't run out and buy a new PC or copy of Windows 95. The file-handling stuff doesn't speed things up much, and you can get a copy of the Microsoft Internet Explorer for free, anyway. (Have a friend download it for you from the Microsoft web site.)

All three versions of Windows 95 look identical. Do you want to know what version you're using? Click your My Computer icon with your right mouse button and choose Properties from the pop-up menu. At the top of the page, the older version of Windows 95 says version 4.00.950. The version currently sold in the stores says version 4.00.950A. The newest version says 4.00.950B. Yawn.

Depending on the version of Windows 95 you're installing — and the software that's currently on your computer — your installation experience may waver slightly from the instructions you read here. In that case, just follow the instructions on the screen. Windows 95 usually gets back on track in a few moments, and you'll be back to the step-by-step instructions shown here.

1. **Start your current version of Windows, put your Windows 95 Installation disk in drive A (or in your CD-ROM drive if you're installing from a compact disc), and then open the Program Manager's Run box.**

   You've never used Program Manager's secret Run box before? Click on File from along the top of Program Manager, shown in Figure 3-1, and choose Run from the menu that drops down.

Figure 3-1:
Click on Eile
in Program
Manager
and choose
Run from
the menu.

If you don't have any version of Windows installed on your computer,
you need to do *two* things. First, bring up a DOS prompt (that C:\>
thing), and second, find your old Windows disks to install it. See,
Windows 95 is an *upgrade* — if you aren't installing it over an old
version of Windows or DOS, you need to buy the expensive, non-
upgrade version of Windows 95. That version costs twice as much as
the upgrade version.

2. **Type** A:\SETUP **in the box that appears, as shown in Figure 3-2, and
click on the OK button.**

Figure 3-2:
Type
A:\SETUP
and click on
OK to
load the
Windows 95
installation
program.

If you're installing Windows 95 from a compact disc, however, you need
to change the drive letter. For example, if your CD-ROM drive is drive E,
type this in the box shown in Figure 3-2:

```
E:\SETUP
```

Or, if you're installing Windows 95 straight from DOS, type this at the DOS prompt and press Enter:

```
A:\>SETUP
```

Your first taste of Windows 95 leaps to the screen. The window merely announces that Windows 95 will check your hard disk for any problems before continuing (see Figure 3-3). It also breaks the news that you may be sitting in front of your computer for anywhere from 30 minutes to an hour, depending on how smoothly the installation process goes.

Figure 3-3:
Before
installing
itself,
Windows 95
checks
your hard
disk for
problems.

3. Click on Continue, and Windows 95 checks your hard disk.

If Windows 95 finds anything wrong with your hard disk, it says so and promptly fixes the problem. Usually, however, everything is fine, and Windows 95 moves on to Step 4.

If Windows 95 said it found something weird, you may want to click on the Details button to see what's up. You can usually get away with clicking on the Continue button and pressing forward, however. Windows 95 prepares its own computerized "computer guru" that helps install itself on your computer. If you're installing Windows 95 from floppy disks, Windows 95 occasionally asks you to insert the next disk, so be prepared by keeping all the disks on the desk in front of you.

But first, be prepared for the legalese Windows 95 tosses in your face, as described in Step 4.

4. Click on Yes on the software agreement.

Here's where Microsoft tosses you a stumper, shown in Figure 3-4. Unless you agree to abide by Microsoft's special Windows 95 terms, the install process simply stops and leaves the room like a surly bellhop who only got a dollar tip. Promise to play by Microsoft's rules and click on the Yes button.

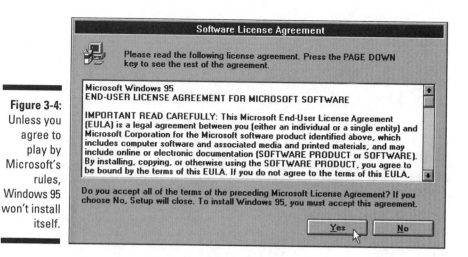

Figure 3-4:
Unless you
agree to
play by
Microsoft's
rules,
Windows 95
won't install
itself.

5. **If Windows 95 asks you to close down any currently running programs, do so. Then click on the OK button.**

The Windows 95 Installation program works hard, and it wants the computer all to itself, as shown in Figure 3-5. If you're running any other programs in the background, shut them down before going further.

Figure 3-5:
Don't run
any other
programs
while
installing
Windows 95.

Don't have an earlier version of Windows on your hard drive? Windows 95 asks you to insert the first disk from your *old* version of Windows into a disk drive so that it can verify that you're merely upgrading an older version of Windows. Without that older version of Windows, you won't be able to install the Windows 95 upgrade, unfortunately. Better head back to the store for the more expensive version of Windows 95 that doesn't require an older version of Windows.

Legal gibberish and licensing terms that leap out during the installation

By clicking on the Yes button, you're essentially telling Microsoft that you agree to the following things:

✔ You won't take Windows 95 apart to see how it works.

✔ You won't rent out your copy of Windows 95, or give copies away to friends.

✔ If you've been using a special preview copy of Windows 95, you promise to destroy that version after a year (or whenever Microsoft tells you, whichever comes first).

✔ Finally, you understand that you're the one punching the keyboard, so Microsoft isn't responsible if the software completely destroys your computer, your business, your data, and your love life.

Welcome to Windows 95!

Don't know whether you're running any other programs? Press Ctrl+Esc, and the Windows 3.1 Task List lists all the currently running programs. The list should contain only Program Manager and Windows 95 Setup. If you see another program listed, click on its name and then click on the Task List's End Task button to shut it down.

6. **When the Windows 95 Setup Wizard appears, press Enter (or click on the button marked Next) to continue.**

As shown in Figure 3-6, Windows 95 explains that installation takes three steps: It gathers information about the computer, copies the files that your particular computer needs, and then restarts the computer to see whether it copied the right files over. Windows 95 replaces your old versions of Windows and DOS in the process.

See the buttons marked Back and Next along the bottom of the window? Throughout the next few steps, you can click the Back button to go back to your last step. So don't feel that you've blown it if you accidentally click on the Next button before you're ready or if you want to go back and change something. Just click on the Back button, and Windows 95 goes back a step.

7. **Click on the Next button to choose the C:\WINDOWS directory.**

Your best bet is to leave the directory at the recommended choice, C:\WINDOWS (see Figure 3-7). This directory is where most programs expect to find Windows, and installing Windows 95 elsewhere can cause problems down the road.

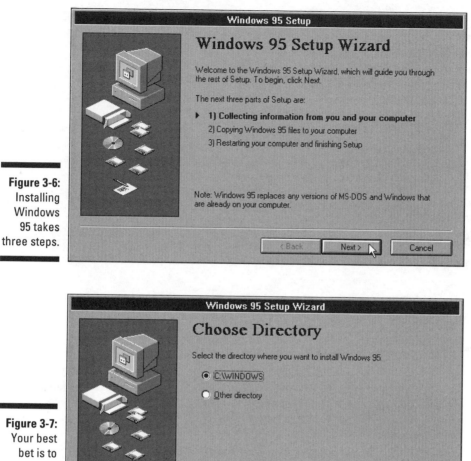

Figure 3-6:
Installing
Windows
95 takes
three steps.

Figure 3-7:
Your best
bet is to
install
Windows 95
in the
C:\WINDOWS
directory.

After you click Next, Windows probes your hard drive, making sure that
it has enough room to fit all the incoming files.

8. **Click on the Next button so that Windows 95 will save your old
   versions of DOS and Windows in case something goes wrong.**

Although Windows 95 replaces your old versions of DOS and Windows,
it doesn't necessarily scrape them off your hard drive. By leaving the
Yes button selected and simply clicking Next (see Figure 3-8), Windows
95 compresses your old versions of DOS and Windows into a 6MB file
and puts them in a hidden place on your hard drive.

(Later on, if you decide Windows 95 really *does* work better than your old versions of Windows and DOS, you can tell Windows 95 to delete that 6MB file for you.)

9. **Click on the Next button to choose the Typical setup.**

   Just clicking on the Next button, shown in Figure 3-9, tells Windows 95 to install the most typical files your computer needs. This decision isn't as difficult as it may seem for one big reason: Windows 95 makes it really easy to go back and add programs you may have left off during the install process.

If you're installing Windows 95 on a laptop, choose the Portable setup. If your hard disk is itty-bitty (less than 60 megabytes), choose the Compact setup. If you're a computer guru who's simply testing this book for a friend, choose Custom for more advanced options.

10. **Type your name, press Tab, type your company name, and click on Next.**

    Type your name and company, as shown in Figure 3-10. Windows 95 registers the software in your name. If you misspell your name or company and Windows 95 jumps to the next page before you can correct it, click on the Back button. Windows 95 gives you a second chance.

Windows 95 Setup Wizard

User Information

Type your name below. If you want, you can also type the name of the company you work for.

Name: Andy Rathbone

Company: Big Expensive Coffee Tbl Books

< Back   Next >   Cancel

Figure 3-10:
Press tab to move from the Name box to the Company box.

---

11. **If you're installing Windows 95 from a compact disc, type the CD's special Key number into the box and click Next, as shown in Figure 3-11.**

12. **Click in the boxes next to any special computer parts you have and then click on Next.**

    Some software puts all the burden on you. *You* have to remember what's installed inside your computer, as well as the equipment's brand name, switch settings, and any other bothersome details. Windows 95 doesn't mind searching inside your computer for all that information, but it needs a little help. If you know that your computer uses any of the equipment listed in the Setup Wizard box, click on the little check box next to that equipment. The box in Figure 3-12, for example, tells Windows 95 that the computer has a sound card installed.

Figure 3-11:
If installing
Windows 95
from a
compact
disc, type
the CD's
special Key
number into
the box and
click on
Next.

Figure 3-12:
Click in the
little box
next to any
special
computer
parts you
have.

After choosing your special parts, click on the Next button. Windows 95
tries to figure out what's inside your computer, a relatively time-
consuming process shown in Figure 3-13.

If Windows 95 gets lost while poking around inside your computer, and
the computer just sits there looking stupid for 10 or 15 minutes, reach
for that off switch. (Don't try the Ctrl+Alt+Delete trick that usually
works.) When you start over at Step 1, Windows 95 lets you choose its
Safe Recovery process, where you both try to figure out what went
wrong.

Windows 95 Setup Wizard

Analyzing Your Computer

Setup is checking to see what kind of hardware is in your computer.

Note: This may take several minutes. If there is no disk activity for a long time, turn your computer off (do not press CTRL+ALT+DEL). Then turn it back on, run Setup, and choose Safe Recovery when prompted.

Progress...

21%

`< Back` `Next >` `Cancel`

Figure 3-13:
Windows 95 usually guesses correctly when trying to figure out what parts are inside your computer.

13. **Click in the appropriate boxes if you want Windows 95 to include The Microsoft Network, Microsoft Mail, or Microsoft Fax. Then click Next.**

    Are you sick of the Information Superhighway yet? If not, you may want to try Microsoft's online entry: The Microsoft Network. Microsoft has its own online service, and it wants you to drop by with your modem.

    Microsoft Fax can send and receive faxes on computers that contain fax modems, and Microsoft Mail software helps people organize their electronic mail (especially if they correspond mostly on The Microsoft Network).

    Not sure whether to install The Microsoft Network, Microsoft Mail, or Microsoft Fax? Then don't bother. Later on down the road, you can head to the Control Panel's Add/Remove Programs button and install the programs (when you have more time on your hands).

14. **Click on Next. Windows 95 installs the recommended components.**

    Let Windows 95 install its recommended components; you can go back later and install some extra goodies, such as a Windows 95 Tour that explains some of the new features in Windows 95. For now, just click on the Next button, shown in Figure 3-14, and concentrate on getting Windows 95 up and running. (*Hint:* To add or remove some of these extra Windows goodies, head for the "Adding and Removing Programs" section in Chapter 10.)

15. **Click on the Next button to tell Windows 95 to create a start up disk.**

    Windows 95 recommends that you create a startup disk, which lets you boot your computer when Windows 95 is giving you grief (see Figure 3-15). It's a wise precaution, so go for it. In fact, when a computer guru comes over to bail you out of a mess, he or she will be relieved to see that start up disk sitting next to the computer. You'll have a better chance of getting your computer back on its feet when talking to the technical support people if you have a start up disk handy.

16. Click on Next to continue, or click on Back to review your settings.

Not sure you've clicked on all the right things so far? Now's your chance to click on the Back buttons to check your past choices. When everything looks good, click on the Next button to continue.

Figure 3-14: Clicking on the Next button tells Windows 95 to install its recommended files; you can always install other files later.

Figure 3-15: Follow Windows 95's recommendation and create a startup disk.

17. Label a disk "Windows 95 startup disk," put it in drive A, and click on OK.

You can get away with labeling the disk something else, but you won't get away with using Drive B. That drive simply doesn't work for startup disks. Click on the OK button to make the disk.

Any existing files on your floppy disk are deleted when Windows 95 makes the startup disk. Don't use a disk with important files on it.

18. After Windows 95 finishes making the startup disk, remove the disk and click on OK.

Not much explanation is needed here. It's a long step, though: Windows 95 now begins copying all the right files onto your computer's hard drive. With more than 20 disks, it's a rather ho-hum process. Feel free to watch the screen so that you won't miss Windows 95 telling you how great it is, as shown in Figure 3-16. Yawn.

19. Click on the Finish button.

When Windows 95 thinks that it has copied enough files onto your computer, it asks you to click on the Finish button. That tells Windows 95 to restart your computer, load Windows 95, and see whether everything works.

If Windows 95 can't even muster up the strength to restart your computer — it just sits there without making noise — wait a good 10 or 15 minutes and then turn it off. Count to 30 slowly, and then turn it back on.

Windows 95 comes back with a screen saying that it's setting up for the first time. Twiddle your thumbs — it takes a while.

20. Click on your time zone and press Enter.

As shown in Figure 3-17, Windows 95 sometimes assumes that everybody lives in Dublin, Edinburgh, or London. If you live somewhere else, click on that spot on the on-screen map. The map moves, listing the appropriate time zone for that area. When it's listing the right time zone, press Enter or click on the Apply button, followed by the OK button.

Oh, and if you're on daylight saving time, click in the box next to "Automatically adjust clock for daylight saving changes."

If you need to set your computer's date and time, click on the Date & Time tab at the top of the screen. Then click on the correct dates and times using the on-screen calendar and clock. Done? Click on the OK button at the bottom of the screen.

Windows makes some last checks to finalize settings and then leaves you with the opening screen, shown in Figure 3-18. (Again, your screen may look a little different depending on the programs Windows 95 installed on your computer.)

Figure 3-16:
Windows 95
flashes a
series of
ads on-
screen
while it
installs
itself.

Figure 3-17:
Click on
your
location
on the
map, and
Windows 95
lists that
area's time
zone.

21. Did you tell Windows 95 to install The Microsoft Network, Microsoft Mail, or Microsoft Fax? Follow the on-screen instructions to make Windows 95 install an Inbox for your online chatter.

Microsoft Exchange puts an Inbox on your Windows 95 desktop, where you can send and receive electronic mail and faxes. Windows 95 can set up Microsoft Fax, Microsoft Mail, and The Microsoft Network to work with the Inbox, but if you want to use any other online services, Microsoft makes you set them up yourself later.

It wants to know what kind of Printer I have!

If you're installing Windows 95 over Windows 3.1, Windows 95 gets your printer information from Windows 3.1. But if you're installing Windows 95 from scratch, you need to enter the Printer's brand name when Windows 95 asks for it during the installation process.

When the Printer Wizard asks for the printer information, push the Page Down key and cursor keys until you've highlighted your printer's manufacturer. Press Tab and then use the Page Down key and cursor keys to highlight your printer's model.

Printer not listed? Check your printer's manual to see what brand of printer it *emulates*, or copies. Many printers say that they're compatible with Hewlett-Packard LaserJet II printers, for example, so you could choose that printer's name from the list. Then click on Next.

Choose the LPT1: option (almost all printers use that LPT1: option) and click on Next again.

Unless you want to change the printer's on-screen name, feel free to click on the Next button on the Printer Name page. See, Windows 95 lists your printer by its brand name in menus. If you're feeling generic — and have only one printer — feel free to change the printer's name to something simple, like "Printer," before clicking on Next. That's especially helpful if your printer has an exceptionally long brand name that may look weird on menus or bump into neighboring icons.

Click on Finish. Windows 95 tests your printer by sending it a sample page. If you have time, go ahead and have Windows 95 test your printer so that you can make sure that everything's set up right. If your toast is starting to burn in the kitchen, don't bother with the test page. You can always test it later.

Windows 95 asks you to insert the appropriate disks so that it can copy the right printer files to your computer, and you are through.

22. **Click on the What's New button for some basic tips on getting Windows 95 to do something.**

   If you've gotten this far, you've done it: You've successfully installed Windows 95.

   Click on the button marked What's New for a quick look at the new goodies in Windows 95 (refer to Figure 3-18). If you have a modem, clicking on the Online Registration button lets you give Microsoft your name and address so that they can send you junk mail about new software.

Leaving Windows 95

After you're finished with Windows 95 and ready to turn off your computer, click on the Start button, located near the lower-left corner of the screen. When the menu sprouts upward, click on the Shut Down option.

Figure 3-18:
The
opening
screen for
Windows 95.

A window pops up, leaving you four options:

✔ **Shut down the computer?:** Choose this option if you want to turn off your computer for the day and do something more constructive.

✔ **Restart the computer?:** This option works well if Windows 95 is acting funny; it tells Windows 95 to shut down and then come back to life, hopefully in a better mood.

✔ **Restart the computer in MS-DOS mode?:** Chances are you'll never have to use this option — unless you're trying to run a DOS program that just won't run when all the Windows 95 graphics are waiting in the background. (Type **exit** at the DOS prompt to make the prompt disappear and the windows reappear.)

✔ **Close all programs and log on as a new user?:** Unless more than one person uses your computer — or the computer's on a network — you won't have to bother with this command. It lets other people log on to the computer and enter passwords. When the computer recognizes them, it gives them predetermined privileges: custom wallpaper, for example, or access to certain files on the network. (See the "It wants me to enter a password!" section in Chapter 5 for more information.)

Turning Off the Computer

If you're finished computing for the day — and you've told Windows 95 to shut down — turn off the computer. Find that switch you used to turn it on and flick it the other way. (Or, if it's a push button, give it another push.)

Never turn off the computer while Windows 95 is running. Use the Windows 95 Shut Down command, described in the preceding section, and wait until Windows 95 flashes a message on-screen saying that it's safe to turn off your computer.

Chapter 4

Windows 95 Stuff Everybody Thinks You Already Know

● ●

In This Chapter

▶ Explanations of the strange terms used in Windows 95

▶ Information on where to look for more details on the topics that are introduced

● ●

*W*hen Windows first hit the market in 1985, it failed miserably. The overpriced, underpowered computer/typewriters of the day burned up their gears over Windows' attempts at fancy graphics. Back then, Windows was not only slow, but it looked dorky and awkward with ugly colors.

Today's best-selling computers come with V8 engines: They can easily whip Windows 95 into shape. With faster computers, perseverance, and a dozen fashionably healthy new color schemes, such as Eggplant, Plum, and Wheat, Windows 95 has turned into a trendy best-seller.

But because Windows has been around for so long, a lot of computer geeks have had a head start. To help you catch up, this chapter is a tourist's guidebook to those Windows words the nerds have been batting around for more than ten years.

Backing Up a Disk

Computers store *bunches* of files on their hard drives. And that multitude of files can be a problem. When the computer's hard drive eventually dies, it takes all your files down with it. Pffffft. Nothing left.

Computer users who don't like anguished *pffffft* sounds *back up* their hard drives religiously. They do so in three main ways.

Some people copy all their files from the hard disk to a bunch of floppy disks. Although custom-written backup programs make this task easier, it's still a time-consuming chore. Who wants to spend half an hour backing up computer files *after* finishing work?

Other people buy a *tape backup* unit. This special computerized tape recorder either lives inside your computer like a floppy disk or plugs into the computer's rear. Either way, the gizmo tape records all the information on your hard disk. Then, when your hard disk dies, you still have all your files. The faithful tape backup unit plays back all your information onto the new hard drive. No scrounging for floppy disks.

Finally, some people buy special *cartridge* storage units. These mechanisms work like hard drives you can slide in and out of your computer. Iomega's $200 Zip drive, for example, can store 100MB of information on a single $20 cartridge. (That can take up a *lot* less space than 70 floppies.)

> ✔ Windows 95 comes with Microsoft Backup, a program that automatically copies files from your hard disk to floppy disks. Unfortunately, that means that you must feed incredible numbers of floppy disks to your computer until it's through copying everything. Yawn. (Chapter 13 describes the process, but you're *much* better off buying a better backup system.)

> ✔ The program can also copy your files to a tape backup unit, if you finally decide to buy one.

> ✔ If your backup program doesn't specifically claim to be "Windows 95 compatible," don't use it. Old backup programs won't know how to back up files using the new Windows 95 file format of more than eight characters. If you try to use an old backup program with Windows 95, the backup won't be reliable.

> ✔ You can't find Microsoft Backup on your Start button? That's because Windows 95 doesn't install it automatically. The Control Panel's Add/Remove Programs icon lets you tell Windows 95 to install the Backup program, however. (You can find more instructions in Chapter 10.)

> ✔ The average cost of a tape backup unit runs from $150 to $400, depending on the size of your computer's hard drive. Some people back up their work every day, using a new tape for each day of the week. If they discover on Thursday that last Monday's report had all the best stuff, they can pop Monday's tape into the backup unit and grab the report.

Clicking

Computers make plenty of clicking sounds, but one click counts the most: the one that occurs when you press a button on a mouse. You'll find yourself clicking the mouse hundreds of times in Windows 95. For example, to push the on-screen button marked Push Me, you move the mouse until the pointer rests over the Push Me button and click the mouse button.

- ✔ When you hear people say, "Press the button on the mouse," they leave out an important detail: *Release* the button after you press it. Press the button with your index finger and release it, just as you press a button on a touch-tone phone.

- ✔ Most mice have 2 buttons; some have 3, and some esoteric models for traffic engineers have more than 32. Windows 95 listens mostly to clicks coming from the button on the *left* side of your mouse. It's the one under your index finger if you're right-handed (or if you're left-handed and lucky enough to find a left-handed mouse). Refer to Chapter 10 for more mouse button tricks.

- ✔ Windows 95 listens to clicks coming from both the left *and* the right buttons on your mouse. Windows 3.1 listens only to clicks coming from the button on the *left* side of your mouse.

- ✔ Like Windows 95, most Windows 95 applications also listen to clicks coming from the *right* button as well as from the *left* button.

- ✔ Don't confuse a *click* with a *double-click*. For more rodent details, see "The Mouse," "Double-Clicking," and "Pointers/Arrows," later in this chapter. The insatiably curious can find even more mouse stuff in Chapter 2, including the new IntelliMouse with the little spinning wheel doohickey.

The Command Line

The *command line* is a macho place where you can type stern code words to boss the computer around. The most famous command line comes with DOS, and it looks like this:

```
C:\> MYPROGRAM
```

When you type a program's name at the command line, DOS rummages around, looking for that program. If DOS succeeds, it loads the program and brings it to the screen for your working pleasure. If it doesn't find it, it burps back with the following bit of ugliness:

```
Bad command or file name
```

✔ The most common reason DOS burps back is because you've spelled the file's name wrong. DOS is more critical than an English teacher with a hair bun. You must be exact.

✔ Don't confuse the command line with the DOS prompt, although the two usually go hand in hand. The *command line* is the information you type next to the DOS prompt. The *DOS prompt* is the thing you can find described if you move your eyes to the section "The DOS Prompt."

✔ For the most part, Windows 95 replaces typing stuff at the command line with a more pleasant way of computing: pressing buttons or clicking on pictures. You can find a command line hidden in the Start button's menu, however, if you want to boss your computer around that way. Just click on the <u>R</u>un button. For more information, see the "Graphical User Interfaces" section of this chapter.

The Cursor

Typewriters have a little mechanical arm that strikes the page, creating the desired letter. Computers don't have little mechanical arms (except in science fiction movies), so they have *cursors:* little blinking lines that show where that next letter will appear in the text.

✔ Cursors appear only when Windows 95 is ready for you to type text, numbers, or symbols — usually when you write letters or reports.

✔ The cursor and the mouse pointer are different things that perform different tasks. When you start typing, text appears at the cursor's location, not at the pointer's location.

✔ You can move the cursor to a new place in the document by using the keyboard's *cursor-control keys* (the keys with little arrows). You can also point to a spot with the mouse pointer and click the button. The cursor leaps to that new spot.

You can distinguish between the cursor and the mouse pointer with one look: Cursors always blink steadily; mouse pointers never do.

For more information, check out "Pointers/Arrows" in this chapter or Table 2-2 in Chapter 2.

Defaults (And the Any Key)

Finally, a computer term that can be safely ignored. Clap your hands and square dance with a neighbor! Here's the lowdown on the, er, hoedown: Some programs present a terse list of inexplicable choices and casually suggest that you select the only option that's not listed: the *default option*.

Don't chew your tongue in despair. Just press Enter.

Those wily programmers have predetermined what option works best for 99 percent of the people using the program. So, if people just press Enter, the program automatically makes the right choice and moves on to the next complicated question.

- ✔ The default option is similar to the oft-mentioned *Any key* because neither of them appears on your keyboard (or on anybody else's, either — no matter how much money they paid).

- ✔ *Default* can also be taken to mean *standard option* or *what to select when you're completely stumped.* For example, "Strangers riding together in elevators stare at their shoes by default."

- ✔ When a program says to press any key, simply press the spacebar. (The Shift keys don't do the trick, by the way.)

Desktop (And Wallpapering It)

To keep from reverting to revolting computer terms, Windows 95 uses familiar office lingo. For example, all the action in Windows 95 takes place on the Windows 95 desktop. The *desktop* is the background area of the screen where all the windows pile up.

Windows 95 comes with a drab green desktop. To jazz things up, you can cover the desktop with pictures, or *wallpaper*. Windows 95 comes with several pictures you can use for wallpaper (and Chapter 10 can help you hang it up).

You can customize the wallpaper to fit your own personality: pictures of little kittens, for example, or eggbeaters. You can draw your own wallpaper with the built-in Windows 95 Paint program. Paint saves your work in the required wallpaper format: a special *bitmap* file ending in the letters BMP. Internet Explorer lets you automatically steal any picture you find on a web site and turn it into your desktop's wallpaper.

Directories

In your everyday paper world, files are stored in folders in a cabinet. In the computer world, files are stored in a *directory* on a disk. Dusty old file cabinets are boring, but directories are even more dreadfully boring: They *never* hold any forgotten savings bonds.

So Windows 95 swapped metaphors. Instead of storing files in directories, Windows 95 holds files in folders. You can see the little pictures of the folders on your monitor.

The folders in Windows 95 are *really* just directories, if you've already grown used to working with directories.

Maintaining files and working with folders can be painful experiences, so they're explained in Chapter 12. In the meantime, just think of folders and directories as separate work areas to keep files organized. Different directories and folders hold different projects; you move from directory to directory as you work on different things with your computer.

- A file cabinet's Vegetables folder could have an Asparagus folder nested inside for organizing material further. In fact, most folders contain several other folders in order to organize information even more. You need to be pretty fastidious around computers; that's the only way of finding your work again.

- Technically, a folder in a folder is a nested *subdirectory* that keeps related files from getting lost. For example, you can have folders for Steamed Asparagus and Raw Asparagus in the Asparagus folder, which lives in the Vegetable folder.

The DOS Prompt

Some people haven't switched to the newer, Windows breed of programs. They're still using the programs they bought several years ago, back when it was trendy to use a DOS program. Luckily, Windows 95 cannot only run DOS programs, but it can provide a DOS prompt for the needy. Click on the Start button, click on the word <u>P</u>rograms, and click on MS-DOS Prompt from the menu.

The DOS prompt rhymes with *the boss chomped,* and it's a symbol that looks somewhat like this:

```
C:\>
```

Type the name of your program at the DOS prompt, press Enter, and the program begins.

If you've been rudely dumped at the DOS prompt, you can scoot quickly to Windows 95 by typing the following no-nonsense word:

```
C:\> EXIT
```

That is, you type **EXIT** (lowercase works too) and follow it with a press of the Enter key.

To appease the DOS hounds, Windows 95 waits in the background while you run a DOS session.

Double-Clicking

Windows 95 places a great significance on something pretty simple: pressing a button on the mouse and releasing it. Pressing and releasing the button once is known as a *click.* Pressing and releasing the button twice in rapid succession is a *double-click.*

Windows 95 watches carefully to see whether you've clicked or double-clicked on its more sensitive parts. The two actions are completely different.

- ✔ A click and a double-click mean two different things to Windows programs. They're not the same.

- ✔ A double-click can take some practice to master, even if you have fingers. If you click too slowly, Windows 95 thinks that you're clicking twice — not double-clicking. Try clicking a little faster next time, and Windows 95 will probably catch on.

- ✔ Can't click fast enough for Windows 95 to tell the difference between a mere click and a rapid-fire double-click? Grab the office computer guru and say that you need to have your Control Panel called up and your clicks fixed. If the guru is at the computer store, tiptoe to the section on tinkering with the Control Panel in Chapter 10.

Dragging and Dropping

Although the term *drag and drop* sounds as if it's straight out of a hitman's handbook, it's really a nonviolent mouse trick in Windows 95. Dragging and dropping is a way of moving something — say, a picture of an egg — from one part of your screen to another.

To *drag,* put the mouse pointer over the egg and *hold down* the mouse button. As you move the mouse across your desk, the pointer drags the egg across the screen. Put the pointer/egg where you want it and release the mouse button. The egg *drops,* uncracked. (If you hold down the *right* mouse button while dragging, Windows 95 tosses a little menu in your face, asking if you're sure that you want to move that egg across the screen.)

For more mouse fun, see "Clicking," "Double-Clicking," "The Mouse," and "Pointers/Arrows" in this chapter and, if you're not yet weak at the knees, the information on the parts of your computer in Chapter 2.

Drivers

Although Windows 95 does plenty of work, it hires help when necessary. When Windows 95 needs to talk to unfamiliar parts of your computer, it lets special *drivers* do the translation. A driver is a piece of software that enables Windows 95 to communicate with parts of your computer.

Hundreds of computer companies sell computer attachables, from printers to sound cards to sprinkler systems. Microsoft requires these companies to write drivers for their products so that Windows 95 knows the polite way to address them.

✔ Sometimes computer nerds say that your *mouse driver* is all messed up. They're not talking about your swerving hand movements. They're talking about the piece of software that helps Windows 95 talk and listen to the mouse.

✔ New versions of Windows 95 often require new drivers. If you send a begging letter to the company that made your mouse, the company may mail you a new, updated driver on a floppy disk. Occasionally, you can get these new drivers directly from Microsoft or from the wild-haired teenager who sold you your computer. Find a computer guru to install the driver, however, or check out the section on installing drivers in Chapter 18.

✔ After you figure out how that darn Internet Explorer works, you can use your computer's modem to call the Microsoft web page. There, you can make a quick copy of just about any driver you need.

Files

A *file* is a collection of information in a form that the computer can play with. A *program file* contains instructions telling the computer to do something useful, like adding up the number of quarters the kids spent on Sweet Tarts last month. A *data file* contains information you've created, like a picture of an obelisk you drew in the Windows 95 Paint program.

✔ Files can't be touched or handled; they're invisible, unearthly things. Somebody figured out how to store files as little magnetic impulses on a round piece of specially coated plastic, or *disk*. (Yep, these are the disks I cover in Chapter 2.)

✔ A file is referred to by its *filename*. DOS makes people call files by a single word containing no more than eight characters. For example, FILENAME could be the name of a file, as could REPORT, SPONGE, or X. Yes, it's difficult to think up descriptive filenames in DOS.

✔ It's so difficult that Windows 95 finally broke the barrier: It lets you call files by bunches of words, as long as they don't total more than 255 characters.

✔ Filenames have optional *extensions* of up to three letters that usually refer to the program that created them. For example, the Windows 95 Paint program automatically saves files with the extension BMP. Microsoft realized that most people don't care about file extensions, so Windows 95 no longer lists a file's extension when it's displaying filenames.

✔ Be careful if you'll be transferring files between a Windows 95 computer and a Windows 3.1 computer. Your Windows 95 file of Kayaking in the Rockies will be automatically renamed KAYAK~1 on the Windows 3.1 computer. The filename's ending is simply truncated, never to be seen again.

✔ Filenames still have more rules and regulations than the Jacuzzi at the condo's clubhouse.

✔ For more information than you'll ever want to know about filenames, flip to Chapter 12.

Graphical User Interfaces

The way people communicate with computers is called an *interface*. For example, the *Enterprise*'s computer used a *verbal interface*. Captain Kirk just told it what to do.

DOS uses a *command line interface*. People type *commands* into the computer, and the computer either digests them or tosses them back in confusion.

Windows 95 uses a *graphical user interface*. People talk to the computer through *graphical symbols,* or pictures. A graphical user interface works kind of like Travel Kiosks at airports — you select some little button symbols right on the screen to find out which hotels offer free airport shuttles.

- ✔ A graphical user interface is called a *GUI,* pronounced *gooey,* as in *Huey, Dewey, Louie,* and *GUI.*

- ✔ Despite what you read in the Microsoft full-page ads, Windows 95 isn't the only GUI for a personal computer. Another GUI, the IBM OS/2 Warp, works like Windows 95. Although still on the shelves, it never took off, effectively killing the sales of my *OS/2 Warp For Dummies* book and leaving everybody stuck with Windows 95.

- ✔ The little graphical symbols or buttons in a graphical user interface are called *icons.*

- ✔ Some computers with sound cards can talk to us. A few of the best software packages can actually speak a few words, but even they stumble when asked to comment on the sacrifice of Isaac in Kierkegaard's *Fear and Trembling.*

Hardware and Software

Alert! Alert! Fasten your seat belt so that you don't slump forward when reading about these two particularly boring terms: hardware and software.

Your CD player is *hardware;* so are the stereo amplifier, speakers, and batteries in the boom box. By itself, the CD player doesn't do anything but hum. It needs music to disturb the neighbors. The music is the *software,* or the information processed by the CD player.

- ✔ Now you can unfasten your seat belt and relax for a bit. Computer *hardware* refers to anything you can touch, including hard things like a printer, a monitor, disks, and disk drives.

- ✔ *Software* is the ethereal stuff that makes the hardware do something fun. A piece of software is called a *program.* Programs come on disks (or CDs, too, if you've anted up for the latest computer gear).

- ✔ Software has very little to do with lingerie.

✔ When somber technical nerds (STNs) say, "It must be a hardware problem," they mean that something must be wrong with your computer itself: its disk drive, keyboard, or central processing unit (CPU). When they say, "It must be a software problem," they mean that something is wrong with the program you're trying to run from the disk.

Here's how to earn points with your computer gurus: When they ask you the riddle, "How many programmers does it take to change a light bulb?," pretend that you don't know this answer: "None; that's a hardware problem."

Icons

An *icon* is a little picture. Windows 95 fills the screen with little pictures, or icons. You choose among them to make Windows 95 do different things. For example, you'd choose the Printer icon, the little picture of the printer, to make your computer print something. Icons are just fancy names for cute buttons.

✔ Windows 95 relies on icons for nearly everything, from opening files to releasing the winged monkeys.

✔ Some icons have explanatory titles, like Open File or Terrorize Dorothy. Others make you guess; for example, the Little Juggling Man Icon opens the network mail system.

✔ For more icon stuff, see "Graphical User Interfaces" earlier in this chapter.

Kilobytes, Megabytes, and So On

Figuring out the size of a real file folder is easy: Just look at the thickness of the papers stuffed in and around it. But computer files are invisible, so their size is measured in bytes (which is pronounced like what Dracula does).

A *byte* is pretty much like a character or letter in a word. For example, the word *sodium-free* contains 11 bytes. (The hyphen counts as a byte.) Computer nerds picked up the metric system much more quickly than the rest of us, so bytes are measured in kilos (1,000), megas (1,000,000), and gigas (way huge).

A page of double-spaced text is about 1,000 bytes, known as 1 kilobyte, which is often abbreviated as 1K. One thousand of those kilobytes is a megabyte, or 1MB. Your computer's hard drive is full of bytes; most hard drives today contain between 500MB and 1,000MB (one gigabyte, or GB).

✔ Just about all floppy disks these days can hold 1.44MB. Today's programs are huge, so they usually come on compact discs, which hold more than 600MB.

✔ All files are measured in bytes, regardless of whether they contain text. For example, that leafy forest background art some people put on their Windows 95 desktop takes up 66,146 bytes. (For information on changing to the forest desktop, see Chapter 10.)

✔ The Windows 95 Explorer or My Computer programs can tell you how many bytes each of your files consumes. To find out more, check out the information on Explorer in Chapter 12. (**Hint for anxious users:** Click on the file's name with your right mouse button and choose Properties from the menu that pops up; you find more information about a file than you want to know.)

One kilobyte doesn't *really* equal 1,000 bytes. That would be too easy. Instead, this byte stuff is based on the number two. One kilobyte is really 1,024 bytes, which is 2 raised to the 10th power, or 2^{10}. (Computers love mathematical details, especially when a 2 is involved.) For more byte-size information, see Table 4-1.

Table 4-1	Ultra-Precise Details from the Slide-Rule Crowd		
Term	*Abbreviation*	*Rough Size*	*Ultra-Precise Size*
Byte		1 byte	1 byte
Kilobyte	K or KB	1,000 bytes	1,024 bytes
Megabyte	M or MB	1,000 kilobytes	1,048,576 bytes
Gigabyte	G or GB	1,000 megabytes	1,073,741,824 bytes

Loading, Running, Executing, and Launching

Files are yanked from a file cabinet and placed onto a desk for easy reference. On a computer, files are *loaded* from a disk and placed into the computer's memory so that you can do important stuff with them. You can't work with a file or program until it has been loaded into the computer's memory.

When you *run, execute,* or *launch* a program, you're merely starting it up so that you can use it. *Load* means pretty much the same thing, but some people fine-tune its meaning to describe when a program file brings in a data file.

> ✔ The Windows 95 Start button enables picture lovers to start programs by using icons. The Windows 95 Explorer enables text-and-word lovers to start programs by clicking the mouse on their names in a list (although Explorer lets you click on icons too, if you prefer).
>
> ✔ If you're feeling particularly bold, you can load programs by using the command line hidden in the Start button as well. For the full dirt, check out the information on the Start button in Chapter 11 and the information on the Explorer in Chapter 12.

Memory

Whoa! How did this complicated memory stuff creep in here? Luckily, it all boils down to one key sentence:

The more memory a computer has available, the more pleasantly Windows 95 behaves.

> ✔ Memory is measured in bytes, just like a file. Most computers have at least 640 kilobytes, or 640K, of memory.
>
> ✔ Windows 95 requires computers to have at least 4 megabytes, or 4MB, of memory, or it won't even bother to come out of the box.

Memory and hard disk space are both measured in bytes, but they're two different things: *Memory* is what the computer uses for quick, on-the-fly calculations when programs are up and running on-screen. *Hard disk space* is what the computer uses to store unused files and programs.

Everybody's computer contains much more hard disk space than memory because hard disks — also known as *hard drives* — are so much cheaper. Also, a hard disk remembers things even when the computer is turned off. A computer's memory, on the other hand, is washed completely clean whenever someone turns it off or pokes its reset button.

The Mouse

A *mouse* is a smooth little plastic thing that looks like Soap on a Rope. It rests on a little roller, or *ball,* and its tail plugs into the back of the PC. When you push the mouse across your desk, the mouse sends its current location through its tail to the PC. By moving the mouse around on the desk, you move a corresponding arrow across the screen.

You can wiggle the mouse in circles and watch the arrow make spirals. Or, to be practical, you can maneuver the on-screen arrow over an on-screen button and click the mouse button to boss Windows 95 around. (Refer to "Clicking," "Double-Clicking," and "Pointers/Arrows," and, if you haven't run out of steam, turn to Chapter 2 for information on the parts of your computer.)

Multitasking and Task Switching

Windows 95 can run two or more programs at the same time, but computer nerds take overly tedious steps to describe the process. So skip this section because you'll never need to know it.

Even though the words *task switching* and *multitasking* often have an exclamation point in computer ads, there's nothing really exciting about them.

When you run two programs, yet switch back and forth between them, you're *task switching*. For example, if Jeff calls while you're reading a book, you put down the book and talk to Jeff. You are task switching: stopping one task and starting another. The process is similar to running your word processor and then stopping to look up a phone number in your handy business card database program.

But when you run two programs simultaneously, you're *multitasking*. For example, if you continue reading your book while listening to Jeff talk about the Natural History Museum's new Grecian urns, you're multitasking: performing two tasks at the same time. In Windows 95, multitasking can be playing its solitaire game or adding a huge spreadsheet while you print something in the background.

These two concepts differ only subtly, and yet computer nerds make a big deal out of the difference. Everybody else shrugs and says, "So what?"

Networks

Networks connect PCs with cables so that employees can share equipment and information. Employees can all send stuff to one printer, for example, or they can send messages back and forth talking about Jane's new hairstyle.

You, as a Windows 95 beginner, are safely absolved from knowing anything about networks. Leave network stuff to that poor person in charge.

> ✔ This book provides more information about networks if you need to know about the subject. Chapter 5, for example, explains logging on and off. Chapter 12 shows how to push and pull files off of other computers that may be networked with your own computer.
>
> ✔ Unless you're working on a computer in an office, however, you probably won't have to worry about networks.
>
> ✔ For information about dial-up networks, like connecting to the Internet through Windows 95's Internet Explorer, head for Chapter 15.

Pointers/Arrows

This idea sounds easy at first. When you roll the mouse around on your desk, you see a little arrow move around on-screen. That arrow is your *pointer,* and it is also called an *arrow.* (Almost everything in Windows 95 has two names.)

The pointer serves as your *electronic index finger.* Instead of pushing an on-screen button with your finger, you move the pointer over that button and click the left button on the mouse.

So what's the hard part? Well, that pointer doesn't always stay an arrow. Depending on where the pointer is located on the Windows 95 screen, it can turn into a straight line, a two-headed arrow, a four-sided arrow, a little pillar, or a zillion other things. Each of the symbols makes the mouse do something slightly different. Luckily, you can find these and other arrow-heads covered in Chapter 2.

Plug and Play

Historically, installing new hardware devices has required substantial technical expertise to configure and load hardware and software. Basically, that means that only geeks could figure out how to fix their computers and add new gadgets to them.

So a bunch of computer vendors hunched together around a table and came up with *Plug and Play* — a way for Windows 95 to set up new gadgets for your computer automatically, with little or no human intervention. You plug in your latest gadget and Windows 95 "interviews" it, checking to see what special settings it needs. Then Windows 95 automatically flips the right switches.

Because Windows 95 keeps track of which switches are flipped, none of the parts argue over who got the best settings. Better yet, users don't have to do anything but plug the darn thing into their computers and flip the On switch.

- ✔ Of course, the process couldn't be *that* simple. Only gadgets that say "Plug and Play" on the box allow for this automatic switch flipping. With the others, you probably need to flip the switches yourself. But at least they still work.

- ✔ Plug-and-play laptops and palmtops often work well with "docking stations." For example, when you plug the laptop into the docking station, Windows 95 automatically detects the new monitor, keyboard, mouse, sound card, and whatever other goodies the owner could afford. Then Windows 95 automatically sets itself up to use those new goodies — without the owner having to fiddle with the settings.

- ✔ Some people call Plug and Play "PNP."

- ✔ Other, more skeptical, people refer to Plug and Play as "Plug and Pray." (It's still rather new technology.)

Quitting or Exiting

When you're ready to throw in the computing towel and head for greener pastures, you need to stop, or quit, any programs you've been using. The terms *quit* and *exit* mean pretty much the same thing: making the current program on-screen stop running so that you can go away and do something a little more rewarding.

Luckily, exiting Windows 95 programs is fairly easy because all of them are supposed to use the same special exit command. You simply click on the little X in the upper-right corner of the program's window. Or, if you prefer using the keyboard, you hold down the Alt key (either one of them, if you have two) and press the key labeled F4. (The F4 key is a *function key;* function keys are either in one row along the top of your keyboard or in two rows along its leftmost edge.)

Don't quit a program by just flicking off your computer's power switch. Doing so can foul up your computer's innards. Instead, you must leave the program responsibly so that it has time to perform its housekeeping chores before it shuts down.

✔ When you press Alt+F4 or click on the little X in the upper-right corner, the program asks whether you want to save any changes you've made to the file. Normally, you click on the button that says something like "Yes, by all means save the work I've spent the last three hours trying to create." (If you've muffed things up horribly, click on the No button. Windows 95 disregards any work you've done and lets you start over from scratch.)

✔ If by some broad stretch of your fingers you press Alt+F4 by accident, click on the button that says Cancel, and the program pretends that you never tried to leave it. You can continue as if nothing happened.

✔ The Alt+F4 trick doesn't work for a DOS program — even if it's running in its own window. You must exit the DOS program by using its own exit keys. Complicated? Well, yes. That's why people are switching to Windows.

✔ Windows 3.1 programs have a square button in their uppermost left corner that looks like an aerial view of a single-slot toaster. Double-clicking on that toaster exits the program. Windows 95 still lets you close most Windows programs by either double-clicking in their uppermost left corner (although the programs don't have that toaster anymore). However, it's usually easier to single-click on the X in the program's uppermost *right* corner. But either action tells the program that you want to close it down.

✔ Save your work before exiting a program or turning off your computer. Computers aren't always smart enough to save it automatically.

Save Command

Save means to send the work you've just created on your computer to a disk for safekeeping. Unless you specifically save your work, your computer thinks that you've just been fiddling around for the past four hours. You need to specifically tell the computer to save your work before it will safely store the work on a disk.

Thanks to Microsoft's snapping leather whips, all Windows 95 programs use the same Save command, no matter what company wrote them. Press and release the Alt, F, and S keys in any Windows 95 program, and the computer saves your work.

If you're saving something for the first time, Windows 95 asks you to think up a filename for the work and pick a folder (which is really a directory) to stuff the new file into. Luckily, this stuff's covered in Chapter 5 in the section, "Saving Your Work."

> ✔ You can save files to a hard disk or a floppy disk. Or, if you're working in a networked office, you can often save files onto other computers.

> ✔ If you prefer using the mouse to save files, click on the word File from the row of words along the top of the program. After a menu drops down, click on the word Save.

> ✔ Choose descriptive filenames for your work. Windows 95 gives you 255 characters to work with, so a file named "June Report on Squeegee Sales" is easier to relocate than one named "Stuff."

> ✔ Some programs, like Microsoft Word for Windows, have an *autosave* feature that automatically saves your work every five minutes or so.

Save As Command

Huh? Save as *what?* A chemical compound? Naw, the Save As command just gives you a chance to save your work with a different name and in a different location.

Suppose that you open the Random Musings file in your Miscellaneous Stuff directory and change a few sentences around. You want to save the changes, but you don't want to lose the original stuff. So you select Save As and type the new name, **Additional Random Musings**.

> ✔ The Save As command is identical to the Save command when you're first trying to save something new: You can choose a fresh name and location for your work.

> ✔ The world's biggest clams can weigh up to 500 pounds.

Shortcuts

The shortcut concept is familiar to most people: Why bother walking around the block to get to school, when a shortcut through Mr. McGurdy's backyard can get you there twice as fast?

It's the same with Windows 95. Instead of wading through a bunch of menus to get somewhere, you can create a shortcut and assign it to an icon. Then, when you double-click on the Shortcut icon, Windows 95 immediately takes you to that location.

You can create a shortcut to your word processor, for example, and leave the shortcut icon sitting on your desktop within easy reach. Double-click on the word processor's shortcut icon, and Windows 95 automatically wades through your computer's folders and files, grabs the word processor, and throws it onto the screen.

A *shortcut* is simply a push button that loads a file or program. You can even make shortcuts for accessing your printer or a favorite folder.

Here's the important thing to remember about Windows 95: Deleting a shortcut doesn't delete the file or program that the shortcut points to. It merely deletes one of the push buttons that quickly brings up that file or program. You can still get to the program by moving through the menus on the Start button or using Windows Explorer.

✔ The ever-helpful Start button automatically makes a shortcut to the last 15 documents you've opened. Click on the Start button, click on the word <u>D</u>ocuments, and you see shortcuts waiting for you to discover them.

✔ Unfortunately, the Start button only keeps track of the last 15 documents you've opened. If you're looking for the *16th* one, you won't find a shortcut waiting. Also, not all programs tell the Start button about recently opened documents; the shortcuts then don't appear on the list. (It's not your fault, if that makes you feel better.)

✔ A shortcut in Windows 95 is the same thing that an icon used to be in Windows 3.1 Program Manager: a push button that starts a program. If you delete a shortcut, you haven't deleted the program; you've just removed a button that started that program.

Temp Files

Like children who don't put away the peanut butter jar, Windows 95 also leaves things lying around. They're called *temp files* — secret files Windows 95 creates to store stuff in while it's running. Windows 95 normally deletes them automatically when you leave the program. It occasionally forgets, however, and leaves them cluttering up your hard drive. Stern lectures leave very little impression.

✔ Temp files usually (but not always) end with the letters TMP. Common temp filenames include ~DOC0D37.TMP, ~WRI3F0E.TMP, the occasional stray ~$DIBLCA.ASD, and similar looking files that usually start with the wavy ~ thing. (Some people call it a *tilde*.)

> ✔ If you exit Windows 95 the naughty way — by just flicking the computer's off switch — Windows 95 won't have a chance to clean up its temp file mess. If you keep doing it, you'll eventually see hundreds of TMP files lying around your hard drive. Be sure to exit Windows 95 the Good Bear way: by clicking the Start button and choosing S̲hut down from the menu that pops up.

The Windows

DOS programs completely fill your screen; only one program fits on-screen at one time. Windows 95, however, enables you to run several programs at the same time by placing them in *windows*. A window is just a little box.

You can move the boxes around. You can make them bigger or smaller. You can make them fill your entire screen. You can make them turn into little icons at the bottom of your screen. You can spend hours playing with windows. In fact, most frustrated new Windows 95 users do.

> ✔ You can put as many windows on-screen as you want, peeping at all of them at the same time or just looking into each one individually. This activity appeals to the voyeur in all of us.

> ✔ For instructions on how to retrieve a lost window from the pile, head immediately to Chapter 8.

> ✔ When a DOS program runs *as a window* in Windows 95, it won't fill the whole screen (unless you push the button that makes the window expand). Windows 95 shrinks the DOS program's window a little so that you can see other windows sitting around it.

Part II
Making Windows 95 Do Something

The 5th Wave   By Rich Tennant

Get the Huggies, hon—she's reaching for the Diaper icon

In this part . . .

Windows 95 is more fun than cheap tattoos from the bottom of a Cracker Jack box. It's especially fun to show friends the built-in screen savers, like the one that straps you into a starship and cruises toward the fifth quadrant's snack shop at warp speed. You can even adjust the ship's speed by using the Control Panel.

Unfortunately, some spoil-sport friend will eventually mutter the words that bring everything back to Earth: "Let's see Windows 95 do something useful, like balance a checkbook or teach the kids to rinse off their plates and put them in the dishwasher."

Toss this eminently practical part at them to quiet 'em down.

Chapter 5

Starting Windows 95

• •

In This Chapter

▶ Revvin' up Windows 95

▶ Starting a program

▶ Finding the secret pull-down menus

▶ Loading a file

▶ Putting two programs on the screen

▶ Using the keyboard

▶ Printing your work

▶ Saving your work

▶ Quitting Windows 95

• •

*H*old on to your hat! Then try to type at the same time. No, let the hat fly by the wayside because this is a hands-on Windows 95 chapter that demonstrates some dazzling special effects. First, you make Windows 95 leap to your screen, ready to load a program!

Then, at the click of the mouse, you launch a second program, running at the same time as the first! Plus, you discover secret magic tricks to bypass the mouse and use the keyboard instead!

Finally, you find out how to print your work so that you'll have some hard copy to show those doubting friends of yours.

Oh, and you find out how to save your work so that you can find it again the next day. So warm up those fingers, shake out your sleeves, and get ready for action.

Revvin' Up Windows 95

If your PC came with Windows 95 already installed (most of them do these days), Windows 95 probably leaps to your screen automatically when you first turn on the computer. If not, perhaps some evil soul left you at a DOS prompt. Try opening the cage door manually by typing the following command at the C:\> prompt:

```
C:\> EXIT
```

That is, you type **EXIT** (lowercase works, too) and follow it with a deft press of the Enter key.

If Windows 95 has been installed on your computer, a chore described in Chapter 3, it pops up on the screen, and its Start button is ready for action. Windows 95 is like an elevator that moves around your computer, and the Start button is like a panel of elevator buttons. By pushing the Start button, you tell Windows 95 where to go and what to do.

✔ When you start Windows 95, you may hear pleasant, Brian Eno-composed synthesizer sounds coming from the computer's sound card. If you don't have a sound card, you don't hear anything but a strong inner urge driving you toward the computer store's sound-card aisles. (Sound cards range in price from $75 to $250.)

✔ Because Big Business doesn't want to hear Brian Eno in the boardroom, Windows 95 may have its sound options turned off. To activate the sounds yourself, choose the Sounds icon from the Control Panel and select a new sound Scheme, a not-too-laborious process described in Chapter 10.

✔ If you're still using Windows 3.1, try starting it up by typing the word **WIN** at the DOS prompt. Microsoft chose the program name WIN because it's such an eager, positive-sounding command, like something from a best-selling *You Can Be a Success Despite Your Chin* paperback.

✔ Windows 95 sends out an annoying Welcome message whenever you start it up. To get rid of this message, click on the check mark in the box labeled <u>S</u>how this Welcome Screen next time you start Windows. The existing check mark disappears, and, after you click the Close button, the Welcome window leaves you alone.

It wants me to enter a password!

Your computer may be part of a *network* — a bunch of computers linked together with cables or through the phone lines. A network lets you sit at your own computer in your own cubicle but swap files with Grace's computer in her cubicle — and neither of you has to get up.

But how do you make sure that nobody else sits down at your computer and starts stealing Grace's files? How can you set up your computer so that nobody else can mess with your own files? Or, if several people share the same computer, how can they make sure that their Windows 95 desktop is customized to their own special needs?

Typing a password solves some of those problems. After Windows 95 wakes up and figures out that it's part of a network, it cautiously sends out the box shown in Figure 5-1.

Figure 5-1:
Type your name in the top box, press Tab, type your password in the bottom box, and click OK to log on to your computer.

By typing your name in the <u>U</u>ser name box and making up a password to type into the <u>P</u>assword box, you enable your computer to immediately recognize you: You're logged on.

- ✔ Depending on your network's level of security, a password can let you do many things. Sometimes entering the password merely lets you use your own computer. Other times, it lets you share files on a network.

- ✔ Because networks can be notoriously difficult to set up, most networked offices have a full-time network administrator who tries to make the darn thing work. (That's the person to bug if something goes wrong.)

✔ If you are not working on a major network where security is an issue, don't type anything in the P̲assword box, shown in Figure 5-1. If you leave the box blank and click the OK button, Windows 95 just lets you type in your name to log on to the computer—nothing to remember, and nothing to forget.

✔ Have you forgotten your password already? Just click on the Cancel button, shown in Figure 5-1. Unless you're on a strict network, Windows 95 still lets you in. Because it doesn't recognize you, however, you won't see your favorite wallpaper.

✔ Keep your password short and sweet: the name of your pet poodle, for example, or the brand of your toothbrush. (See your network adminis-trator if Windows 95 doesn't accept your password.)

✔ Passwords are case sensitive. That term means that a password of **caviar** is different from **Caviar**. The computer notices the capital C and considers them to be two different words.

Starting your favorite program with the Start button

When Windows 95 first takes over your computer, it turns your screen into a desktop. However, the desktop is merely a fancy name for a plate of buttons with labels underneath them. Click on a button, and programs hop to the screen in their own little windows. Click on the Start button in the bottom-left corner of the screen, and you'll have even more buttons to choose from, as shown in Figure 5-2.

Because the buttons have little pictures on them, they're called *icons.* (No relation to the icons favored by the Byzantine emperors in the eighth and ninth centuries A.D. They still used DOS back then.)

Icons offer clues to the program they represent. For example, the icon of the Inbox with mail stands for Microsoft Exchange, a program that lets people send and receive mail on their computers.

See the dark bar shading the Windows Explorer icon's title in Figure 5-2? The bar means that the Windows Explorer program is *highlighted:* It's queued up and ready to go. If you press the Enter key while Windows Explorer is highlighted, Explorer hops to the forefront. (Don't press Enter, though, because Explorer is too boring to play with right now.)

Look at the little arrow sitting by itself in the corner of your screen. Roll your mouse around until that arrow hovers over the button that says Start.

Figure 5-2:
The Start
button in
Windows 95
hides
dozens of
menus for
starting
programs.

Click your mouse button, and the Start menu pops up on the screen, shown
in Figure 5-3. Next, click on the Programs button, and another menu full of
buttons shoots out, as shown in Figure 5-4. Click on Accessories to see yet
another menu, shown in Figure 5-5. Click on Games to see the last menu on
the chain (see Figure 5-6). And, if you're not too exhausted, click on FreeCell
to check out Windows 95's great solitaire game.

Figure 5-3:
To start a
program in
Windows 95,
click on
the Start
button . . .

Figure 5-4:
. . . and then
click on
Programs
and follow
the menu
as it grows.

Figure 5-5:
Click on the
type of
program
you'd like to
load. . .

Figure 5-6:
. . . and then
click on
your
program's
name to
load it.

✔ The Start button is just a big panel of buttons. When you press one of the buttons by pointing at it and clicking with the mouse, the program assigned to that button heads for the top of the screen and appears in a little window.

✔ You don't have to click your way through all those buttons hiding beneath the Start button. Click on the Start button and then just hover your mouse pointer over the other menu areas you want to open. Windows 95 opens them without even waiting for your clicks.

✔ Icons can stand for files as well as for programs. Clicking on the Documents button usually brings up shortcut buttons that take you to 15 of your most recently used documents.

✔ Microsoft has already set up the Start button to include icons for the most popular programs and files Windows 95 found as it installed itself on your computer — stuff like 1-2-3 and WordPerfect. If you want to add some other programs and files, however, check out the section in Chapter 11 on customizing your Start button.

- If you're kind of sketchy about all this *double-click* stuff, head back to the section in Chapter 2 on your mouse and that double-click stuff.

- Do you despise mice? You don't need a mouse for the Start button. Hold down Ctrl and press Esc to make the Start menu appear. Then push your arrow keys to navigate the various menus. Highlighted the program you want? Press Enter, and the program begins to run.

- If the icon you're after in the Start menu has a little black bar around its name, it's *highlighted.* If you just press Enter, the highlighted program loads itself into a little window. Or you can still double-click on it to load it. Windows 95 lets you do things in a bunch of different ways.

- This chapter gives you just a quick tour of Windows 95. You can find glowing descriptions of the Start button in Chapter 11.

Pull-Down Menus

Windows 95, bless its heart, makes an honest effort toward making computing easier. For example, the Start button puts a bunch of options on the screen in front of you. You just choose the one you want, and Windows 95 takes it from there.

But if Windows 95 put all its options on the screen at the same time, it would look more crowded than a 14-page menu at the House of Hui restaurant. To avoid resorting to fine print, Windows 95 hides some menus in special locations on the screen. When you click the mouse in the right place, more options leap toward you, like Sparky, the friendly Dalmatian.

For example, load Windows multimedia player program, Media Player, by clicking on the Start button. When the Start menu pops up, choose Programs, click on Accessories, and choose Multimedia. When you spot Media Player on the last pop-out menu, click on it to bring it to the screen.

See the row of words beginning with File that rests along the top edge of Media Player? You find a row of words across the top of just about every Windows 95 program. Move your mouse pointer over the word File and click.

A menu opens from beneath File. This menu is called a *pull-down menu,* if you're interested, and it looks somewhat like what you see in Figure 5-7.

- Pull-down menus open from any of those key words along the top of a window. Just click the mouse on the word, and the menu tumbles down like shoeboxes falling off a closet shelf.

- To close the menu, go back up and click the mouse again, but click it someplace away from the menu.

✔ Different Windows 95 programs have different words across the menu bar, but almost all of the bars begin with the word File. The File pull-down menu contains file-related options, like Open, Save, Print, and Push Back Cuticles.

✔ You find pull-down menus sprinkled liberally throughout Windows 95.

Figure 5-7:
Click on a word along the top of any window to reveal a secret pull-down menu.

Loading a file

First, here's the bad news: Loading a file into a Windows 95 program can be a mite complicated sometimes. Second, *loading* a file means the same thing as *opening* a file.

Now that those trifles have been dispensed with, here's the good news: All Windows 95 programs load files in the exact same way. So, after you know the proper etiquette for one program, you're prepared for all the others!

Here's the scoop: To open a file in any Windows 95 program, look for the program's *menu bar,* that row of important-looking words along its top. Because you're after a *file,* click on File.

A most-welcome pull-down menu descends from the word File. The menu has a list of important-looking words. Because you're trying to *open* a file, move the mouse to the word Open and click once again.

Yet another box hops onto the screen, shown in Figure 5-8, and you see this box named *Open* appear over and over again in Windows 95.

See the list of filenames inside the box? Point at one of them with the mouse, click the button, and that file's name shows up in the box called File name. Click on the Open button, and Media Player opens the file and displays it on the screen. If you don't have a mouse, press the Tab key until a little square appears around one of the file's names. Then press the arrow keys until the file you want is highlighted, and press Enter.

Figure 5-8:
Almost
every
Windows 95
program
tosses this
box at you
when you
load or
save a file.

Open	? X
Look in:	Media

The Microsoft Sound

| File name: | | Open |
| Files of type: | All files (*.*) | Cancel |

You've done it! You've loaded a file into a program! Those are the same stone steps you'll walk across in any Windows 95 program, whether it was written by Microsoft or by the teenager down the street. They all work in the same way.

✓ Sometimes you won't spot the file you're after. It's just not listed in that little box. That means that you'll have to do a little spelunking. Just like most people store their underwear and T-shirts in different dresser drawers, most computers store their files in different places called folders. If you're having trouble finding a file for your program to open, head for the "Getting the Lowdown on Folders" section in Chapter 12.

✓ You can speed things up by simply double-clicking on a file's name right from a menu; that action tells Windows 95 to load the file as well. Or you can click on the name once to highlight it (it turns black) and then press the Enter key. Windows 95 is full of multiple options like that (different strokes for different folks and all).

✓ If you've changed an open file, even by an accidental press of the spacebar, Windows 95 takes it for granted that you've changed the file for the better. When you try to load another file into a program, Windows 95 cautiously asks whether you want to save the changes you've made to the current file. Click on the No button unless you do, indeed, want to save that version you've haphazardly changed.

✓ The Open box has a bunch of options in it. You can open files that are stored in different folders or on other disk drives. You can also call up files that were created by certain programs, filtering out the ones you won't be needing. Chapter 6 explains all this Open box stuff.

✓ Now here's some more bad news: Only Windows 95 programs can handle long filenames. If you're using Windows 3.1 programs in Windows 95, you are still stuck with the old versions of the Open and Save boxes, and the long filenames won't work right in these programs.

✓ If you're still a little murky on the concepts of *files, folders, directories,* and *drives,* flip to Chapter 12 for an explanation of Windows Explorer.

Putting two programs on-screen simultaneously

After spending all your money for Windows 95 and a computer powerful enough to cart it around, you're not going to be content with only one program on your screen. You want to *fill* the screen with programs, all running in their own little windows.

How do you put a second program on the screen? Well, if you've opened Media Player by double-clicking on its icon in the Start button's menu, you're probably already itching to load FreeCell, the solitaire game. Simply click on the Start button and start moving through the menus, as described in the "Starting your favorite program with the Start button" section earlier in this chapter.

✔ This section is intentionally short. When working in Windows 95, you almost always have two or more programs on the screen at the same time. There's nothing really special about it, so there's no need to belabor the point here.

✔ The special part comes when you move information between the two programs, which is explained in Chapter 9.

✔ If you want to move multiple windows around on the screen, move yourself to Chapter 7.

✔ If you've started up FreeCell, you're probably wondering where the Media Player window disappeared to. It's now hidden behind the FreeCell window. To get it back, check out the information on retrieving lost windows in Chapter 8. (Or, if you see a button called Media Player along the bottom of your screen, click on it.)

✔ To switch between windows, just click on them. When you click on a window, it immediately becomes the *active* window — the window where all the activity takes place. For more information on switching between windows, switch to Chapter 7.

✔ Can't find FreeCell? Unfortunately, Windows 95 doesn't automatically install FreeCell on everybody's computers. To correct this oversight, use the Control Panel's Add/Remove Programs icon, as described in Chapter 10.

Using the Keyboard

It's a good thing Microsoft doesn't design automobiles. Each car would have a steering wheel, a joystick, a remote control, and handles on the back for people who prefer to push. Windows 95 offers almost a dozen different ways for you to perform the most simple tasks.

For example, check out the top of any window where that important-looking row of words hides above secret pull-down menus. Some of the words have certain letters underlined. What gives? Well, it's a secret way for you to open their menus without using the mouse. This sleight of hand depends on the Alt key, that dark key resting next to your keyboard's spacebar.

Press (and release) Alt and keep an eye on the row of words in the Media Player *menu bar.* The first word, File, darkens immediately after you release Alt. You haven't damaged it; you've selected it, just as if you'd clicked on it with the mouse. The different color means that it's highlighted.

Now, see how the letter F in File is underlined? Press the letter F, and the pull-down menu hidden below File falls recklessly down, like a mushroom off a pizza.

That's the secret underlined-letter trick! And pressing Alt and F is often faster than plowing through a truckload of mouse menus — especially if you think that the whole mouse concept is rather frivolous, anyway.

- ✔ You can access almost every command in Windows 95 by using Alt rather than a mouse. Press Alt, and then press the key for the under-lined letter. That option, or command, then begins to work.

- ✔ If you accidentally press Alt and find yourself trapped in Menu Land, press Alt again to return to normal. If that doesn't work, try pressing Esc.

- ✔ As pull-down menus continue to appear, you can keep plowing through them by selecting underlined letters until you accomplish your ultimate goal. For example, pressing Alt and then F brings down the File pull-down menu. Pressing O subsequently activates the Open files option from the File menu and immediately brings the Open file box to the front of the screen.

When you see a word with an underlined letter in a menu, press and release Alt. Then press that underlined letter to choose that menu item.

Printing Your Work

Eventually, you'll want to transfer a copy of your finely honed work to the printed page so that you can pass it around. Printing something from any Windows 95 program (or application, or applet, whatever you want to call it) takes only three keystrokes. Press and release Alt and then press the letters F and P. What you see on your screen will be whisked to your printer.

Pressing Alt activates the words along the top, known as the *menu bar.* The letter F wakes up the File menu, and the letter P tells the program to send its stuff to the printer — pronto.

- ✔ Alternatively, you can use the mouse to click on the word File and then click on the word Print from the pull-down menu. Depending on the RPM of your mouse ball and the elasticity of your wrist, both the mouse and the keyboard method can be equally quick.

- ✔ If nothing comes out of the printer after a few minutes, try putting paper in your printer and making sure that it's turned on.

- ✔ When you print something in Windows 95, you're actually activating yet another program, which sits around and feeds stuff to your printer. You may see the program as a little icon at the bottom of your screen. If you're curious about the new printing process, check out the section in Chapter 9 that covers it.

- ✔ Some programs, such as WordPad, have a little picture of a printer along their top. Clicking on that printer icon is a quick way of telling the program to shuffle your work to the printer.

Saving Your Work

Anytime you create something in a Windows 95 program, be it a picture of a spoon or a letter to the *New York Times* begging for a decent comics page, you'll want to save it to disk.

Saving your work means placing a copy of it onto a disk, either the mysterious hard disk inside your computer or a floppy disk, one of those things you're always tempted to use as beverage coasters. (Don't try it, though.)

Luckily, Windows 95 makes it easy for you to save your work. You need only press three keys, just as if you were printing your work or opening a file. To save your work, press and release Alt, press F, and then press S.

If you prefer to push the mouse around, click on File from the Windows 95 menu bar. When the secret pull-down menu appears, click on Save. Your mouse pointer turns into an hourglass, asking you to hold your horses while Windows 95 shuffles your work from the program to your hard disk or a floppy disk for safekeeping.

That's it!

- ✔ If you're saving your work for the first time, you see a familiar-looking box: It's the same box you see when opening a file. See how the letters in the File name box are highlighted? The computer is always paying attention to the highlighted areas, so anything you type appears in that box. Type in a name for the file and press Enter.

- ✔ If Windows 95 throws a box in your face saying something like This filename is not valid, you haven't adhered to the ridiculously strict filename guidelines discussed in Chapter 12.

> ✔ Just as files can be loaded from different directories and disk drives,
> they can be saved to them as well. You can choose between different
> directories and drives by clicking on various parts of the Save box. All
> this stuff is explained in Chapter 6.

Quitting Windows 95

Ah! The most pleasant thing you'll do with Windows 95 all day could very
well be to stop using it. And you do that the same way you started: by using
the Start button, that friendly little helper that popped up the first time you
started Windows 95.

Other Windows 95 programs come and go, but the Start button is always on
your screen somewhere. (Sometimes you have to press Ctrl+Esc to bring it
out of hiding.)

First, make the Start menu pop to the forefront by clicking on the Start
button. Keyboard buffs can hold down Ctrl and press Esc at the same time.
Next, click on the Shut down the computer command from the Start button's
menu. Windows 95, tearful that you're leaving, sends out one last plea,
shown in Figure 5-9.

Figure 5-9:
Be sure to
shut down
Windows 95
before
turning off
your
computer.

Shut Down Windows	✕
Are you sure you want to:	
⦿ Shut down the computer?	
○ Restart the computer?	
○ Restart the computer in MS-DOS mode?	
○ Close all programs and log on as a different user?	
[Yes] [No] [Help]	

If you mean business, click on the Yes button or press Enter. Windows 95
starts to put all of its parts away, preparing to leave the screen of your
computer. If, by some odd mistake, you've clicked on the Shut Down button
in error, click on the No button, and Windows 95 ignores your faux pas.
(Keyboard users must press Tab to highlight the No button and then
press Enter.)

Finally, if you want to run a cranky DOS program that doesn't like to run with
Windows 95, select the last option, Restart the computer in MS-DOS mode.
(To return to Windows 95 from DOS, type **EXIT** at the C:\> prompt thing.)

✔ Be sure to shut down Windows 95 through its official Shut Down program before turning off your computer. Otherwise, Windows 95 can't properly prepare your computer for the event, leading to future troubles.

✔ Holding down Alt and pressing F4 tells Windows 95 that you want to stop working in your current program and close it down. If you press Alt+F4 while no programs are running, Windows 95 figures that you've had enough for one day, and it acts as though you clicked on its Shut Down button.

✔ When you tell Windows 95 that you want to quit, it searches through all your open windows to see whether you've saved all your work. If it finds any work you've forgotten to save, it tosses a box your way, letting you click on the OK button to save it. Whew!

✔ If you happen to have any DOS programs running, Windows 95 stops and tells you to quit your DOS programs first. See, Windows 95 knows how to shut down Windows 95 programs because they all use the same command. But all DOS programs are different. You have to shut the program down manually, using whatever exit sequence you normally use in that program.

✔ If you have a sound card, you hear a pleasant wind-chimes sound telling you that it's time to go home and relax (or time to *buy* a sound card if you haven't yet succumbed to the urge).

✔ You don't *have* to shut down Windows 95. In fact, some people leave their computers on all the time. Just be sure to turn off your monitor; those things like to cool down when they're not being used.

Chapter 6

Field Guide to Windows 95 Buttons, Bars, Boxes, Folders, and Files

● ●

In This Chapter

▶ Looking at a typical window

▶ Getting into bars

▶ Changing borders

▶ Getting to know the button family

▶ Disregarding the dopey Control-menu button

▶ Exploring dialog box stuff: text boxes, drop-down list boxes, list boxes, and other gibberish

▶ Finding out how to open a file

▶ Knowing when to click and when to double-click

▶ Knowing when to use the left mouse button and when to use the right mouse button

● ●

*A*s children, just about all of us played with elevator buttons until our parents told us to knock it off. An elevator gave such an awesome feeling of power: Push a little button, watch the mammoth doors slide shut, and feel the responsive push as the spaceship floor begins to surge upward. . . .What fun!

Part of an elevator's attraction still comes from its simplicity. To stop at the third floor, you merely press the button marked 3. No problems there. Okay, the parking levels sometimes get a little weird — especially when they're named after fruits or vegetables. Still, the push-and-stand-back-while-the-door-closes concept is classic in its simplicity.

Windows 95 takes the elevator button concept to an extreme, unfortunately, and it loses something in the process. First, some of the Windows 95 buttons don't even *look* like buttons (unless you're heading down to the parking garage). Most of the Windows 95 buttons have ambiguous little pictures rather than clearly marked labels. And the worst part is the Windows 95 terminology: The phrase *push the button* becomes *click the scroll bar above or below the scroll box on the vertical scroll bars.* Yuck!

When braving your way through Windows 95, don't bother learning all these dorky terms. Instead, treat this chapter as a field guide, something you can grab when you stumble across a confusing new button or box that you've never encountered before. Just page through until you find its picture. Read the description to find out whether that particular creature is deadly or just mildly poisonous. Then read to find out where you're supposed to poke it with the mouse pointer.

You'll get used to the critter after you've clicked on it a few times. Just don't bother remembering the scientific name *vertical scroll bar,* and you'll be fine.

A Typical Window

Nobody wants a field guide without pictures, so Figure 6-1 shows a typical window with its parts labeled.

Just as boxers grimace differently depending on where they've been punched, windows behave differently depending on where they've been clicked. The following sections describe the correct places to click and, if that doesn't work, the best places to punch.

Figure 6-1:
Here's how the ever-precise computer nerds label the different parts of a window.

🖒 Windows 95 is full of little weird-shaped buttons, borders, and boxes. You don't have to remember their Latin or Greek etymologies. The important part is just finding out what part you're supposed to click. Then you can start worrying about whether you're supposed to single-click or double-click. (And that little dilemma is explained near the end of this chapter.)

🖒 After you click on a few windows a few times, you realize how easy it really is to boss them around. The hard part is finding out everything for the first time, just like when you stalled the car while learning how to use the stick shift.

Bars

Windows 95 is filled with bars; perhaps that's why some of its programs seem a bit groggy and hung over. Bars are thick stripes along the edges of a window. You find several different types of bars in Windows 95.

The title bar

The title bar is that topmost strip in any window (see Figure 6-2). It lists the name of the program, as well as the name of any open file. For example, the title bar in Figure 6-2 comes from the Windows 95 Notepad. It contains an untitled file because you haven't had a chance to save the file yet. (For example, the file may be full of notes you've jotted down from an energetic phone conversation with Ed McMahon.)

Figure 6-2:
A title bar
lists the
program's
name along
the top of a
window.

You choose a name for that file when you save it for the first time. That new filename then replaces the admittedly vague Untitled in the title bar.

🖒 The title bar merely shows the name of the current program and file. If you've just started to create a file, the title bar refers to that file's name as Untitled.

> ✔ The title bar can serve as a *handle* for moving a window around on-screen. Point at the title bar, hold down the mouse button, and move the mouse around. An outline of the window moves as you move the mouse. When you've placed the outline in a new spot, let go of the mouse button. The window leaps to that new spot and sets up camp.
>
> ✔ When you're working on a window, its title bar is *highlighted,* meaning that it's a different color from the title bar of any other open window. By glancing at all the title bars on-screen, you can quickly tell which window is currently being used.

To enlarge a window so that it completely fills the screen, double-click on its title bar. It expands to full size, making it easier to read and covering up everything else. No mouse? Then press Alt, the spacebar, and then X.

The menu bar

Windows 95 has menus *everywhere.* But if menus appeared all at once, everybody would think about deep-fried appetizers rather than computer commands. So Windows 95 hides its menus in something called a *menu bar* (see Figure 6-3).

Figure 6-3:
A menu bar
provides a
handy
place for
Windows 95
to hide its
cluttersome
menus.

| File   Edit   Search   Appetizers   Help |

Lying beneath the title bar, the menu bar keeps those little menus hidden behind little words. To reveal secret options associated with those words, click on one of those words.

If you think that mice are for milksops, use the brawny Alt key instead. A quick tap of the Alt key activates the menu words across the top of the window. Press the arrow keys to the right or left until you've selected the word you're after and then press the down-arrow key to expose the hidden menu. (You can also press a word's underlined letter to bring it to life, but that tip is explained later in more detail.)

For example, to see the entrees under Edit, click your mouse button on Edit (or press Alt and then E). A secret menu tumbles down from a trap door, as shown in Figure 6-4, presenting all sorts of *edit-related* options.

Figure 6-4: Select any word in the menu bar to reveal its secret hidden menu.

📄 Untitled - Notepad
File   Edit   Search   Appetizers   Help
Undo   Ctrl+Z
Cut   Ctrl+X
Copy   Ctrl+C
Paste   Ctrl+V
Delete   Del
Select All
Time/Date   F5
✓ Word Wrap

✔ When you select a key word in a menu bar, a menu comes tumbling down. The menu contains options related to that particular key word.

✔ Just as restaurants sometimes run out of specials, a window sometimes isn't capable of offering all its menu items. Any unavailable options are *grayed out,* as the Cut, Copy, Paste, and Delete options are in Figure 6-4.

✔ If you accidentally select the wrong word, causing the wrong menu to jump down, just sigh complacently. (S-i-i-i-igh.) Then select the word you *really* wanted. The first menu disappears, and the new one appears below the new word.

✔ If you want out of Menu Land completely, click the mouse pointer back down on your work in the window's *workspace* — usually the area where you've been typing stuff. (Or press your Alt key, whichever method comes to mind sooner.)

✔ Some menu items have *shortcut keys* listed next to them, such as the Ctrl+Z key combination next to the Undo option in Figure 6-4. Just hold down the Ctrl key and press the letter Z to undo your last effort. The Undo option takes place immediately, and you don't have to wait for the menu to tumble down.

If you find yourself performing the same task on a menu over and over, check to see whether a shortcut key is next to it. By pressing the shortcut key, you can bypass the menu altogether, performing that task instantly.

The scroll bar

The scroll bar, which looks like an elevator shaft, is along the edge of a window (see Figure 6-5). Inside the shaft, a little freight elevator (the *scroll box*) travels up and down as you page through your work. In fact, by glancing at the little elevator, you can tell whether you're near the top of a document, the middle, or the bottom.

Figure 6-5:
Scroll bars
enable you
to page
through
everything
that's in the
window.

For example, if you're looking at stuff near the *top* of a document, the elevator box is near the top of its little shaft. If you're working on the bottom portion of your work, the elevator box dangles near the bottom. You can watch the little box travel up or down as you press the PgUp or PgDn key. (Yes, it's easy to get distracted in Windows 95.)

Here's where the little box in the scroll bar comes into play: By clicking in various places on that scroll bar, you can quickly move around in a document without pressing the PgUp or PgDn key.

✔ Instead of pressing the PgUp key, click in the elevator shaft *above* the little elevator (the *scroll box*). The box jumps up the shaft a little bit, and the document moves up one page, too. Click *below* the scroll box, and your view moves down, just as with the PgDn key.

✔ To move your view up line by line, click on the boxed-in arrow (*scroll arrow*) at the top of the scroll bar. If you hold down the mouse button while the mouse pointer is over that arrow, more and more of your document appears, line by line, as it moves you closer to its top. (Holding down the mouse button while the pointer is on the bottom arrow moves you closer to the bottom, line by line.)

✔ Scroll bars that run along the *bottom* of a window can move your view from side to side rather than up and down. They're handy for viewing spreadsheets that extend off the right side of your screen.

✔ If the scroll bars don't have a little scroll box inside them, you have to use the little arrows to move around. There's no little elevator to play with. Sniff. Sniff.

✔ Want to move around in a hurry? Then put the mouse pointer on the little elevator box, hold down the mouse button, and *drag* the little elevator box up or down inside the shaft. For example, if you drag the box up toward the top of its shaft and release it, you can view the top of the document. Dragging it and releasing it down low takes you near the end.

✔ Windows 95 adds another dimension to some scroll bars: the little elevator's *size.* If the elevator is swollen up so big that it's practically filling the scroll bar, the window is currently displaying practically all the information the file has to offer. But if the elevator is a tiny box in a huge scroll bar, you're only viewing a tiny amount of the information contained in the file. Don't be surprised to see the scroll box change size when you add or remove information from a file.

✔ Clicking or double-clicking on the little elevator box itself doesn't do anything, but that doesn't stop most people from trying it anyway.

✔ If you don't have a mouse, you can't play on the elevator. To view the top of your document, hold down Ctrl and press Home. To see the bottom, hold down Ctrl and press End. Or press the PgUp or PgDn key to move one page at a time.

Undoing what you've just done

Windows 95 offers a zillion different ways for you to do the same thing. Here are three ways to access the Undo option, which unspills the milk you've just spilled:

✔ Click on <u>E</u>dit and then click on <u>U</u>ndo from the menu that falls down. (This approach is known as *wading through the menus.*) The last command you made is undone, saving you from any damage.

✔ Press and release the Alt key, and then press the letter E (from <u>E</u>dit), and then press the letter U (from <u>U</u>ndo). (This *Alt key method* is handy when you don't have a mouse.) Your last bungle is unbungled, reversing any grievous penalties.

✔ Hold down the Ctrl key and press the Z key. (This little quickie is known as the *shortcut key method.*) The last mistake you made is reversed, sparing you from further shame.

Don't feel like you have to learn all three methods. For example, if you can remember the Ctrl+Z key combination, you can forget about the menu method or the Alt key method.

Or, if you don't want to remember *anything,* stick with the menu method. Just pluck the Undo command as it appears on the menu.

Finally, if you don't have a mouse, you'll have to remember the Alt key or Ctrl key business until you remember to buy a mouse.

The taskbar

Windows 95 converts your computer monitor's screen into a desktop. But because your newly computerized desktop is probably only 15 inches wide, all your programs and windows cover each other up like memos tossed onto a spike.

To keep track of the action, Windows 95 introduces the taskbar. It lies along the bottom of your screen and simply lists what windows are currently open. If you've found the Start button, you've found the taskbar — the Start button lives on the taskbar's left end.

- ✔ Whenever you open a window, Windows 95 tosses that window's name onto a button on the taskbar. If you open a lot of windows, the taskbar automatically shrinks all its buttons so they'll fit.

- ✔ To switch from one window to another, just click on the desired window's name from its button on the taskbar. Wham! That window shoots to the top of the pile.

- ✔ Are all those open windows looking too crowded? Click on the taskbar with your right mouse button and choose the <u>M</u>inimize All Windows option. All your currently open windows turn into buttons on the taskbar.

- ✔ In Windows 3.1, double-clicking on the desktop in the background brought up the Task List, a taskbar-like program that listed open windows, let you choose between them, and tiled them across your screen for easy access. In Windows 95, clicking on the taskbar with the right mouse button brings up the Task List's equivalent — a menu for organizing your open windows.

- ✔ You can't find your taskbar? Try pointing off the edge of your screen, slowly, trying each of the four sides. If you hit the correct side, some specially configured taskbars will stop goofing around and come back to the screen.

- ✔ You can find more information about the taskbar in Chapter 11.

Borders

A *border* is that thin edge enclosing a window. Compared with a bar, it's really tiny.

- ✔ You use borders to change a window's size. I discuss how to do that in Chapter 7.

- ✔ You can't use a mouse to change a window's size if the window doesn't have a border.

✔ If you like to trifle in details, you can make a border thicker or thinner through the Windows 95 Control Panel, which is discussed in Chapter 10. In fact, laptop owners often thicken their windows' borders to make them a little easier to grab with those awkward trackballs.

✔ Other than that, you won't be using borders much.

The Button Family

Three basic species of buttons flourish throughout the Windows 95 environment: command buttons, option buttons, and minimize/maximize buttons. All three species are closely related, and yet they look and act quite differently.

Command buttons

Command buttons may be the simplest to figure out — Microsoft labeled them! Command buttons are most commonly found in *dialog boxes,* which are little pop-up forms that Windows 95 makes you fill out before it will work for you.

For example, when you ask Windows 95 to open a file, it sends out a form in a dialog box. You have to fill out the form, telling Windows 95 what file you're after, where it's located, and equally cumbersome details.

Table 6-1 identifies some of the more common command buttons that you encounter in Windows 95.

Table 6-1	Common Windows 95 Command Buttons	
Command Button	**Habitat**	**Description**
OK	Found in nearly every pop-up dialog box	A click on this button says, "I'm done filling out the form, and I'm ready to move on." Windows 95 then reads what you've typed into the form and processes your request. (Pressing the Enter key does the same thing as clicking on the OK button.)

(continued)

Table 6-1 (continued)

Command Button	Habitat	Description
Cancel	Found in nearly every pop up dialog box	If you've somehow loused things up when filling out a form, click on the Cancel button. The pop up box disappears, and everything returns to normal. Whew! (The Esc key does the same thing.)
Help	Found in nearly every pop-up dialog box	Stumped? Click on this button. Yet another box pops up, this time offering help on your current situation. (The F1 function key does the same thing.)
Setup... Pizza... Settings...	Found less often in pop-up dialog boxes	If you encounter a button with ellipsis dots (. . .) after the word, brace yourself: Selecting that button brings yet *another* box to the screen. From there, you must choose even *more* settings, options, or toppings.

> ✔ By selecting a command button, you're telling Windows 95 to carry out the command that's written on the button. (Luckily, no command buttons are labeled Explode.)
>
> ✔ See how the OK button in Table 6-1 has a slightly darker border than the others? That darker border means that the button is highlighted. Anything in Windows 95 that's highlighted takes effect as soon as you press the Enter key; you don't *have* to select it.
>
> ✔ Some command buttons have underlined letters that you don't really notice until you stare at them. An underlined letter tells you that you can press that command button by holding down the Alt key while pressing the underlined letter. (That way you don't have to click or double-click if your mouse is goofing up.)
>
> ✔ Instead of scooting your mouse to the Cancel button when you've goofed in a dialog box, just press your Esc key. It does the same thing.

If you've clicked on the wrong command button but *haven't yet lifted your finger from the mouse button,* stop! There's still hope. Command buttons take effect only *after* you've lifted your finger from the mouse button. So keep your finger pressed on the button and scoot the mouse pointer away from the button. When the pointer no longer rests on the button, gently lift your finger. Whew! Try *that* trick on any elevator.

Did you stumble across a box that contains a confusing command button or two? Click on the question mark in the box's upper-right corner (if there is a question mark, that is). Then, when you click on the confusing command button, a helpful comment appears to explain that button's function in life.

Option buttons

Sometimes Windows 95 gets ornery and forces you to choose just a single option. For example, you can elect to *eat* your brussels sprouts or *not* eat your brussels sprouts. You can't choose both, so Windows 95 doesn't let you select both of the options.

Windows 95 handles this situation with an *option button*. When you choose one option, the little dot hops over to it. If you choose the other option, the little dot hops over to it instead. You find option buttons in many dialog boxes. Figure 6-6 shows an example.

Figure 6-6:
When you
choose an
option, the
black dot
hops to it.

| Brussels Sprouts Quandary | ? X |

Should you
- ○ Eat brussels sprouts
- ◉ Let brussels sprouts rot

OK   Cancel

✔ Although Windows 95 tempts you with several choices in an option box, it lets you select only one of them. It moves the dot (and little dotted border line) back and forth between the options as your decision wavers. Click on the OK button when you've reached a decision. The *dotted* option then takes effect.

✔ If you *can* select more than one option, Windows 95 doesn't present you with option buttons. Instead, it offers the more liberal *check boxes,* which are described in the "Check boxes" section later in this chapter.

✔ Option buttons are round. Command buttons, described earlier, are rectangular.

Some old-time computer engineers refer to option buttons as radio buttons, after those push buttons on car radios that switch from station to station, one station at a time.

Minimize/maximize buttons

All the little windows in Windows 95 often cover each other up like teenage fans in the front row of a Pearl Jam concert. To restore order, you need to separate the windows by using their minimize/maximize buttons.

These buttons enable you to enlarge the window you want to play with or shrink all the others so they're out of the way. Here's the scoop.

The *minimize button* is one of three buttons in the upper-right corner of every window. It looks like that little button in the margin next to this paragraph.

A click on the minimize button makes its window disappear and then reappear as a tiny button on the taskbar along the bottom of your screen. (Click on the button to return the window to its normal size.) Keyboard users can press Alt, the spacebar, and then N to minimize a window.

- ✔ Minimizing a window doesn't destroy its contents; it just transforms the window into a little button on the bar that runs along the bottom of the screen.

- ✔ To make the button turn back into an on-screen window, click on it. It reverts to a window in the same size and location as before you shrank it. (Keyboard users can press Alt, the spacebar, and then R.)

- ✔ Closing a window and minimizing a window are two different things. Closing a window purges it from the computer's memory. To reopen it, you need to load it off your hard drive again. Turning a window into an icon keeps it handy, loaded into memory, and ready to be used at an instant's notice.

The *maximize button* is in the upper-right corner of every window, too. It looks like the one in the margin.

A click on the maximize button makes the window swell up something fierce, taking up as much space on-screen as possible. Keyboard users can press Alt, the spacebar, and then X to maximize their windows.

- ✔ If you're frustrated with all those windows that are overlapping each other, click on your current window's maximize button. The window muscles its way to the top, filling the screen like a *real* program.

- ✔ Immediately after you maximize a window, its little maximize button turns into a *restore button* (described momentarily). The restore button lets you shrink the window back down when you're through giving it the whole playing field.

You don't *have* to click on the maximize button to maximize a window. Just double-click on its *title bar,* the thick strip along the window's top bearing its name. That double-click does the same thing as clicking on the maximize button, and the title bar is much easier to aim for.

 In the upper-right corner of every maximized window is the restore button, which looks like the button in the margin.

After a window is maximized, a click on this button returns the window to the size it was before you maximized it. (Keyboard users can press Alt, the spacebar, and then R.)

> ✔ Restore buttons appear only in windows that fill the entire screen (which is no great loss because you need a restore button only when the window is maximized).

> ✔ DOS programs can run in a window. But when they're in a window, they can't fill the entire screen, even if you click the maximize button. DOS windows just can't grow as large as normal windows. Perhaps they smoked cigarettes in their youth. (Or maybe they didn't read the "Changing Fonts in a DOS Window" trick, described in Chapter 14.)

> ✔ If DOS programs *aren't* running in a window, they can fill the entire screen. Windows 95 hides in the background, tapping its toes until the programs finish and it can grab the screen again. For more information on this confusing DOS stuff, troop to Chapter 14.

Don't bother with this Control-menu button stuff

The Control-menu button provides a quick exit from any window: Just give the little ornament a quick double-click. Other than that feature, however, the Control-menu button is pretty useless, redundant, and repetitive.

For example, by clicking once on the Control-menu button, you get a pull-down menu with a bunch of options. Choose the Move option, and you can move around the window with the keyboard's arrow keys. (But it's much easier to move a window by using the mouse, as you find out in Chapter 7.)

Choosing the Size option lets you change a window's size. (But that's much easier with a mouse, too, as you find out in Chapter 7.)

Don't bother with the menu's Minimize and Maximize options, either. Those two options have their own dedicated buttons, right in the window's other top corner. Click on the minimize button (the button with the little line on it) to minimize the window; click on the maximize button (the button with the big square on it) to maximize the window. Simple. You don't need to bumble through a menu for the Minimize and Maximize options when minimize and maximize buttons are already staring you in the face.

The Close option is redundant. You can close the window by double-clicking on the Control-menu button in the first place and

(continued)

(continued)

avoid the hassle of going through a menu. Or, click once on the dedicated Close button — the button with the X on it in the window's far, upper-right corner.

So don't bother messing with the Control-menu button because it's just a waste of time.

(You may need to play with it if you use a laptop and don't have a mouse, however. But even then, you should invest in a trackball, as described in Chapter 2. Until then, press Alt and the spacebar to bring up the Control menu and then press any of the underlined letters to access the function.)

The Dopey Control-Menu Button

Just as all houses have circuit breakers, all windows have *Control-menu buttons*. These buttons hide in the top-left corner of almost every window, where they look like an inconspicuous hood ornament. (Sharp-eyed readers will notice that the button is actually a miniature icon representing the program.)

That little hood ornament hides a menu full of functions, but they're all pretty dopey, so ignore them all except for this one: Double-click on the Control-menu button whenever you want to leave a window.

✔ You can get by without using the Control-menu button at all. Just hold down the Alt key and press the F4 key to close an application and exit the window. Or click on the Close button, that button with the X on it in the window's far, upper-right corner.

✔ If you click on the Control-menu button, a secret hidden menu appears, but it's pretty useless. So ignore it, skip the technical chatter in the sidebar about the Control-menu button, and move along to the more stimulating dialog boxes that follow.

Dialog Box Stuff (Lots of Gibberish)

Sooner or later, you'll have to sit down and tell Windows 95 something personal. You'll want to tell Windows 95 the name of a file to open, for example, or the name of a file to print. To handle this personal chatter, Windows 95 sends out a dialog box.

A *dialog box* is merely another little window. But instead of containing a program, it contains a little form or checklist for you to fill out. These forms can have bunches of different parts, which are discussed in the following sections. Don't bother trying to remember the names of the parts, however. It's more important to figure out how they work.

Text boxes

A *text box* works just like a fill-in-the-blanks test in history class. You can type anything you want into a text box — even numbers. For example, Figure 6-7 shows a dialog box that pops up when you want to search for some words or characters in WordPad.

Figure 6-7:
This dialog
box from
WordPad
contains a
text box.

When you type words or characters into this box and press the Enter key, WordPad searches for them. If it finds them, WordPad shows them to you on the page. If it doesn't find them, WordPad sends out a robotic dialog box saying it's finished searching.

✔ Two clues let you know whether a text box is *active,* that is, ready for you to start typing stuff into it: The box's current information is high-lighted, or a cursor is blinking inside it. In either case, just start typing the new stuff. (The older, highlighted information disappears as the new stuff replaces it.)

✔ If the text box *isn't* highlighted or there *isn't* a blinking cursor inside it, it's not ready for you to start typing. To announce your presence, click inside it. Then start typing. Or press Tab until the box becomes high-lighted or contains a cursor.

✔ If you click inside a text box that already contains words, you must delete the information with the Delete or Backspace key before you can start typing in new information. (Or you can double-click on the old information; that way the incoming text automatically replaces the old text.)

Regular list boxes

Some boxes don't let you type stuff into them. They already contain information. Boxes containing lists of information are called, appropriately enough, *list boxes.* For example, WordPad brings up a list box if you're bored enough to want to change its font (see Figure 6-8).

Figure 6-8:
By selecting
a font from
the list box,
you change
the way
letters look
in WordPad.

✔ See how the Times New Roman font is highlighted? It's the currently selected font. Press Enter (or click on the OK command button), and WordPad uses that font in your current paragraph.

✔ See the scroll bars along the side of the list box? They work just as they do anywhere else: Click on the little scroll arrows (or press the up or down arrow) to move the list up or down, and you can see any names that don't fit in the box.

✔ Many list boxes have a text box above them. When you click on a name in the list box, that name hops into the text box. Sure, you could type the name into the text box yourself, but it wouldn't be nearly as much fun.

✔ When confronted with a bunch of names in a list box, type the first letter of the name you're after. Windows 95 immediately scrolls down the list to the first name beginning with that letter.

Drop-down list boxes

List boxes are convenient, but they take up a great deal of room. So Windows 95 sometimes hides list boxes, just as it hides pull-down menus. Then, if you click in the right place, the list box appears, ready for your perusal.

So, where's the right place? It's that downward-pointing arrow button, just like the one shown next to the box beside the Font option in Figure 6-9.

Figure 6-10 shows the drop-down list.

When one just isn't enough

Because Windows 95 can display only one pattern on your desktop at a time, you can select only one pattern from the desktop's list box. Other list boxes, like those in Windows Explorer, let you select a bunch of names simultaneously. Here's how:

✔ To select more than one item, hold down the Ctrl key and click on each item you want. Each item stays highlighted.

✔ To select a bunch of adjacent items from a list box, click on the first item you want. Then hold down Shift and click on the last item you want. Windows 95 immediately highlights the first item, last item, and every item in between. Pretty sneaky, huh?

✔ Finally, when grabbing bunches of icons, try using the "rubber band" trick: Point at an area of the screen next to one icon, and, while holding down the mouse button, move the mouse until you've drawn a lasso around all the icons. After you've highlighted the icons you want, let go of the mouse button, and they remain highlighted. Fun!

Figure 6-9:
Click on the downward-pointing arrow next to the Font box to see a drop-down list box.

Character Map	☐☐☒

Shows available characters in the selected font.   *Keystroke: Spacebar*

Figure 6-10:
A list box
drops down
to display
all the fonts
that are
available.

To make a drop-down list box drop down without using a mouse, press the Tab key until you've highlighted the box next to the little arrow. Hold down the Alt key and press the down-arrow key, and the drop-down list starts to dangle.

✔ Unlike regular list boxes, drop-down list boxes don't have a text box above them. That thing that *looks* like a text box just shows the currently selected item from the list; you can't type anything in there.

✔ To scoot around quickly in a drop-down list box, press the first letter of the item you're after. The first item beginning with that letter is instantly highlighted. You can press the up- or down-arrow key to see the ones nearby.

✔ Another way to scoot around quickly in a drop-down list box is to click on the scroll bar to its right. (Scroll bars are discussed earlier in this chapter, if you need a refresher.)

✔ You can choose only *one* item from the list of a drop-down list box.

✔ The program in Figure 6-10 is called Character Map, and Windows 95 usually doesn't install that handy little accessory. To slap the hand of Windows 95 and make it install the Character Map, use the Control Panel's Add/Remove Program feature, as described in Chapter 10.

Check boxes

Sometimes you can choose from a whopping number of options in a dialog box. A check box is next to each option, and if you want that option, you click in the box. If you don't want it, you leave the box blank. (Keyboard users can press the up- or down-arrow key until a check box is highlighted and then press the space bar.) For example, with the check boxes in the dialog box shown in Figure 6-11, you pick and choose how the Windows 95 taskbar behaves.

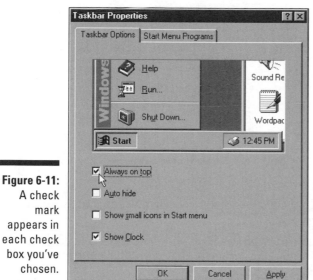

Figure 6-11:
A check
mark
appears in
each check
box you've
chosen.

✔ By clicking in a check box, you change its setting. Clicking in an empty square turns on that option. If the square already has a check mark in it, a click turns off that option, removing the check mark.

✔ You can click next to as many check boxes as you want. With *option buttons,* those things that look the same but are round, you can select only *one* option.

Sliding controls

Rich Microsoft programmers, impressed by track lights and sliding light switches in luxurious model homes, have added sliding controls to Windows 95, as well. These "virtual" light switches are easy to use and don't wear out nearly as quickly as the real ones do. To slide a control in Windows 95 — to adjust the volume level, for example — just drag and drop the sliding lever, like the one shown in Figure 6-12.

Point at the lever with the mouse and, while holding down the mouse button, move the mouse in the direction you want the sliding lever to move. As you move the mouse, the lever moves, too. When you've moved the lever to a comfortable spot, let go of the mouse button, and Windows 95 leaves the lever at its new position. That's it.

Figure 6-12:
To slide a lever, point at it, hold down the mouse button, and move your mouse.

✔ Some levers slide to the left and right, others move up and down. None of them move diagonally.

✔ To change the volume in Windows 95, click on the little speaker near the clock in the bottom-right corner. A sliding volume control appears, ready to be dragged up or down.

✔ No mouse? Then go buy one. In the meantime, press Tab until a little box appears over the sliding lever; then press your arrow keys in the direction you want the lever to slide.

Just Tell Me How to Open a File

Enough with the labels and terms. Forget the buttons and bars. How do you load a file into a program? This section gives you the scoop. You follow these steps every time you load a file into a program.

Opening a file is a *file-related* activity, so start by finding the word File in the window's menu bar (see Figure 6-13).

Figure 6-13:
To open a file, you first choose the word File in the window's menu bar.

Then simply do the following:

1. **Click on File (or press Alt and then F) to knock down that word's hidden little menu.**

   Figure 6-14 shows the File pull-down menu.

Figure 6-14: When you choose File, the File pull-down menu appears.

2. **Click on Open (or press O) to bring up the Open dialog box.**

   You can predict that Open will call up a dialog box because of the trailing . . . things beside Open on-screen. (Those . . . things are called an *ellipsis,* or *three dots,* depending on the tightness of your English teacher's hair bun.)

   Figure 6-15 shows the Open dialog box that leaps to the front of the screen. In fact, a similar dialog box appears almost any time you mess with the File pull-down menu in any program.

Figure 6-15: This Open dialog box appears whenever you open a file in any Windows program.

✔ If you find your filename listed in the first list box, in this case, the one listing the SHARP.TXT file, you're in luck. Double-click on the file's name, and it automatically jumps into the program. Or hold down Alt and press N, type the file's name, and press Enter. Or click on the file's name once and press Enter. Or curse Windows 95 for giving you so many options for such a simple procedure.

✔ If you don't find the file's name, it's probably in a different folder, also known as a *directory.* Click on the little box along the top that is labeled Look in, and Windows 95 displays a bunch of other folders to rummage through. Each time you click on a different folder, that folder's contents appear in the first list box.

✔ Can't find the right folder or directory? Perhaps that file is on a different drive. Click on one of the other drive icons listed in the Look in box to search in a different drive. Drive icons are those little gray box things; folder icons, well, look like folders.

✔ Could the file be named something strange? Click on the Files of type drop-down list box (or hold down Alt and press T) to select a different file type. To see *all* the files in a directory, select the All Files (✔.✔) option. Then all the files in that directory show up.

✔ Don't know what those little icons along the top are supposed to do? Rest your mouse pointer over the one that has you stumped. After a second or so, the increasingly polite Windows 95 brings a box of explanatory information to the screen. For example, rest the mouse pointer over the folder with the explosion in its corner, and Windows 95 tells you that clicking on that icon creates a new folder.

✔ Still using Windows 3.1 programs? You may still run across the older, Windows 3.1-style boxes for opening files.

✔ This stuff is incredibly mind-numbing, of course, if you've never been exposed to directories, drives, folders, wild cards, or other equally painful carryovers from the DOS days of Windows 95. For a more rigorous explanation of this scary file-management stuff, troop to Chapter 12.

Hey! When Do I Click, and When Do I Double-Click?

That's certainly a legitimate question, but Microsoft only coughs up a vague answer. Microsoft says that you should *click* when you're *selecting* something in Windows 95 and you should *double-click* when you're *choosing* something. Huh?

Well, you're *selecting* something when you're *highlighting* it. For example, you may select a check box, an option button, or a filename. You click on it to *select* it, and then you look at it to make sure that it looks okay. If you're satisfied with your selection, you click on the OK button to complete the job.

To *select* something is to set it up for later use.

When you *choose* something, however, the response is more immediate. For example, if you double-click on a filename, that file immediately loads itself into your program. The double-click says, "I'm choosing this file, and I want it now, buster." The double-click alleviates the need to confirm your selection by clicking on the OK button.

You *choose* something you want to have carried out immediately.

✔ All right, this explanation is still vague. So always start off by trying a single-click. If clicking once doesn't do the job, try a double-click. It's usually much safer than double-clicking first and asking questions later.

✔ If you accidentally double-click rather than single-click, it usually doesn't matter. But, if something terrible happens, hold down the Ctrl key and press the letter Z. You can usually undo any damage.

✔ If Windows 95 keeps mistaking your purposeful double-click as two disjointed single-clicks, head for the section in Chapter 10 on tinkering with the Control Panel. Adjusting Windows 95 so that it recognizes a double-click when you make one is pretty easy.

When Do I Use the Left Mouse Button, and When Do I Use the Right Mouse Button?

When somebody tells you to "click" something in Windows 95, it almost always means that you should "click with your left mouse button." That's because most Windows 95 users are right-handed, and their index finger hovers over the mouse's left button, making it an easy target.

Windows 95, however, also lets you click your *right* mouse button, and it regards the two actions as completely different.

Pointing at something and clicking the right button often brings up a secret hidden menu with some extra options. Right-click on a blank portion of your desktop, for example, and a menu pops up allowing you to organize your desktop's icons or change the way your display looks. Right-clicking on an icon often brings up a hidden menu, as well.

Or hold down your right mouse button while dragging a folder across the desktop. Windows 95 brings up a menu, asking whether you're sure that you want to move the folder over there. If you drag the folder while holding down your left mouse button, Windows 95 doesn't ask; it simply moves the folder there.

✔ The right mouse button is designed more for advanced users, who like to feel that they're doing something sneaky, so clicking the right mouse button often brings up a hidden menu of extra options.

✔ Confused about something on the screen? Try clicking it with your right mouse button, just for kicks. The result may be unexpectedly helpful.

Chapter 7

Moving the Windows Around

. . . .

. . . .

*A*h, the power of Windows 95. Using separate windows, you can put a spreadsheet, a drawing program, and a word processor on-screen *at the same time.*

You can copy a hot-looking graphic from your drawing program and toss it into your memo. Stick a chunk of your spreadsheet into your memo, too. And why not? All three windows can be on-screen *at the same time.*

You have only one problem: With so many windows on-screen at the same time, you can't see anything but a confusing jumble of programs.

This chapter shows how to move those darn windows around on-screen so that you can see at least *one* of them.

Moving a Window to the Top of the Pile

Take a good look at the mixture of windows on-screen. Sometimes you can recognize a tiny portion of the window you're after. If so, you're in luck. Move the mouse pointer until it hovers over that tiny portion of the window and click the mouse button. Shazam! Windows 95 immediately brings the clicked-on window to the front of the screen.

That newly enlarged window probably covers up strategic parts of other windows. But at least you'll be able to get some work done, one window at a time.

- ✔ Windows 95 places a lot of windows on-screen simultaneously. But unless you have two heads, you'll probably use just one window at a time, leaving the remaining programs to wait patiently in the background. The window that's on top, ready to be used, is called the *active* window.

- ✔ The active window is the one with the most lively title bar along its top. The active window's title bar is a brighter color than all the others.

- ✔ The last window you've clicked on is the active window. All your subsequent keystrokes and mouse movements will affect that window.

- ✔ Some programs can run in the background, even if they're not in the currently active window. Some communications programs can keep talking to other computers in the background, for example, and some spreadsheets can merrily crunch numbers, unconcerned with whether they're the currently active window. Imagine!

Although many windows may be on-screen, you can enter information into only one of them: the active window. To make a window active, click on any part of it. It rises to the top, ready to do your bidding.

Another way to move to a window is by clicking on its name in the Windows 95 taskbar. See "The Way-Cool Taskbar" section later in this chapter.

Moving a Window from Here to There

Sometimes you want to move a window to a different place on-screen (known in Windows 95 parlance as the *desktop*). Maybe part of the window hangs off the edge of the desktop, and you want it centered. Or maybe you want to put two windows on-screen side by side so that you can compare their contents.

In either case, you can move a window by grabbing its *title bar,* that thick bar along its top. Put the mouse pointer over the window's title bar and hold down the mouse button. Now use the title bar as the window's handle. When you move the mouse around, you tug the window along with it.

When you've moved the window to where you want it to stay, release the mouse button to release the window. The window stays put and on top of the pile.

- ✔ The process of holding down the mouse button while moving the mouse is called *dragging*. When you let go of the mouse button, you're *dropping* what you've dragged.

- ✔ When placing two windows next to each other on-screen, you usually need to change their sizes as well as their locations. The very next section tells how to change a window's size, but don't forget to read "The Way-Cool Taskbar" later in this chapter. It's full of tips and tricks for resizing windows as well as moving them around.

- ✔ Stuck with a keyboard and no mouse? Press Alt, the spacebar, and M. Then use the arrow keys to move the window around. Press Enter when it's in the right place.

Making a Window Bigger or Smaller

Sometimes, moving the windows around isn't enough. They still cover each other up. Luckily, you don't need any special hardware to make them bigger or smaller. See that thin little border running around the edge of the window? Use the mouse to yank on a window's corner border, and you can change its size.

First, point at the corner with the mouse arrow. When it's positioned over the corner, the arrow turns into a two-headed arrow. Now hold down the mouse button and drag the corner in or out to make the window smaller or bigger. The window's border expands or contracts as you tug on it with the mouse, so you can see what you're doing.

When you're done yanking, and the window's border looks about the right size, let go of the mouse button. The window immediately redraws itself, taking the new position.

Here's the procedure, step by step:

1. **Point the mouse pointer at the edge of the corner.**

   It turns into a two-headed arrow, shown in Figure 7-1.

2. **Hold down the mouse button and move the two-headed arrow in or out to make the window bigger or smaller.**

   Figure 7-2 shows how the new outline takes shape when you pull the corner inward to make the window smaller.

Figure 7-1:
When the
mouse
points
at the
window's
bottom
corner, the
arrow
grows a
second
head.

Figure 7-2:
As you
move the
mouse, the
window's
border
changes to
reflect its
new shape.

3. Release the mouse button.

The window shapes itself to fit into the border you've just created (see Figure 7-3).

That's it!

✔ This procedure may seem vaguely familiar because it is. You're just *dragging and dropping* the window's corner to a new size. That *drag and drop* concept works throughout Windows 95. For example, you can *drag and drop* a title bar to move an entire window to a new location on-screen.

✔ You can grab the side border of a window and move it in or out to make it fatter or skinnier. You can grab the top or bottom of a window and move it up or down to make it taller or shorter. But grabbing for a corner is always easiest because then you can make a window fatter, skinnier, taller, or shorter, all with one quick flick of the wrist.

Figure 7-3:
Let go of
the mouse
button, and
the window
fills its
newly
adjusted
border.

If a window is hanging off the edge of the screen, and you can't seem to position it so that all of it fits on screen, try shrinking it first. Grab a visible corner and drag it toward the window's center. Release the mouse button, and the window shrinks itself to fit in its now smaller border. Then grab the window's title bar and hold down the mouse button. When you drag the title bar back toward the center of the screen, you can see the whole window once again.

Making a Window Fill the Whole Screen

Sooner or later, you get tired of all this New Age, multiwindow mumbo jumbo. Why can't you just put *one* huge window on-screen? Well, you can.

To make any window grow as big as it gets, double-click on its *title bar,* that topmost bar along the top of the window. The window leaps up to fill the screen, covering up all the other windows.

To bring the pumped-up window back to normal size, double-click on its title bar once again. The window shrinks to its former size, and you can see everything that it was covering up.

✔ When a window fills the entire screen, it loses its borders. That means that you can no longer change its size by tugging on its title bar or dragging its borders. Those borders just aren't there anymore.

✔ If you're morally opposed to double-clicking on a window's title bar to expand it, you can expand it another way. Click on the window's *maximize button,* the middle-most of the three little boxes in its top right corner. The window hastily fills the entire screen. At the same time, the maximize button turns into a *restore* button; click on the restore button when you want the window to return to its previous size.

✔ Refer to Chapter 6 for more information on the maximize, minimize, and restore buttons.

✔ If you don't have a mouse, you can make the window bigger by holding down Alt, pressing the spacebar, and pressing X. But for goodness sake, buy a mouse so that you don't have to try to remember these complicated commands!

✔ DOS programs running in on-screen windows don't usually fill the screen. When you double-click on their title bars, they get bigger, but Windows 95 still keeps 'em relatively small. If you take them out of the window, however, they fill the screen completely and shove Windows 95 completely into the background. To take a DOS program out of a window, click on the DOS window to make it active and then hold down Alt and press Enter. The DOS program suddenly lunges for the entire screen, and Windows 95 disappears. To bring it back, hold Alt and press Enter again. (For more of this DOS stuff, see Chapter 14.)

Shrinking Windows to the Taskbar

Windows spawn windows. You start with one window to write a letter to Mother. You open another window to check her address, for example, and then yet another to see whether you've forgotten any recent birthdays. Before you know it, four more windows are crowded across the desktop.

To combat the clutter, Windows 95 provides a simple means of window control: You can transform a window from a screen-cluttering square into a tiny button at the bottom of the screen.

See the three buttons lurking in just about every window's top-right corner? Click on the *minimize button* — the button with the little line in it. Whoosh! The window disappears, and a little button appears on the bar running along the bottom of your screen. Click on that new button on the bar, and your window hops back onto the screen, ready for action.

The difference can be dramatic. Figure 7-4 shows a desktop with a bunch of open windows.

Figure 7-5 shows that same desktop after all windows but one have been turned into buttons along the taskbar. Those other windows are still readily available, mind you. Just click on a window's button from the taskbar along the bottom of the screen, and that window instantly leaps back to its former place on-screen.

✔ To shrink an open window so that it's out of the way, click on the leftmost of the three buttons in the window's top-right corner. The window *minimizes* itself into a button and lines itself up on the bar along the bottom of the screen.

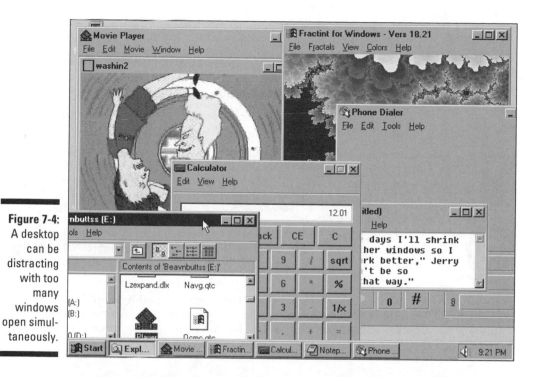

Figure 7-4:
A desktop can be distracting with too many windows open simultaneously.

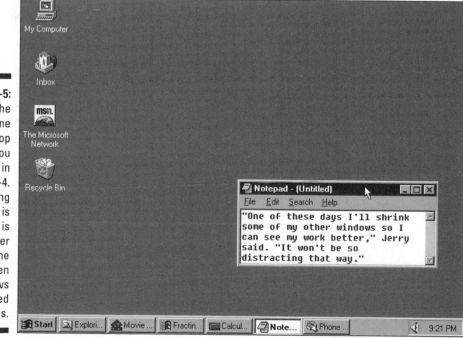

Figure 7-5:
Here's the same desktop that you saw in Figure 7-4. Seeing what is going on is easier when the open windows are turned into icons.

- ✔ The buttons on the taskbar all have a label so that you can tell which program each button represents.

- ✔ When you minimize a window, you neither destroy its contents nor close it. You merely change its shape. It is still loaded into memory, waiting for you to play with it again.

- ✔ To put the window back where it was, click on its button on the taskbar. It hops back up to the same place it was before.

- ✔ Whenever you load a program by using the Start button or Explorer, that program's name automatically appears on the taskbar. If one of your open windows ever gets lost on your desktop, click on its name on the taskbar. The window immediately jumps to the forefront.

- ✔ Do you want to shrink all your open windows into buttons, and in a hurry? Click on a blank area of your taskbar with your right mouse button and choose <u>M</u>inimize All Windows from the menu that pops up. Slurp. Windows 95 sucks all the open windows off the screen, tidying things up quickly.

- ✔ Keyboard users can press Alt, the spacebar, and N to minimize a window. Holding down Alt and pressing the Tab key restores the window to its former glory. (That fun little tip gets its own section, titled "The Alt+Tab trick," later in this chapter.)

Turning Taskbar Buttons into Windows

To turn a minimized window at the bottom of the screen back into a useful program in the middle of the screen, just click on its name on the taskbar. Pretty simple, huh?

- ✔ If you prefer wading through menus, just click on the shrunken window's button with your *right* mouse button. A Control menu shoots out the top of its head. Click on the menu's <u>R</u>estore option, and the program leaps back to its former window position.

- ✔ In addition to using a click, you can use a few other methods to turn icons back into program windows. The very next section describes one way, and "The Way-Cool Taskbar" section later in this chapter describes another.

Keeping your icons straight

Don't be confused by a program's icon on your desktop and a program's button on the taskbar along the bottom of your screen. They're two different things. The button at the bottom of the screen stands for a program that has already been loaded into the computer's memory. It's ready for immediate action. The icon on your desktop or in Windows 95 Explorer stands for a program that is sitting on the computer's hard disk waiting to be loaded.

If you mistakenly click on the icon in the Windows Explorer or desktop rather than the button on the taskbar at the bottom of the screen, you load a *second* copy of that program. Two versions of the program are loaded: one running as a window and the other running as a taskbar button waiting to be turned back into a window.

Running two versions can cause confusion — especially if you start entering stuff into both versions of the same program. You won't know which window has the *right* version!

Switching from Window to Window

Sometimes switching from window to window is easy. If you can see any part of the window you want — a corner, a bar, or a piece of dust — just click on it. That's all it takes to bring that window to the front of the screen, ready for action.

You can also just click on that window's button on the taskbar along the bottom of your screen. The following sections give a few extra tricks for switching from window to window to window.

The Alt+Tab trick

This trick is so much fun that Microsoft should have plastered it across the front of the Windows 95 box instead of hiding it in the middle of the manual.

Hold down Alt and press Tab. A most welcome box pops up in the center of the screen, naming the last program you've touched (see Figure 7-6).

Figure 7-6:
When you
hold down
Alt and
press Tab,
Windows 95
displays the
name of
the last
program
you used.

If the program you're after is named, rejoice! And remove your finger from the Alt key. The window named in that box leaps to the screen.

If you're looking for a *different* program, keep your finger on the Alt key and press Tab once again. At each press of Tab, Windows 95 displays the name of another open program. When you see the one you want, release the Alt key, and then hoot and holler. The program leaps to the screen, ready for your working pleasure.

✔ The Alt+Tab trick works even if you're running a DOS program with Windows 95 lurking in the background. The DOS program disappears while the pop-up box has its moment in the sun. (And the DOS program returns when you're done playing around, too.)

✔ The Alt+Tab trick cycles through all the currently open programs, whether the programs are in on-screen windows or living their lives as buttons on the taskbar. When you release the Alt key, the program currently listed in the pop-up window leaps to life.

✔ The first time you press Tab, the little pop-up window lists the name of the program you last accessed. If you prefer to cycle through the program names in the opposite direction, hold down Shift *and* Alt while pressing Tab. If you agree that this is a pretty frivolous option, rub your stomach and pat your head at the same time.

The Alt+Esc trick

The concept is getting kind of stale with this one, but here goes: If you hold down Alt and press Esc, Windows 95 cycles through all the open programs but in a slightly less efficient way.

Instead of bringing its name to a big box in the middle of the screen, Windows 95 simply highlights the program, whether it's in a window or sitting as a button on the taskbar. Sometimes this method can be handy, but usually it's a little slower.

If Windows 95 is currently cycling through a program on the taskbar, the Alt+Esc trick simply highlights the button at the bottom of the screen. That's not much of a visual indicator, and most of the time it won't even catch your eye.

When you see the window you want, release the Alt key. If it's an open window, it becomes the active window. But if you release the Alt key while a button's name is highlighted, you need to take one more step: You need to click on the button to get the window on-screen.

The Alt+Esc trick is a little slower and a little less handy than the Alt+Tab trick described in the preceding section.

The Way-Cool Taskbar

This section introduces one of the handiest tricks in Windows 95, so pull your chair in a little closer. Windows 95 comes with a special program that keeps track of all the open programs. Called the *taskbar,* it always knows what programs are running and where they are. Shown in Figure 7-7, the taskbar normally lives along the bottom of your screen, although Chapter 11 shows how to move it to any edge you want. (***Hint:*** Just "drag" it there.)

From the taskbar, you can perform powerful magic on your open windows, as shown in the next few sections.

Figure 7-7:
Always handy, the taskbar lists your currently running programs and lets you bring them to the forefront by clicking on their names.

| Start | FreeCell Game #25958 | Calculator | Hydrator Inspection - Word... | 11:49 AM |

✔ See how the button for Calculator looks "pushed in" in Figure 7-7? That's because Calculator is the currently active window on the desktop. One of your taskbar's buttons always looks "pushed in" unless you close or minimize all the windows on your desktop.

✔ Don't see the taskbar? Then hold down Ctrl and press Esc. Windows 95 instantly brings the taskbar and Start menu to the surface, ready to do your bidding. If the taskbar merely lurks along the edge, grab the visible part with your mouse and drag it toward the center of the screen until the entire taskbar is visible.

Switching to another window

See a window you want to play with listed on the taskbar? Just click on its name, and it rises to the surface. Simple. (Especially if you've ever labored under earlier versions of Windows.) If the taskbar isn't showing for some reason, pressing Ctrl+Esc calls it to the forefront.

Ending a task

Mad at a program? Then kill it. Click on the program's name on the taskbar with your *right* mouse button and then click on the word Close from the menu that pops up (or press C). The highlighted program quits, just as if you'd chosen its Exit command from within its own window.

The departing program gives you a chance to save any work before it quits and disappears from the screen.

Cascading and tiling windows

Sometimes those windows are scattered *everywhere*. How can you clean up in a hurry? By using the Cascade and Tile commands. Click on a blank spot on the taskbar with the *right* mouse button — the spot on or near the clock is usually good — and the cascade and tile commands appear.

The two commands organize your open windows in drastically different ways. Figure 7-8 shows what your screen looks like when you choose the Cascade command.

Talk about neat and orderly! The taskbar grabs all the windows and deals them out like cards across the desktop. When you choose the taskbar's Cascade command, all the open windows are lined up neatly on-screen with their title bars showing.

Figure 7-8:
The
taskbar's
Cascade
command
piles all the
open
windows
neatly
across the
screen. It's
a favorite
command
of blackjack
players.

The Tile Horizontally and Tile Vertically commands rearrange the windows, too, but in a slightly different way (see Figure 7-9).

The tile commands arrange all the currently open windows across the screen, giving each one the same amount of space. This arrangement helps you find a window that has been missing for a few hours.

Note: Both the tile and cascade commands arrange only open windows. They don't open up any windows currently shrunken into buttons on the taskbar.

If you have only two open windows, the tile commands arrange them side by side, making it easy for you to compare their contents. The Tile Vertically command places them side by side *vertically,* which makes them useless for comparing text: You can only see the first few words of each sentence. Choose the Tile Horizontally command if you want to see complete sentences.

Arranging icons on the desktop

The taskbar can be considered a housekeeper of sorts, but it *only* does windows. It arranges the open windows neatly across the screen, but it doesn't touch any icons living on your desktop.

Figure 7-9:
The
taskbar's
title
commands
organize
the open
windows
like tiles on
the shower
floor. You
can see
them all, but
they're too
small to be
of much
use.

If the open windows look fine but the desktop's icons look a little shabby, click on a blank area of your desktop with your right mouse button. When the menu pops up from nowhere, click the Arrange Icons command and choose the way you want Windows 95 to line up your icons: by Name, Type, Size, or Date.

Or, simply choose the Auto Arrange option from the same menu. Then your desktop's icons always stay in neat, orderly rows.

The taskbar is an easily accessible helper. Take advantage of it often when you're having difficulty finding windows or when you want to clean up the desktop so that you can find things.

Finding the taskbar

Is the taskbar not along the bottom of your screen? Hold down Ctrl and press Esc, and the taskbar instantly appears. If you'd prefer that the taskbar not disappear sometimes, head for Chapter 11. It explains how to customize your taskbar so that it doesn't bail on you.

Chapter 8

I Can't Find It!

Sooner or later, Windows 95 gives you that head-scratching feeling. "Golly," you say, as you frantically tug on your mouse cord, "that window was *right there* a second ago. Where did it go?"

When Windows 95 starts playing hide-and-seek with your programs, files, windows, or other information, this chapter tells you where to search and how to make it stop playing foolish games. Then when you find your Solitaire window, you can get back to work.

Plucking a Lost Window from the Taskbar

Forget about that huge, 1940s roll-top mahogany desk in the resale shop window. The Windows 95 peewee desktop can't be any bigger than the size of your monitor.

In a way, Windows 95 works more like those spike memo holders than like an actual desktop. Every time you open a new window, you're tossing another piece of information onto the spike. The window on top is relatively easy to see, but what's lying directly underneath it?

If you can see a window's ragged edge protruding from any part of the pile, click on it. The window magically rushes to the top of the pile. But what if you can't see *any* part of the window at all? How do you know it's even on the desktop?

You can solve this mystery by calling up your helpful Windows 95 detective: the taskbar. The taskbar keeps a master list of everything that's happening on your screen (even the invisible stuff).

If the taskbar isn't squatting along one edge of your screen, just hold down your Ctrl key and press Esc. The taskbar pops into action (see Figure 8-1).

Figure 8-1:
The mighty taskbar always contains an up-to-date list of all open windows.

See the list of programs stamped onto buttons on the taskbar? Your missing window is *somewhere* on the list. When you spot it, click on its name, and the taskbar instantly tosses your newfound window to the top of the pile.

✔ Most of the time, the taskbar performs admirably in tracking down lost windows. If your window isn't on the list, you've probably closed it. Closing a window, also known as *exiting* a window, takes it off your desktop and out of your computer's memory. To get that window back, you need to open it again, using the services of the Start button (see Chapter 11), the Windows Explorer (see Chapter 12), or the My Computer program (also in Chapter 12).

✔ I lied. Sometimes a window can be running and yet *not* be listed on the taskbar. Some utility programmers figure that people don't *need* to see their programs or their icons. Berkeley Systems' After Dark screen saver, for example, can be running on your screen and yet not show up on the taskbar. It simply runs in the background.

✔ Sometimes you see your missing program listed on the taskbar, and you click on its name to dredge it from the depths. But even though the taskbar brings the missing program to the top, you *still* can't find it on your desktop. The program may be hanging off the edge of your desktop, so check out the very next section.

Finding a Window That's off the Edge of the Screen

Even a window at the top of the pile can be nearly invisible. A window can be moved anywhere on the Windows 95 desktop, including off the screen. In fact, you can inadvertently move 99 percent of a window off the screen, leaving just a tiny corner showing (see Figure 8-2). Clicking on the window's name in the taskbar won't be much help in this case, unfortunately. The window's already on top, but it's still too far off the screen to be of any use.

✔ If you can see any part of the rogue window's *title bar,* that thick strip along its top, hold the mouse button down and *drag* the traveler back to the center of the screen.

✔ Sometimes a window's title bar can be completely off the screen. How can you drag it back into view? Start by clicking on any part of the window that shows. Then hold down your Alt key and press the spacebar. A menu appears from nowhere. Select the word Move, and a mysterious four-headed arrow appears. Press your arrow keys until the window's border moves to a more manageable location and then press Enter. Whew! Don't let it stray that far again!

Figure 8-2: Microsoft Word is almost completely off the bottom-right corner of the screen, making it difficult to locate.

> ✔ For an easier way to make Windows 95 not only track down all your criminally hidden windows but also line them up on the screen in *mug shot* fashion, check out the next two sections.

Cascading Windows (The "Deal All the Windows in Front of Me" Approach)

Are you ready to turn Windows 95 into a personal card dealer who gathers up all your haphazardly tossed windows and deals them out neatly on the desktop in front of you?

Then turn the taskbar into a card dealer. Click on a blank area of your taskbar — near the clock is good — with your *right* mouse button, and a menu pops up. Click on the Cascade option, and the taskbar gathers all your open windows and deals them out in front of you, just like in a game of blackjack.

Each window's title bar is neatly exposed, ready to be grabbed and reprimanded with a quick click of the mouse.

> ✔ If the missing window doesn't appear in the stack of neatly dealt windows, perhaps it has been minimized. The Cascade command gathers and deals only the open windows; it leaves the minimized windows resting as buttons along the taskbar. The solution? Click on the missing window's button on the taskbar *before* cascading the windows across the screen.
>
> ✔ For more about the Cascade command, check out Chapter 7.

Tiling Windows (The "Stick Everything on the Screen at Once" Approach)

Windows 95 can stick all your open windows onto the screen at the same time. You'll finally be able to see all of them — no overlapping corners, edges, or menu flaps. Sound too good to be true? It is. Windows 95 *shrinks* all the windows so that they fit on the screen. And some of the weird-shaped windows still overlap. But, hey, at least you can see most of them.

Click on a blank area of the taskbar with your right mouse button and choose Tile Vertically or Tile Horizontally from the pop-up menu.

✔ The Tile command pulls all the open windows onto the screen at the same time. If you have two open windows, each of them takes up half the screen. With three windows, each window gets a third of the screen. If you have 12 windows, each window takes up one-twelfth of the available space. (They're *very* small.)

✔ The Tile Vertically command arranges the windows vertically, like socks hanging from a clothesline. Tile Horizontally arranges the windows horizontally, like a stack of folded sweatshirts. The difference is the most pronounced when you're tiling only a few windows, however.

✔ You can find more information about the Tile command in Chapter 7. The minimize button is covered in Chapter 6.

DOS without Getting Lost

Windows 95 gets tricky when you start running DOS programs. Unlike Windows programs, hoggy DOS programs expect to have the entire computer to themselves. Windows 95 has to trick them into thinking everything is normal.

As part of one trick, Windows 95 enables you to run a DOS program so that it takes up the whole screen, just as if you weren't using Windows 95 at all. All you see on the screen is the DOS program. Windows 95 gives no clue that it is lurking somewhere in the background.

This trick makes the DOS program happier, but it can cause headaches for you. You can have a hard time remembering exactly what's happening. Are you running a DOS program under Windows? Did some nasty person boot up an old version of DOS on your computer? Sometimes, Windows 95 waits in the background while a DOS prompt sits on the screen with no program showing at all. With all these options, getting lost is easy.

✔ If you think that you may be lost at the DOS prompt, type the following command and then press Enter:

```
C:\> EXIT
```

That is, type **exit** and then press Enter. If Windows 95 is waiting in the background, it lurches back to life, banishing the DOS prompt in the process. If you want to return to the DOS prompt for some bizarre reason, click on the Start button and then click on MS-DOS Prompt from the Programs menu.

✔ If you're stuck in a DOS program and want to get back to another window, hold down Alt and press Esc. If Windows 95 is lurking in the background, it leaps back to the screen, turning your DOS program into a button along the taskbar. Then, because you're back to Windows 95, you can grab the window you *really* want.

✔ For more soothing salves to treat DOS-program confusion, check out Chapter 14.

Finding Lost Files, Folders, or Computers (But Not Misplaced Laptops)

Windows 95 has gotten much better at finding lost files and folders. And it should; after all, it's the one who's hiding the darn things. When one of your files, folders, or programs (or computers, if you're on a network) disappears into the depths of your computer, make Windows 95 do the work in getting the darn thing back.

Click on the Start button, click on the Find option, and choose either On The Microsoft Network or Files or Folders from the pop-up menu, shown in Figure 8-3.

Figure 8-3: Windows 95 can search your computer for lost files, folders, and, if you're on a network, lost computers.

An incredibly detailed program pops up, letting you search for files meeting the most minute criteria. Best yet, it can simply search for missing files by their names. For example, suppose that your file called HYDRATOR INSPEC-TION disappeared over the weekend. To make matters worse, you're not even sure you spelled *Hydrator* correctly when saving the file.

What's the solution? Type in any part of the filename you can remember. In this case, type **drat** into the Named box, and click on the Find Now button. The Find program lists any file or folder with a name that contains *drat,* as shown in Figure 8-4 — quick and simple.

Figure 8-4:
Here, the Windows 95 Find program sniffed out a file with *drat* as part of its name.

✔ Of course, you don't *have* to keep things quick and simple. For example, the Find program normally searches drive C — your computer's hard drive. If you'd prefer that it search every nook and cranny — all your hard drives and even any floppy disks or CD-ROM drives —click on the little downward-pointing arrow near the Look in box. When a menu drops down, click on the My Computer setting. That tells the Find program to look *everywhere* on your computer.

✔ Make sure that a check mark appears in the Include subfolders box, shown in Figure 8-4. If that option's not checked, the Find program searches through only your first layer of folders — it doesn't look inside any folders living inside of other folders.

✔ Can't remember what you called a file but know the time and date you created it? Click on the Date Modified tab along the program's top. That step lets you narrow down the search to files created only during certain times. (It's especially handy for finding files you know you created yesterday.)

✔ For a quick peek inside some of the files the Find program turned up, click on the file's name with your right mouse button and choose Quick View from the menu that pops up. Windows 95 shows you the file's contents *without* making you load the program that created the file.

> ✔ The Advanced option lets people search for specific types of files: Bitmap files, Faxes, Configuration settings, and other more complicated options. To be on the safe side, leave the option set for All Files and Folders, so you know that the Find command is searching through *everything*.

> ✔ If you're searching for a computer on a network, click on the Start button and choose Computer from the Find menu. Type two backslashes followed by the computer's name, and Windows 95 ferrets out that computer on the network. For example, you'd type **\\yachtclub** to find the computer named YachtClub. After the program lists the computer, double-click on its icon to begin browsing its files.

Finding Snippets of Stored Information

Help! You remember how much Mr. Jennings *loved* that wine during lunch, so you stealthily typed the wine's name into your computer. Now, at Christmas time, you don't remember the name of the file where you saved the wine's name. You don't remember the date you created the file, either, or even the folder where you stashed the file. In fact, the only thing you remember is how you described the wine's bouquet when typing it into your computer: "Like an alligator snap from behind a barge."

Luckily, that description is all Windows 95 needs in order to find your file. Click on the Start button and choose Files or Folders from the Find menu, shown in Figure 8-3. After the Find program pops up, click on the tab marked Advanced, click in the box marked Containing text, and type **barge**, as shown in Figure 8-5.

Figure 8-5:
The Windows 95 Find program searches the entire computer for a file containing the word barge.

![Screenshot of the Find: Files containing text barge window. Menu bar shows File, Edit, View, Options, Help. Tabs: Name & Location, Date Modified, Advanced (selected). Of type: All Files and Folders. Containing text: barge. Size is: KB. Buttons: Find Now, Stop, New Search. Columns: Name, In Folder, Size, Type, Mo... Status bar: Searching C:\WINDOWS]

Just like in the preceding section, the Find program searches the computer, looking for files meeting your specifications. This time, however, it searches inside the files themselves, looking for the information you're after.

- ✔ Feel free to limit your search, using any of the tips and examples discussed in the preceding section; they apply here as well.

- ✔ CD-ROM discs take a *long* time to search. You can speed things up by telling the Find program to limit its search to hard disks. (Just popping the CD out of the drive is one way to keep the Find program from searching it.)

- ✔ When searching for files containing certain words, type in the words *least* likely to turn up in other files. For example, the word *barge* is more unique than *like, an, snap,* or *behind;* therefore, it's more likely to bring up the file you're searching for. And if *barge* doesn't work, try *alligator.*

Peeking into Icons with Quick View

When you open a *real* manila folder, it's easy to separate the food coupons from the letters to a congressperson; the pieces of paper look completely different. But although Windows 95 sticks titles beneath all the icons in its folders, the icons often look like one big blur, as shown in Figure 8-6. Which icon stands for what? And where is that letter to the congressperson, anyway?

Figure 8-6:
Even with their labels, the icons in Windows 95 are sometimes hard to tell apart from each other.

[Screenshot: Boring College Term Papers window with File, Edit, View, Help menus. Icons labeled: Bicamerl, Kafbor, Kafbosch, Kafka1, Mindbody, Skiing. Status bar reads "6 object(s)" and "1.43MB".]

You can double-click on an icon to see what file it stands for — a double-click tells Windows 95 to load the file into the program that created it and bring them both to the screen. But there's a faster way to get a sneak peek of what's inside many Windows 95 icons. Here's how the Quick View feature works:

1. While pointing at an icon, click your right mouse button.

A menu pops up, as shown in Figure 8-7. If Windows 95 recognizes the type of file, you see the Quick View option on the menu.

Figure 8-7: Click on an icon with your right mouse button to see if Windows 95 offers the Quick View option.

2. Choose Quick View from the menu.

The Quick View option shows you what's inside the file without taking the time to load the program that created it. The option is a quick way to sort through files with similar-looking icons.

- Windows 95 lets you use up to 255 characters when naming files. When you first install Windows 95, however, all your old files still have their eight-character filenames. By using Quick View, you can peek into your old files and give them better names. First, peek into the file to see what's in there. When you've decided on a longer, more descriptive name, choose the Rename command. (It's on the same menu as the Quick View command.)

- The Quick View command works with a few dozen of the most popular formats, including Lotus 1-2-3, Bitmap, WordPad, Microsoft Word for Windows, and WordPerfect. A company called Inso Corporation (800-333-1395 or 312-329-0700) sells a special "add-on" Quick View utility that enables you to peek inside more than 100 types of files. (Can't find the Quick View option? Add it by double-clicking the Control Panel's Add/Remove Programs option.)

- Once you've found the file you're after, you can open it easily from within Quick View: Click on the little icon in the upper-left corner — the icon beneath the word File. Quick View immediately opens the file for editing.

Chapter 9

That "Cut and Paste" Stuff (Moving Around Words, Pictures, and Sounds)

*U*ntil Windows came along, IBM-compatible computers had a terrible time sharing anything. Their programs were rigid, egotistical things, with no sense of community. Information created by one program couldn't always be shared with another program. Older versions of programs passed down this selfish system to newer versions, enforcing the segregation with *proprietary file formats* and *compatibility tests*.

To counter this bad trip, the Windows programmers created a communal workplace where all the programs could groove together peacefully. In the harmonious tribal village of Windows, programs share their information openly in order to make a more beautiful environment for all.

In the Windows co-op, all the windows can beam their vibes to each other freely, without fear of rejection. Work created by one Windows program is accepted totally and lovingly by any other Windows program. Windows programs treat each other equally, even if one program is wearing some pretty freaky threads or, in some gatherings, *no threads at all*.

This chapter shows you how easily you can move those good vibes from one window to another.

Examining the Cut and Paste Concept (And Copy, Too)

Windows 95 took a tip from the kindergartners and made *cut and paste* an integral part of all its programs. Information can be electronically *cut* from one window and *pasted* into another window with little fuss and even less mess.

Just about any part of a window is up for grabs. You can highlight an exceptionally well-written paragraph in your word processor, for example, or a spreadsheet chart that tracks the value of your Indian-head pennies. After *highlighting* the desired information, you press a button to *copy* or *cut* it from its window.

At the press of the button, the information heads for a special place in Windows 95 called the *Clipboard.* From there you can paste it into any other open window.

The beauty of Windows 95 is that with all those windows on-screen at the same time, you can easily grab bits and pieces from any of them and paste all the parts into a new window.

✔ Unlike DOS programs, Windows programs are designed to work together, so taking information from one window and putting it into another window is easy. Sticking a map onto your party fliers, for example, is *really* easy.

✔ Cutting and pasting works well for the big stuff, like sticking big charts into memos. But don't overlook it for the small stuff, too. For example, copying someone's name and address from your address book program is quicker than typing it by hand at the top of your letter. Or, to avoid typographical errors, you can copy an answer from the Windows 95 Calculator and paste it into another program.

✔ Cutting and pasting is different from that new *Object Linking and Embedding* stuff you may have heard people raving about. That more powerful (and, naturally, more confusing) *OLE* stuff gets its own section later in this chapter.

✔ When you cut or copy some information, it immediately appears in a special Windows program called the *Clipboard Viewer.* From the Clipboard, it can be pasted into other windows. The Clipboard has its own bag of tricks, so it gets its own section later in this chapter.

✔ Although the Clipboard Viewer comes installed with Windows 3.1, Microsoft doesn't automatically install the Clipboard Viewer program with Windows 95. That means you need to head for the Control Panel's Add/Remove Programs icon and tell Windows 95 to copy the Clipboard Viewer to your hard drive, a process described in Chapter 10. (If you installed Windows 95 over Windows 3.1, your faithful old Clipboard Viewer is still on your hard drive.)

Highlighting the Important Stuff

Before you can grab information from a window, you have to tell the window exactly what parts you want to grab. The easiest way to tell it is to *highlight* the information with a mouse.

You can highlight a single letter, an entire novel, or anything in between. You can highlight pictures of water lilies. You can even highlight sounds so that you can paste belches into other files (see the OLE section later in this chapter).

In most cases, highlighting involves one swift trick with the mouse: Put the mouse arrow or cursor at the beginning of the information you want and hold down the mouse button. Then move the mouse to the end of the information and release the button. That's it! All the stuff lying between your mouse moves is highlighted. The information usually turns a different color so that you can see what you've grabbed. An example of highlighted text is shown in Figure 9-1.

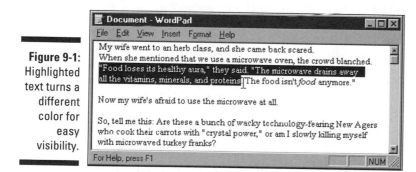

Figure 9-1:
Highlighted text turns a different color for easy visibility.

If you're mouseless, use the arrow keys to put the cursor at the beginning of the stuff you want to grab. Then hold down Shift and press the arrow keys until the cursor is at the end of what you want to grab. You see the stuff on-screen become highlighted as you move the arrow keys. This trick works with almost every Windows 95 program. (If you're after text, hold down Ctrl, too, and the text is highlighted word by word.)

Some programs have a few shortcuts for highlighting parts of their information:

- To highlight a single *word* in Notepad, WordPad, or most text boxes, point at it with the mouse and double-click. The word turns black, meaning that it's highlighted. (In WordPad, you can hold down the button on its second click, and then, by moving the mouse around, you can quickly highlight additional text word by word.)

- To highlight a single *line* in WordPad, click next to it in the left margin. Keep holding down the mouse button and move the mouse up or down to highlight additional text line by line.

- To highlight a *paragraph* in WordPad, double-click next to it in the left margin. Keep holding down the mouse button on the second click and move the mouse to highlight additional text paragraph by paragraph.

- To highlight an entire *document* in WordPad, hold down Ctrl and click anywhere in the left margin. (To highlight the entire document in Notepad, press and release Alt and then press E and then A. So much for consistency between Windows 95 programs.)

- To highlight a portion of text in just about any Windows 95 program, click at the text's beginning, hold down Shift, and click at the end of the desired text. Everything between those two points becomes highlighted.

- To highlight part of a picture or drawing while in Paint, click on the little tool button with the dotted lines in a square. (The button is called the Select tool, as Windows 95 informs you if you rest your mouse pointer over the tool for a second.) After clicking on the Select tool, hold down the mouse button and slide the mouse over the desired part of the picture.

After you've highlighted text, you must either cut it or copy it *immediately.* If you do anything else, like absentmindedly click the mouse someplace else in your document, all your highlighted text reverts to normal, just like Cinderella after midnight.

Be careful after you highlight a bunch of text. If you press any key — the spacebar, for example — Windows 95 immediately replaces your highlighted text with the character that you type — in this case, a space. To reverse that calamity and bring your highlighted text back to life, hold down Alt and press the Backspace key.

DOS windows have their own methods of highlighting information. Check out the section "Using Copy and Paste with a DOS Program," later in this chapter, for the real dirt.

Deleting, Cutting, or Copying What You Highlighted

After you've highlighted some information (which is described in the preceding section, in case you just entered the classroom), you're ready to start playing with it. You can delete it, cut it, or copy it. All three options differ drastically.

Deleting the information

Deleting the information just wipes it out. Zap! It just disappears from the window. To delete highlighted information, just press the Delete or Backspace key.

- ✔ If you've accidentally deleted the wrong thing, panic. Then hold down Ctrl and press the letter Z. Your deletion is graciously undone. Any deleted information pops back up on-screen. Whew!

- ✔ Holding down Alt and pressing Backspace also undoes your last mistake. (Unless you've just said something dumb at a party. Then use Ctrl+Z.)

Cutting the information

Cutting the highlighted information wipes it off the screen, just as the Delete command does, but with a big difference: When the information is removed from the window, it is copied to a special Windows 95 storage tank called the *Clipboard*.

When you're looking at the screen, cutting and deleting look identical. In fact, the first few times you try to cut something, you feel panicky, thinking that you may have accidentally deleted it instead. (This feeling never really goes away, either.)

To cut highlighted stuff, hold down Shift and press Delete. Whoosh! The highlighted text disappears from the window, scoots through the underground tubes of Windows 95, and waits on the Clipboard for further action.

- ✔ One way to tell whether your Cut command actually worked is to paste the information back into your document. If it appears, you know that the command worked, and you can cut it out again right away. If it doesn't appear, you know that something has gone dreadfully wrong. (For the Paste command, discussed a little later, hold down Shift and press Insert, that 0 on the numeric keypad.)

✔ Microsoft's lawyers kicked butt in the Apple lawsuit, so Windows 95 uses the same cut keys as the Macintosh. You can hold down Ctrl and press the letter *X* to cut. (Get it? That's an *X*, as in *you're crossing,* or *X-ing, something out.*)

Copying the information

Compared with cutting or deleting, *copying* information is quite anticlimactic. When you cut or delete, the information disappears from the screen. But, when you copy information to the Clipboard, the highlighted information just sits there in the window. In fact, it looks as if nothing has happened, so you repeat the Copy command a few times before giving up and just hoping it worked.

To copy highlighted information, hold down Ctrl and press Insert (the 0 on the numeric keypad or Ins on some keyboards). Although nothing seems to happen, that information really does head for the Clipboard.

✔ Windows 95 uses the same Copy keys as the Macintosh does. If you don't like the Ctrl+Insert combination, you can hold down Ctrl and press C to copy. That combination is a little easier to remember, actually, because C is the first letter of *copy*.

✔ To copy an image of your entire Windows 95 desktop (the *whole screen*) to the Clipboard, press the Print Screen key, which is sometimes labeled PrtSc or something similar. (Some older keyboards make you hold down Shift simultaneously.) A snapshot of your screen heads for the Clipboard, ready to be pasted someplace else. Computer nerds call this snapshot a *screen shot.* All the pictures of windows in this book are screen shots. (And, no, the information doesn't also head for your printer.)

✔ To copy an image of your currently active window (just one window — nothing surrounding it), hold down Alt while you press Print Screen. The window's picture appears on the Clipboard. (You usually don't have to hold down Shift with this one, even for wacky keyboards. But if Alt+Print Screen doesn't work, hey, try holding down Shift anyway.)

Finding out more about cutting, copying, and deleting

Want to know more about cutting, copying, and deleting? Read on (you really should read this stuff).

✔ Windows 95 often puts *toolbars* across the tops of its programs. Figure 9-2 shows the toolbar buttons that stand for cutting, copying, and pasting things.

Figure 9-2:
From left to right, clicking on these toolbar buttons cuts, copies, or pastes.

Paste

Cut

Copy

✔ The cut, copy, and paste process works differently in DOS windows. See "Using Copy and Paste with a DOS Program" in this chapter for a dose of DOS details.

✔ If you prefer to use menus, the Cut, Copy, and Paste commands tumble down when you select the word Edit on any menu bar.

✔ When you're using the Print Screen key trick to copy a window or the entire screen to the Clipboard (see the preceding section), one important component is left out: The mouse arrow is *not* included in the picture, even if it was in plain sight when you took the picture. (Are you asking yourself how all the little arrows got in this book's pictures? Well, I drew most of 'em in by hand!)

✔ Sometimes figuring out whether the Cut or Copy commands are really working is difficult. To know for sure, keep the Windows Clipboard Viewer showing at the bottom of the screen. Then you can watch the images appear on it when you press the buttons. (The Clipboard Viewer is listed on the Start menu under Accessories, which is listed in the Programs section. Not listed? Head for Chapter 10; you must tell Windows 95 to install the Clipboard Viewer program.)

✔ Don't keep screen shots or large graphics on the Clipboard any longer than necessary. They consume a lot of memory that your other programs could be using. To clear off any memory-hogging detritus, copy a single word to the Clipboard or call up the Clipboard Viewer and press Delete.

Pasting Information into Another Window

After you've cut or copied information to the special Windows 95 Clipboard storage tank, it's ready for travel. You can *paste* that information into just about any other window.

Pasting is relatively straightforward compared with highlighting, copying, or cutting: Click the mouse anywhere in the destination window and click in the spot where you want the stuff to appear. Then hold down Shift and press Insert (the 0 key on the numeric keypad). Presto! Anything that's sitting on the Clipboard immediately leaps into that window.

- ✔ Another way to paste stuff is to hold down Ctrl and press V. That combination does the same thing as Shift+Insert. (It also is the command those funny-looking Macintosh computers use to paste stuff.)

- ✔ You can also choose the Paste command from a window's menu bar. Select the word Edit and then select the word <u>P</u>aste. But don't select the words Paste <u>S</u>pecial. That command is for the Object Linking and Embedding stuff, which gets its own section later in this chapter.

- ✔ Some programs have toolbars along their top. Clicking on the Paste button, shown in Figure 9-2, pastes the Clipboard's current contents into your document.

- ✔ The Paste command inserts a *copy* of the information that's sitting on the Clipboard. The information stays on the Clipboard, so you can keep pasting it into other windows if you want. In fact, the Clipboard's contents stay the same until a new Cut or Copy command replaces them with new information.

Using Copy and Paste with a DOS Program

DOS programs all behave a little strangely under Windows 95. Likewise, the Copy and Paste commands work a little differently. DOS gets kind of complicated, so you should really think about ditching your DOS programs and switching to Windows programs if you're serious about copying and pasting.

You must remember certain rules when you use the Copy and Paste commands with DOS programs:

Rule 1: You can't cut text or anything else from a DOS program in Windows 95. You can only *copy* stuff. The original information always remains in your DOS program.

Rule 2: You can't paste anything but text into most DOS programs.

Rule 3: You can't paste text into a DOS program when it's running in *full-screen mode,* meaning that it's taking up the entire screen.

Rule 4: Before you copy information from a DOS program, you need to decide whether you want to copy a *picture* from the DOS window or copy *text* — actual words. You can't copy a picture out of a DOS program unless the DOS program is running in a window. The upcoming two sections explain the procedures for copying pictures and text from a DOS program.

Rule 5: Copying and pasting from DOS programs is decidedly complicated and tedious, as evidenced by Rules 1 through 4.

Copying a picture from a DOS program

To copy a picture from a DOS program, run the program in its own window on-screen. Then hold down Alt while pressing Print Screen.

The Alt+Print Screen trick copies a *graphic image* of the DOS window to the Windows 95 Clipboard. From there you can paste the picture into the Windows 95 graphics program, Paint, and clean it up a little before copying it to its final destination.

✔ This method gives you a snapshot of the DOS program that is running in the window. It is surrounded by typical window dressing, like menu bars, title bars, scroll bars, and the like. You can erase these extraneous elements in Paint to make the picture look better.

✔ If you use this trick to copy a DOS program that's showing only text, you get just a *picture* of that text. You can't copy the text into a word processor or arrange it into paragraphs. It's just a picture, like a Polaroid snapshot of an open book.

Copying text from a DOS program

If the DOS program is running full-screen, press Print Screen. (Some keyboards make you hold down Shift simultaneously.) Even though Windows 95 is running invisibly in the background, it dredges all the text showing in the DOS program and copies it onto the Clipboard. (Not to the printer, though. Print Screen doesn't do that in Windows 95.)

If the DOS program is running in a *window* on-screen, here's how to grab that text using a mouse:

1. **Click on the DOS program's Mark button — the button with a little square made of dotted lines along the window's top.**

A tiny flashing square appears in the upper-left corner of the screen, as barely visible in Figure 9-3.

Figure 9-3:
Click on the Mark button, and a tiny flashing square appears in the window's upper-left corner.

2. **Hold down the mouse button when you're at the beginning of what you want to grab, move the mouse to the end of the text, and then release the mouse button.**

   Your screen looks similar to the one shown in Figure 9-4.

Figure 9-4:
As you slide the mouse over the text, it changes color.

3. **When the information you're after changes color, press Enter.**

   Wham! Windows 95 copies that highlighted text to the Clipboard.

   ✔ When you grab text from a DOS application in a window, you can grab it only in square- or rectangular-shaped chunks. That limitation is not as bad as it seems, though, because Windows 95 tosses out any extraneous spaces at the ends of lines.

✔ You can't retain any of the special formatting the DOS text may have had, such as boldface or underline. Any adjacent graphics are also left out. In addition, if the text itself is in graphics form, like fancy letters or something, you can't grab it as text.

✔ This *Select mode* stuff can be confusing: Your DOS application is frozen on-screen and doesn't respond. It's frozen because you're picking chunks out of it. And you can tell that you're picking chunks out of it by looking at the title bar: The word *Select* is in front of the program's name.

✔ If you change your mind and don't want to grab information out of there, press Esc, and everything goes back to normal—as normal as a computer can be, anyway.

✔ Trying to do all this with a keyboard instead of a mouse? Then you'll have to do all of this: Press Alt+Spacebar, and choose Mar<u>k</u> from the <u>E</u>dit menu. The DOS window goes into Select mode. Tap the arrow keys until the cursor rests at the beginning of the text you want to grab; then, while holding down Shift, press the arrow keys until the cursor rests at the end of the text you want to grab. When the text you're after is highlighted, press Enter. Whew! Windows 95 then copies it to the Clipboard.

Pasting text into a DOS program

Most DOS programs are text-based critters. You can't copy any graphics into most of them. You can dump some words into them, however, by doing this: With the program running in a window, move the cursor to the spot where you want the text to appear. Next, click on the little Paste icon from the DOS window's toolbar. (The Paste icon, shown in Figure 9-2, has a little Clipboard on it.)

Any text on the Clipboard is instantly poured into the DOS program, starting where you left the cursor sitting.

Note: You'll probably have to reformat the text after you pour it into the DOS program. The sentences usually break in all the wrong places. Plus you lose any special formatting, such as boldface or underline. Hey, that's what you get for still clinging to your stubborn old DOS programs!

Stuck with a DOS program that refuses to run in a window? Windows 95 can still paste some text into it. When the program is running full-screen, click where you want the text to appear. Then hold down Alt and press Esc. The DOS program turns into a button on the taskbar at the bottom of your screen. Click on the DOS program's button with your right mouse button and watch as its Control menu rises eerily from the top of its head. Click on the word <u>E</u>dit and then on the word <u>P</u>aste. Presto! The text on the Clipboard jumps into your DOS program, right where you left the cursor sitting.

Using the Clipboard Viewer

Windows 95 employs a special program to let you see all the stuff that's being slung around by cutting and copying. Called the *Clipboard Viewer* (sometimes called the ClipBook Viewer), it's merely a window that displays anything that has been cut or copied to the Clipboard.

To see the Clipboard Viewer, click on the Start button and click on Clipboard Viewer from the Accessories menu (which pops up when you rest the mouse pointer over the <u>P</u>rograms area). Inside the Clipboard Viewer, you see any information you've cut or copied recently. Figures 9-5, 9-6, and 9-7 show some examples.

Figure 9-5:
This Clipboard contains a recently copied picture of a chip.

Figure 9-6:
This Clipboard contains text recently copied from a DOS program.

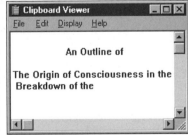

✔ Sometimes the Clipboard Viewer can't show you exactly what you've copied. For example, if you copy a sound from the Windows 95 Sound Recorder, you just see a picture of the Sound Recorder's icon. And, at the risk of getting metaphysical, what does a sound look like anyway?

✔ The Clipboard functions automatically and transparently. Unless you make a special effort, you don't even know it's there. (That's why the Clipboard Viewer is handy — it lets you see what the Clipboard is up to.)

Figure 9-7:
This
Clipboard
contains a
sound
copied
from the
Windows 95
Sound
Recorder.

The *Clipboard* is a special area inside memory where Windows 95 keeps track of information that's been cut or copied. The *Clipboard Viewer* is a program that lets you see the information that's currently on the Clipboard.

✔ To better track what's being cut and pasted, some people leave the Clipboard Viewer sitting open at the bottom of the screen. Then they can actually *see* what they've cut or copied.

✔ Most of the time, the Clipboard is used just for temporary operations — a quick cut here, a quick paste there, and then on to the next job. But the Clipboard Viewer lets you save the Clipboard's contents for later use. Choose File from the menu bar and then choose Save As from the pull-down menu. Type in a filename and click on the OK command button (or just press Enter).

Keeping the Clipboard clear

Whenever you cut or copy something, that information heads for the Clipboard. And it stays there, too, until you cut or copy something else to replace it. But while that information sits there on the Clipboard, it uses up memory.

Windows 95 needs all the memory it can get, or it begins running slowly or balking at opening more windows. Big chunks of text, pictures, and sounds can consume a lot of memory, so clear off the Clipboard when you're through cutting and pasting to return the memory for general Windows use.

To clear off the Clipboard quickly, just copy a single word to the Clipboard: Double-click on a word in a text file, hold down Ctrl, and press C.

Or, if the Clipboard Viewer is up on-screen, click on it to bring it to the forefront and then press Delete. You clear the Clipboard off, enabling Windows 95 to use the memory for more-pressing matters.

✔ The Clipboard can hold only one thing at a time. Each time you cut or copy something else, you replace the Clipboard's contents with something new. If you want to collect a bunch of *clips* for later pasting, use the Save <u>A</u>s option described in the preceding paragraph. The Clipboard also starts up empty each time you start Windows 95.

✔ No Clipboard Viewer on your Start menu? Windows 95 doesn't always install it automatically. Head for the Add/Remove Programs section in Chapter 10 for ways to add the Windows accessories that Windows 95 left out.

Looking at Funky Object Linking and Embedding Stuff

Because the concepts of cutting and pasting are so refreshingly simple, Microsoft complicated them considerably with something called *Object Linking and Embedding,* known as *OLE.* It sounds complicated, so I'll start with the simple part: the object.

The *object* is merely the information you want to paste into a window. It can be a sentence, a road map, a sneeze sound, or anything else that you can cut or copy from a window.

Normally, when you paste an object into a window, you're pasting the same kind of information. For example, you paste text into a word processor and pictures into the Windows 95 Paint program. But what if you want to paste a sound into WordPad, the Windows 95 word processor?

That's where Object Linking and Embedding comes in, offering subtle changes to the paste concept. You'll probably never use them, but they can be fun to fiddle around with on cloudy days. Beware, however: OLE awareness is the first step down those ever-spiraling stairs toward computer-nerd certification.

Embedding

On the surface, *embedding* an object looks just like pasting it. The object shows up in the window. Big deal. But, when you embed an object, you're also embedding the name of the program that created that object. When you double-click on the object, poof! The program that created it jumps to the top of the screen, ready to edit it.

For example, you can embed a spreadsheet chart showing your current net worth in a letter you're writing to an old high-school friend. Then if the stock market changes before you mail the letter, you can easily update the letter's chart. Just call up the letter in your word processor and double-click on the chart. The spreadsheet that created the chart pops up, ready for you to make the changes. After you're done, you close the spreadsheet. The spreadsheet disappears, leaving the updated chart in your letter.

Embedding is really pretty handy. You don't have to remember the chart's filename. You don't even have to call up your spreadsheet. Windows 95 does all that grunt work automatically. Just double-click on the chart, make the changes when your spreadsheet appears, and then quit the spreadsheet to return to the letter.

As with most things in Windows 95, the OLE concept is easier to use than its name implies.

Linking

Linking looks just like embedding or pasting. Your chart appears in your letter, just as before. But here's where things get weird: You're not really pasting the chart. You're pasting the chart's *filename*.

The word processor runs over to the file containing the chart, sees what the chart looks like, and then puts a copy of it in the letter.

What's the point? Well, unlike pasting or embedding, you're keeping only one copy of the chart around. When you call up the chart in your spreadsheet and change it, those changes are automatically reflected in your word processor the next time you load that letter. With only one *real* version of the object lying around, every copy is always the right version.

- ✔ Not all Windows 95 programs can handle Object Linking and Embedding. In fact, of the programs that come in the Windows 95 box, only WordPad and the obtuse Object Packager are really OLE savvy.

- ✔ *Dynamic Data Exchange* was an earlier method for sharing information between Windows-based programs. It never really worked all that well, and OLE pretty much replaces it. So don't bother trying to learn what it was or, actually, used to be.

- ✔ Object Linking and Embedding can get pretty complex, so the vast majority of Windows 95 users simply acknowledge that their computer can do that stuff and let the technicians play with it.

Should you paste, embed, or link your important objects? Here's what to do:

- ✔ Use *Paste* for objects you'll never want to change.

- ✔ *Embed* objects if you want to be able to edit them easily at a later date.

- ✔ Choose the *Link* option if you want several programs to share the same version of a single object.

Leaving Scraps on the Desktop Deliberately

The Clipboard is a handy way to copy information from one place to another, but it has a major limitation: Every time you copy something new to the Clipboard, it replaces what was copied there before. What if you want to copy a *bunch* of things from a document?

If you were cutting and pasting over a real desktop, you could leave little scraps lying everywhere, ready for later use. The same *scraps* concept works with Windows 95: You can move information from window to window, using the desktop as a temporary storage area for your scraps of information.

For example, suppose that you have some paragraphs in a WordPad document you want to copy to some other places. Highlight the first paragraph, drag it out of the WordPad window, and drop it onto the desktop. Poof! A small Scrap icon appears on your desktop. See another interesting paragraph? Drag it onto the desktop, as well: Another Scrap icon appears.

Eventually, you'll have copies of your report's best paragraphs sitting in little scraps on your desktop. To move any of the scraps into another document, just drag them into that other document's window and let go.

Any remaining, unused scraps can be dumped into the Recycling Bin, or simply left on the desktop, adding a nice, comfortable layer of clutter.

To make a scrap, highlight the information you want to move, usually by running the mouse pointer over it while holding down the mouse button. Then, point at the highlighted information and, while holding down the mouse button, point at the Desktop. Let go of the mouse button, and a scrap containing that information appears on the Desktop.

Note: Not all Windows 95 applications support Scraps. In fact, WordPad is the only program in the Windows 95 box that can use Scraps.

Controlling the Printer

Many of the Windows 95 features work in the background. You know that they're there *only* when something is wrong and weird messages start flying around. The Windows 95 print program is one of those programs.

When you choose the Print command in a program, you may see the little Windows 95 printer icon appear at the bottom corner of your screen. When your printer stops spitting out pages, the little printer icon disappears.

When everything is running smoothly, the printer icon looks like this in the corner of your taskbar:

◁ ◑ 10:35 PM

Your printer can print only one thing at a time. If you try to print a second memo before the first one is finished, Windows 95 jumps in to help. It intercepts all the requests and lines them up in order, just like a harried diner cook.

To check up on what is being sent to the printer, double-click on the taskbar's little printer icon and you see the print program in all its glory, as shown in Figure 9-8.

Figure 9-8:
See what files are about to be printed.

Document Name	Status	Owner	Progress	Started At
NETLOG - Notepad	Printing		11.6KB	10:51:23 PM 2/12/95
MAIL			91.2KB	10:51:31 PM 2/12/95
Egyptian Stone			15.0KB	10:51:42 PM 2/12/95

Mr. Printer
Printer Document View Help
3 jobs in queue

✔ When the printer is through with NETLOG, it moves to the second file in the lineup, which, in this case, is MAIL.

✔ Changing the order of the files as they're about to be printed is easy. For example, to scoot EGYPTIAN STONE ahead of MAIL, click on its name and hold down the mouse button. Then *drag* the file up so that it cuts in front of MAIL. Release the button, and the Print Manager changes the printing order. (The printing order is called a *queue,* pronounced *Q.*)

✔ To cancel a print job, click on the filename you don't like with your right mouse button and then choose Cancel Printing from the menu that pops up.

✔ If the boss is walking by the printer while you're printing your party flier, choose Document from the menu and select Pause Printing from the menu that drops down. The printer stops. After the boss is out of sight, click on Pause Printing again to continue.

✔ If you're on a network (shudder), you may not be able to change the order in which files are being printed. You may not even be able to pause a file.

✔ If your printer is not hooked up, Windows 95 will probably try to send your file to the printer anyway. When it doesn't get a response, it sends you a message that your printer isn't ready. Plug the printer in, turn it on, and try again. Or hit Chapter 18 for more printer troubleshooting tips.

Chapter 10

Customizing Windows 95 (Fiddling with the Control Panel)

• •

In This Chapter

▶ Exploring the Control Panel

▶ Customizing the display

▶ Changing colors

▶ Changing video modes

▶ Understanding TrueType fonts

▶ Making Windows 95 recognize your double-click

▶ Setting the computer's time and date

▶ Changing to a different printer

▶ Assigning cool multimedia sounds to your computer's tasks

▶ Installing new computer parts

▶ Installing or removing programs

▶ Avoiding dangerous icons

• •

*I*n a way, working with Windows 95 is like remodeling a bathroom. You can spend time on the practical things, like calculating the optimum dimensions for piping or choosing the proper brand of caulking to seal the sink and tub. Or you can spend your time on the more aesthetic options, like adding an oak toilet-paper holder, a marble countertop, or a rattan cover for the tissue box.

You can remodel Windows 95, too, and in just as many ways. On the eminently practical side, head for the Windows 95 Control Panel, call up the System icon, and spend laborious hours optimizing the cache sizes for your disk drives.

Or check out the Control Panel's more refined options: Change the color of the title bars to teal, for example, or cover the Windows 95 desktop with daisy patterns or pinstripe wallpaper.

This chapter shows you how to turn Windows 95 into that program you've always dreamed of owning someday. (Although you *still* can't have *bay* windows.)

Finding the Control Panel

The Control Panel is the cupboard that holds most of the Windows 95 switches. Flip open the Control Panel, and you can while away an entire workday adjusting all the various Windows 95 options.

To find it, click on the Start button, choose Settings, and click on Control Panel. The Control Panel window pops up, as shown in Figure 10-1. Each icon in the window represents a switch that controls part of the computer.

Figure 10-1:
Double-click on an icon in the Control Panel to reveal hidden switches controlling that particular area.

Everybody's Control Panel looks different because everybody can afford different computer toys. For example, some modem hounds have special icons that control the way their modems collect mail from all their electronic mailboxes. Others have icons that help them agonize over settings for their networks or sound cards. Table 10-1 takes a quick look at some of the icons you may come across in your copy of Windows 95.

Each of these options is discussed in more glowing detail later in this chapter.

For a quick way to access your Control Panel, double-click on the My Computer icon on the corner of your desktop. You can find a Control Panel folder inside, waiting to be opened with a double-click.

Table 10-1	Deciphering the Control Panel Icons
This Icon	*Does This*
Accessibility Options	Windows 95 can be customized to work more easily for people with physical limitations. The screen can be made more readable, for example, or the numeric keypad can be converted into a makeshift mouse (which is also handy for laptop users).
Add New Hardware	Installed that new (insert name of expensive computer gadget here)? Head for this area to summon the Hardware Installation Wizard. The Wizard handles the messy chores of introducing Windows 95 to new computer parts.
Add/Remove Programs	Installed that new (insert name of expensive software here)? Double-click here to make Windows 95 automatically install your new software. Use this icon to tell Windows 95 to add on any optional components, too, like the FreeCell card game or Backup program. (You still have to insert the disks, though.) Finally, this icon lets you uninstall software you've grown tired of — provided that the software manufacturer listed the program on the uninstallable programs list.
Date/Time	This area lets you change your computer's date, time, and time zone settings.
Display	Double-click the Display icon to change your screen's wallpaper, color scheme, number of available colors, resolution, screen-saver, and other display-oriented settings.
Fonts	Windows 95 comes with fonts like Arial and Courier. If you head back to the software store and buy more, like Lucida-Blackletter and Lucida Handwriting, install them by double-clicking on this icon. (***Nerdly Note:*** This icon is actually a *shortcut* to the real Fonts setting area. Chapters 4 and 11 cover shortcuts.)
Internet	When you're ready to join the Internet and surf the World Wide Web, this icon's waiting for you. It opens a Pandora's box of buttons that let you customize your Internet lifestyle. (Chapter 15 shows how to point and click your way through the Internet.)
Joystick	Finally! Windows games can now use a joystick. Here's where you can calibrate and test your joystick if you're losing.

(continued)

Table 10-1 *(continued)*

This Icon	*Does This*
Keyboard	Here you can change how long the keyboard takes to repeat a letter when you hold down a key. Yawn. Rarely used. Or, if you pack up the computer and move to Sweden, double-click here to switch to the Swedish language format (or Belgian, Finnish, Icelandic, and a bunch of other countries' formats). Finally, here's where you tell Windows 95 whether you've upgraded from an older 83- or 84-key keyboard to a newer 101- or 102-key keyboard — the ones with the numeric keypads.
Mail	E-mail junkies with pen pals from several different sources — Office networks, CompuServe, The Microsoft Network, or even a fax program — can stick all their mail into one big Inbox through this program. You need a computer nerd to set this one up, however — it has some wacky stuff.
Microsoft Mail Postoffice	Save this one for the office Network guru. You aren't missing much, just the mechanics of linking computers so that people can swap information.
Modems	Before you can talk to other computers over the phone lines, you need a modem. Double-click here, and Windows 95 tries to figure out what sort of modem you have so that it can start bossing it around.
Mouse	Make that mouse scoot faster across the screen, change it from right-handed to left-handed, fine-tune your double-click, choose between brands, and change all sorts of mouse-related behaviors.
Multimedia	Sound-card owners can drop by here to tweak their gear settings, adjust playback/record volumes, fiddle with MIDI instruments, and play with other goodies, like video capture cards and laser disc players.
Network Neighborhood	Yech. Let your network folks mess with this one. They're getting paid extra for it.
Passwords	More network stuff for the weary. This setting is where your office network guru makes an agonizing decision: Should different users of a single PC be allowed to set up their own wallpaper, or should everybody in the office be stuck with the same boring picture?

This Icon	Does This
Power	On some computers, Windows 95 is very PC: power conscious. On laptops, for example, a double-click of this icon brings up ways to save battery power. You can make it turn off the screen when you haven't touched the keyboard in a specified number of minutes. Some desktop computers can turn off the hard drives when they haven't been used in a while, too.
Printers	Come here to tell Windows 95 about your new printer, adjust the settings on your old printer, or choose which printer (or fax card) you want Windows 95 to use. ***Technical Note:*** This isn't really an icon; it's a shortcut that leads to the Printer setup program.
Regional Settings	Used mostly by laptoppers with Frequent Flyer cards, this area changes the way Windows 95 displays and sorts numbers, currency, the date, and the time. (If you've simply changed time zones, just double-click on the date/time display on the bottom-right corner of the taskbar, a process described in Chapter 11.)
Sounds	The most fun! Make Windows 95 play different sounds for different events. For example, hear a cool Pink Floyd riff whenever a Windows 95 error message pops up on-screen. (Windows 95 comes with a few sounds, but you'll have to record Pink Floyd yourself, unfortunately.)
System	Like race-car mechanics, computer gurus can fiddle around in here for hours. Don't play in here unless a nearby computer guru can serve as Safety Patrol. This is scary stuff.

Customizing the Display

Display

The most-often-used part of the Control Panel is probably the Display icon, which looks like the icon in the margin.

When you open this door, you can change the wallpaper, screen saver, and other visual aspects of the Windows 95 desktop (see Figure 10-2).

Unlike several other switches in the Control Panel, the Display icon doesn't control anything too dangerous. Feel free to fiddle around with all the settings. You can't cause any major harm. If you do want to play, however, be sure to write down any original settings. Then you can always return to normal if something looks odd.

Display Properties   [?][X]

Background | Screen Saver | Appearance | Settings

Pattern
[(None)   ]
[50% Gray   ]
[Boxes   ]
[Bricks   ]
[Buttons   ]
        Edit Pattern...

Wallpaper
[(None)   ]
[256COLOR   ]
[Arcade   ]
[Arches   ]
[Argyle   ]
        Browse...
Display: ⦿ Tile   ○ Center

[OK]   [Cancel]   [Apply]

Figure 10-2:
The Display icon lets you change your desktop's colors, resolution, wallpaper, screen saver, and other display-oriented options.

You don't have to root through the Start button and the Control Panel to get to the Display icon's contents. Instead, just click on a blank part of your desktop by using your right mouse button. When the menu pops up out of nowhere, click on Properties. That bypasses the Control Panel and takes you straight to the Display settings area.

The next few sections describe how to customize different parts of your display after you double-click on the Control Panel's Display icon.

The display's background (hanging new wallpaper)

When Windows 95 first installs itself, it paints a dull green background across the screen and then starts sprinkling windows and icons over it. Windows 95 *has* to choose that dull green in the beginning, or nobody would think it's a *serious business application*.

However, Microsoft snuck other backgrounds, known as *wallpaper,* into the Windows 95 box. Those pieces of wallpaper are hiding on the hard drive, just waiting to be installed. Different wallpaper can reflect different personalities (see Figure 10-3). For example, you can turn the window's background into a pile of fallen autumn leaves. You can choose an argyle pattern that matches your socks. Or you can create your own wallpaper in Paint, the Windows 95 graphics program, and hang your new wallpaper yourself.

Figure 10-3:
Windows
wallpaper,
the
backdrop
beneath
all the
windows
and icons,
can match
your mood
for the day.

To change the wallpaper, double-click on the Display icon from the Control Panel. (Or click on a blank spot of your desktop with your right mouse button and choose Properties from the menu that appears from nowhere.)

A rather large dialog box appears (refer to Figure 10-2). Look for the word Wallpaper hovering over a list of names and click on one of the names. (Try the name Forest for soothing pine boughs.) Wham! Windows 95 displays a small preview of how your selection would look as wallpaper (see Figure 10-4).

To see more names on the list, click on the little arrows on the bar next to the names. If you aren't using a mouse, you can select a listed item by using the arrow keys to highlight the item you want and then pressing Enter. In a long list, you can find a certain name more quickly by pressing the name's first letter.

When you see the name of the wallpaper you want, select it. Then click on the Apply button to make Windows 95 install it. Like the way your new wallpaper looks on-screen? Click on the OK command button. The dialog box disappears, and you are back at your desktop (with the new wallpaper displayed proudly in the background).

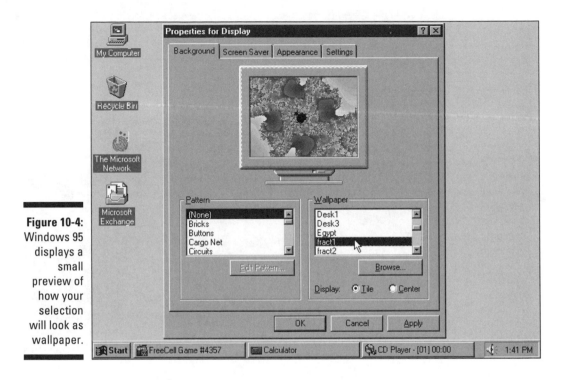

Figure 10-4:
Windows 95
displays a
small
preview of
how your
selection
will look as
wallpaper.

✔ Wallpaper can be *tiled* across the screen or *centered.* Small pictures should be *tiled,* or painted repeatedly across the screen. Larger pictures look best when they're centered. Select the option button next to your preference; the buttons lurk beneath the list of wallpaper names. Or try them both and then choose the one you like best.

✔ Wallpaper files are merely *bitmaps,* or files created in Windows 95 Paint. (Bitmap files end with the letters BMP.) Anything you create in Windows 95 Paint can be used as wallpaper. In fact, you can even use Paint to alter the wallpaper Microsoft provided with Windows 95.

✔ Windows 95 only lists wallpaper that's stored directly in the Windows directory. If you create a potential wallpaper in Paint, you have to move the file to the Windows directory before it shows up in the Desktop dialog box's master list; or you have to choose the file by clicking on the Browse button. If this concept seems strange, foreign, confusing, or all three, check out Chapter 12 for more information about directories and moving files between them.

Wallpaper looks like a lot of fun, but it may be *too much* fun if your computer doesn't have more than 8MB of RAM. Fancy, colorful wallpaper files can use up a great deal of the computer's memory, consistently slowing Windows 95 down. If you find yourself running out of memory, change the wallpaper to the (None) option. The screen won't look as pretty, but at least Windows 95 works.

Small files that are *tiled* across the screen take up much less memory than large files that are *centered* on-screen. If Windows 95 seems slow or it sends you furtive messages saying that it's running out of memory, try tiling some smaller bits of wallpaper. Also, try black-and-white wallpaper; it doesn't slow down Windows 95 as much.

✔ The Pattern option sprinkles tiny lines and dots across the screen, providing a low-budget alternative to wallpaper. To add or change those sprinkles, click on one of the names listed in the Pattern section, right next to the list of wallpaper names (refer to Figure 10-2). Choose from the patterns Microsoft provided; or if you're desperate for something to do, click on the Edit Pattern button to create your own little patterns.

✔ Patterns are a poor-man's wallpaper. They're only one color, and they don't vary much. If Windows 95 keeps complaining about needing more memory, however, dump your wallpaper and switch to patterns. They don't eat up nearly as much memory.

✔ To see patterns across the back of the desktop, you need to change the wallpaper option to (None); otherwise, the patterns won't show up.

✔ Did you happen to spot an eye-catching picture while web surfing with Internet Explorer? Click on that web site's picture with your right mouse button and select the Set as Wallpaper option. Sneaky Microsoft copies that picture to your desktop and leaves it there as your new wallpaper.

The display's screen saver

In the dinosaur days of computing, computer monitors were permanently damaged when an oft-used program burned its image onto the screen. The program's faint outlines showed up even when the monitor was turned off.

To prevent this *burn-in,* people installed a *screen saver* to jump in when a computer hadn't been used for a while. The screen saver would either blank the screen or fill it with wavy lines to keep the program's display from etching itself into the screen.

Today's monitors don't really have this problem, but people use screen savers anyway — mainly because they look cool.

✔ Windows comes with several screen savers built in, although none of them is activated at first. To set one up, click on the Screen Saver tab along the top of the Display Properties dialog box (refer to Figure 10-2). Then click on the downward-pointing arrow in the Screen Saver box. Finally, select the screen saver you want.

✔ Immediately after choosing a screen saver, click on the Preview command button to see what the screen saver looks like. Wiggle the mouse or press the spacebar to come back to Windows 95.

✔ Fiddlers can click on Settings for more options. For example, you can control the colors and animation speed.

✔ Click in the Password protected box to set a password, then when the screen saver kicks in, you won't be able to see the screen again until you type in the password.

✔ Forgot your password? Push your computer's reset button. (Yep, you lose any work you didn't save before the screen saver kicked in.) After Windows 95 returns to life, click on the desktop with your right mouse button, choose Properties from the pop-up menu, and click on the Screen Saver tab. Whew. Now, assign a new password before your screen saver kicks in again. (And make this password a little easier to remember.)

✔ Click on the up or down arrows next to Wait to tell the screen saver when to kick in. If you set the option to 5, for example, Windows 95 waits until you haven't touched the mouse or keyboard for five minutes before letting the screen saver out of its cage.

✔ Windows 95 comes with more screen savers than it initially installs. To make Windows 95 install *all* its screen savers, use the Control Panel's Add/Remove Programs icon, described later in this chapter, and make Windows 95 install more of itself. (***Hint:*** The Flying through Space screen saver looks cool.)

The display's appearance (getting better colors)

If you paid extra for a fancy color monitor and video card, the time has come to put them to use. You can make Windows 95 appear in any color you want by clicking on the tab marked Appearance, found along the top of the Display menu.

The Appearance dialog box opens, enabling you to choose between several Microsoft-designed color schemes or to create your own. (Tell your boss that a more pleasant color scheme will enhance your productivity.) Figure 10-5 shows the Appearance dialog box.

To choose among previously designed color schemes, click on the arrow next to the box beneath Scheme. After the list drops down, click on the name of the scheme you want to try out. Each time you select a new color scheme, the sample window shows you how the colors will look.

Figure 10-5:
Windows 95
lets you
personalize
your
computer
by choosing
different
color
schemes.

If you want to change one of the color schemes slightly, go for it: Click on the box beneath Item to see a list of areas you can fiddle with. For example, to change the font Windows 95 uses for icon titles, select Icon from the list and select a different font from the ones listed in the Font box.

And, if you want even more choices, you can mix your own colors by choosing Other from the Color menu and clicking on the Define Custom Colors command button.

Feel free to play around with the colors by trying out different schemes or designing your own combinations. Playing with the colors is an easy way to see what names Windows 95 uses for its different components. It's also a fun way to work with dialog boxes. But if you goof something awful, and all the letters suddenly disappear, click on the Cancel button. (It's the middle of the three buttons along the bottom.) Letters disappear when they've been changed to white on a white background.

✔ Color schemes don't refer to color alone; they can change the appearance of Windows 95 in other ways. For example, the horizontal Icon Spacing setting determines how closely your icons sit next to each other. The Scrollbar setting determines the width of the scroll bars and their elevator-like buttons you click on to move around in a document.

✔ Created an outstanding new color scheme? Click on the Save As button and type in a new name for your creation. If you ever grow weary of your creative new color scheme, you can always return to the Windows 95 original colors by selecting Windows Standard.

✔ Windows 95 continues to display your newly chosen colors until you head back to the Appearance menu and change them again.

✔ Is all this talk of "dialog boxes," "command buttons," and "funny arrow things" getting you down? Head to Chapter 6 for a field guide to figuring out Windows 95 menus.

Display settings (playing with new video modes)

Just as Windows 95 can print to hundreds of different brands of printers, it can accommodate zillions of different monitors, too. It can even display different *video modes* on the same monitor.

For example, Windows 95 can display different numbers of color on-screen, or it can shrink the size of everything, packing more information onto the screen. The number of colors and the size of the information on-screen comprise a *video mode,* or *video resolution.*

Some Windows 95 programs only work in a specific video mode, and those programs casually ask you to switch to that mode. Huh?

Here's what's happening: Monitors plug into a special place on the back of the computer. That special place is an outlet on a *video card* — the gizmo that translates your computer's language into something you can *see* on the monitor. That card handles all the video-mode switches. By making the card switch between modes, you can send more or fewer colors to your monitor or pack more or less information onto the screen.

To make a video card switch to a different video mode, click on the Settings tab, one of the four tabs along the top of the Control Panel's Display menu, shown in Figure 10-2. (Can't find the Display menu? Click on a blank part of your desktop by using the right mouse button and choose Properties from the menu that springs up.)

As shown in Figure 10-6, the Settings menu lets you select the video mode you want Windows 95 to display on-screen. (Click on the arrow next to the Color palette box to change the number of colors Windows 95 is currently displaying; click in the Desktop area box to change the current resolution.) Windows 95 gives you a chance to back out if you choose a video mode your computer can't handle, thank goodness.

Figure 10-6:
Selecting
the video
mode you
want to
display
on-screen.

When Windows 95 switches to the new resolution, it gives you 15 seconds to click on a button saying that you approve of the change. If your card or monitor can't handle the new resolution, you won't be able to see the button on-screen. Then because you didn't click on the button, Windows 95 automatically changes back to the original resolution. Whew!

Monitors and cards can display Windows 95 in different *resolutions*. The higher the resolution, the more information Windows 95 can pack onto the screen. (And the smaller the windows become, too.) Windows 95 refers to resolution as *Desktop area*. For more information about this monitor/card/resolution stuff, troop over to Chapter 2 and read the section about computer parts that I told you to ignore.

To switch to a higher resolution, use your mouse to slide the little bar in the Desktop area box. Then watch how the screen changes. The more you slide the bar to the right, the more information Windows 95 can pack onto the screen. Unfortunately, the information also gets smaller. Click on the Apply button after you select a new resolution to see it in action.

✔ Earlier versions of Windows made users shut down Windows when changing resolution. Windows 95 isn't nearly as rude. You can change resolution while all your programs are still running. (Make sure that you've saved your work anyway, however. Who *really* trusts their computer to be polite these days?) Also, Windows 95 sometimes still needs to shut down and restart when switching the number of colors it can display.

✔ Want to change the number of colors Windows 95 can throw onto the screen? Click on the little arrow in the <u>C</u>olor palette box. After the list drops down, select the number of colors you want.

✔ New video cards usually come with a disk that contains special information called a *driver*. If Windows 95 doesn't recognize your breed of video card, it may ask you to insert this disk when you're changing video modes.

✔ The more colors you ask Windows 95 to display, the slower it runs. Usually, it's best to stick with 256 colors unless you have a fancy video card, own a fancy monitor to go with it, and want to look at ultra-realistic photos on-screen.

✔ If you'll be looking at pictures stored through the Kodak PhotoCD technology, you'll probably want Windows 95 to display as many colors as possible — often 65,000 (16-bit) or 1.6 million (24-bit). Switch back to fewer colors when you're done, however, if Windows 95 starts running too slowly.

✔ If Windows 95 acts goofy with your video card or monitor — or you've recently installed new ones — head for the "Installing New Hardware" section later in this chapter. Windows 95 probably needs to be formally introduced to your new equipment before it will talk to it.

Understanding the Fuss about TrueType Fonts

In the first few versions of Windows, the *fonts,* or sets of letters, numbers, and other characters, produced individual letters and numbers that looked kind of jagged. A capital A, for example, didn't have smooth, diagonal lines. Instead, the sides had rough ridges that stuck out. They usually looked fine on the printer but pretty awful on-screen, especially when the headlines were in large letters.

Windows 3.1 introduced a new font technology called TrueType fonts to eliminate the jaggies and make the screen match more closely what comes out of the printer. The technology is still around in Windows 95.

Fonts

Double-click on the Control Panel's Fonts icon to see what fonts come with Windows 95, to install additional fonts, or to delete the ugly ones you don't like anymore.

Double-click on any of the font icons, and you see what that particular font looks like. For example, a double-click on the icon marked Courier New Italic brings up an eye chart displaying how that font would look on the printed page, as shown in Figure 10-7.

Figure 10-7:
Double-click on a font icon to see what it looks like.

[Courier New Italic (True Type) window]

Courier New Italic (True Type)

Done   Print

Courier New Italic (True Type)
Typeface name: Courier New
File size: 80 KB
Version: MS core font:v1.00
Typeface © The Monotype Corporation plc. Data © The
Monotype Corporation plc/Type Solutions Inc. 1990-1992. All
Rights Reserved

abcdefghijklmnopqrstuvwxyz
ABCDEFGHIJKLMNOPQRSTUVWXYZ
1234567890.:,;("*!?')

12 The quick brown fox jumps over t.
18 The quick brown fox jum
24 The quick brown f

Fonts
File Edit Vie

TT
Courier New

✔ Icons marked with the letters "TT" are TrueType fonts, so they'll always look better than the fonts marked with the letter A.

✔ *Note:* You'll probably never need to fiddle with the Fonts icon. Just know that it's there in case you ever want to get fancy and install more fonts on your computer. So pretend that the technical sidebar about TrueType stuff doesn't even exist.

To be on the safe side, don't delete any fonts that come with Windows 95; only delete fonts that you've installed yourself. Windows programs often borrow Windows 95 fonts for menus. If you delete those fonts, your menus mysteriously vanish. And for goodness sake, don't delete any fonts beginning with the letters **MS**. (Don't delete the fonts that have red lettering in their icons, either.)

Just what is this TrueType stuff, anyway?

In early versions of Windows, people with fancy fonts had a problem. They could create some fine-looking documents that would have raised a smile from Gutenberg himself. But when they copied a document to a disk and gave it to somebody else, that person couldn't see those same fancy fonts. Only people who had those same fancy fonts already *installed* on their computer could see the document the way it was supposed to look.

TrueType fixes that problem handily by *embedding* the font in the document itself. You can create a letter in WordPad by using fancy True Type fonts; when you give a disk with the letter on it to a friend, that person can see the

same fonts in the letter, even if those fonts aren't installed on their computer.

At least, the TrueType fonts included with Windows 95 work that way; some other TrueType fonts don't embed themselves.

Also, TrueType fonts are *scalable.* You can make them bigger or smaller, and they still look nice. Earlier font technology required a different set of fonts for each size. The files were pretty hoggy compared with TrueType technology.

Most people get along fine with the fonts that are included with Windows 95, so they never have to worry about TrueType or how it works.

Fonts can eat up a lot of hard drive space. If you've installed some fonts that you no longer use, delete them. Double-click on the Control Panel's Fonts icon, click with your right mouse button on the name of the font you no longer use, and then choose Delete from the pop-up menu. A box appears, asking whether you're sure that you want to remove that font; click the Yes button if you *really* want to give it the purge.

Making Windows 95 Recognize Your Double-Click

Mouse

Clicking twice on a mouse button is called a double-click; you do a lot of double-clicking in Windows 95. But sometimes you can't click fast enough to suit Windows 95. It thinks that your double-clicks are just two single clicks. If you have this problem, head for the Control Panel's Mouse icon.

When you double-click on the Mouse icon, the Mouse dialog box pops up (see Figure 10-8). If your mouse dialog box doesn't look like the one in Figure 10-8, the company that made your mouse slipped its own software into the Control Panel. The following instructions may not work for you, but you can generally access the same types of options for any mouse. If your menu looks weird, try pressing F1 for help.

Figure 10-8:
Double-
click in the
Test area
box to
check your
current
settings.

To check the double-click speed, double-click in the box marked Test area. Each time Windows 95 recognizes your double-click, a little puppet with water-buffalo horns pops out of the Jack in the Box. Double-click again, and the puppet disappears.

Slide the scroll box toward the words Fast or Slow until Windows 95 successfully recognizes your double-click efforts. Click on the OK command button when you're through, and you're back in business.

✔ Can't double-click on the Mouse icon quickly enough for Windows 95 to open the darn thing up? Just click once, and poke the Enter key with your finger. Or, click once with the right button and choose Open from the menu that shoots out of the mouse icon's head. Yep, there are a lot of ways to do the same thing in Windows 95.

✔ If you're left-handed, click in the little circle marked Left-handed, shown along the top of Figure 10-8, and click on the Apply button. Then you can hold the mouse in your left hand and still click with your index finger.

✔ For a psychedelic experience, click on the tab marked Motion along the window's top and then click in the box marked Show pointer trails. Windows 95 makes *ghost arrows* follow the mouse pointer. Laptop users can spot the arrow more easily when it is followed by ghosts. The more you slide the little box toward the long side of the bar, the longer your trail of mouse ghosts grows.

✔ The mouse arrow doesn't have to move at the same speed as the mouse. To make the arrow *zip* across the screen with just a tiny push, click on the Motion tab along the top. Then, in the Pointer speed box, slide the little box toward the side of the scroll bar marked Fast. To slow down the mouse, allowing for more precise pointing, slide the box toward the Slow side.

✔ Some brands of mice come with fancier features and a different settings page. The new Microsoft IntelliMouse, described in the mouse section of Chapter 2, brings a wide variety of mouse fun. An odometer tracks the distance your mouse pointer has traveled across the screen, for example. Or, you can make the pointer automatically reappear on the opposite side when you push it off the edge of the screen. Add in a bunch of fun animated mouse pointers (martini glasses, piano keyboards, clam shells, and other goodies), and you'll be too busy playing to work.

Setting the Computer's Time and Date

Many computer users don't bother to set the computer's clock. They just look at their wristwatches to see when it's time to stop working. But they're missing out on an important computing feature: Computers stamp new files with the current date and time. If the computer doesn't know the correct date, it stamps files with the *wrong* date. Then how can you find the files you created yesterday? Last week?

Also, Windows 95 sometimes does some funny things to the computer's internal clock, so you may want to reset the date and time if you notice that the computer is living in the past.

To reset the computer's time or date, choose the Control Panel's Date/Time icon.

A double-click on the Date/Time icon brings a little calendar to the screen, shown in Figure 10-9. To change the date, just click on the correct date as listed on the on-screen calendar. If the date's off by a month or more, click on the little arrow next to the currently listed month. A list drops down, letting you choose a different month. To change the year or the hour, click on the number you want to change and then click on the up or down arrows to make the number bigger or smaller. When the number is correct, click on the OK button for Windows 95 to make the changes.

Figure 10-9:
To change
the time,
click on the
numbers
beneath the
clock; then
click on the
little arrows
next to the
numbers.

✔ Moved to a new time zone? Click on the Time Zone tab along the top of the window. Click on the downward-pointing arrow next to the currently listed time zone. A *long* list of countries and locations appears; click on the one where you're currently hanging your hat.

✔ Windows 95 has a Find program, described in Chapter 11, that can locate files by the time and date they were created — but *only* if you keep your computer's date and time set correctly.

✔ Most computers have an internal clock that automatically keeps track of the time and date. Nevertheless, those clocks aren't always reliable, especially among laptops with "power-saving" features. Check your $2,000 computer's clock against your $20 wristwatch every few weeks to make sure that the computer is on the mark.

For an even quicker way to change your computer's time or date, double-click on the little clock Windows 95 puts on the taskbar that lives along the edge of the screen. Windows 95 brings up the Date/Time menu, just as if you'd waded through the Control Panel and double-clicked on the Date/Time icon.

Fiddling with the Printer

Most of the time, the printer will work fine. Especially after you turn it *on* and try printing again. In fact, most people will never need to read this section.

Printers

Occasionally, however, you may need to tweak some printer settings. You'll need to install a new printer or remove an old one that you've sold (so it won't keep cluttering up the list of printers). Either way, start by choosing the Control Panel's Printers icon.

The Printers dialog box surfaces, as shown in Figure 10-10.

Figure 10-10:
Double-
clicking the
Add Printer
icon tells
Windows 95
about your
new printer.

Is the My Computer window open? Double-click on the Printers icon hiding in there. That step takes you to the same Printers dialog box as the Control Panel does.

If you're installing a new printer, grab the Windows 95 compact disc or floppy disks that came in the box; you'll need them during the installation.

1. **To add a new printer, double-click on the Add Printer icon.**

   Déjà vu! You see the same list of printers as when you first installed Windows 95.

2. **Just as before, click on the Next button and then use the PgUp and PgDn keys to select your printer's manufacturer and model number.**

   The Add Printer Wizard box lists the names of printer manufacturers on the left; click on the name of your printer's manufacturer, and the right side of the box lists the models of printers that manufacturer makes.

3. **When you see your printer listed, press Enter or double-click on the printer's name. Windows 95 asks you to stick the appropriate setup disks into a drive, and the drive makes some grinding noises.**

   After a moment, you see the new printer listed in the box.

4. **Click on the new printer's icon and choose the Set As Default Printer option from the window's File menu.**

   That's it. If you're like most people, your printer will work like a charm. If it doesn't, you may have to wade through the technical stuff in the sidebar about printer ports and such.

If you have more than one printer attached to your computer, select your most-oft-used printer as the *default* printer. That choice tells Windows 95 to assume that it's printing to that oft-used printer.

✔ To remove a printer you no longer use, click on its name and then click on the <u>D</u>elete command button. That printer's name no longer appears as an option when you try to print from a Windows 95-based program.

✔ You can change most of the printer options in the program you're printing from. Choose <u>F</u>iles in the menu bar and then choose P<u>r</u>int Setup. From there, you can often access the same box of printer options as you find in the Control Panel.

✔ Some printers offer a variety of options. For example, you can print from different paper trays or print at different resolutions. To play with these options, click on the Printer's icon with the right mouse button and choose P<u>r</u>operties from the menu that pops up. Although different models of printers offer different options, most let you change paper size, fonts, and types of graphics.

✔ If your printer isn't listed in the Windows 95 master list, you have to contact the printer's manufacturer for a *driver.* When it comes in the mail, repeat the process for adding a printer, but click on the Have <u>D</u>isk button. Windows 95 asks you to stick in the manufacturer's disk so that it can copy the *driver* onto the hard disk. (For more information, check out the section "Adding New Hardware," later in this chapter.)

✔ Working with printers can be more complicated than trying to retrieve a stray hamster from under the kitchen cupboards. Feel free to use any of the Help buttons in the dialog boxes. Chances are they'll offer some helpful advice, and some are actually customized for your particular brand of printer. Too bad they can't catch hamsters.

Windows 95 is a little better at housekeeping than Windows 3.1, especially when it comes to deleting old files. When you delete a printer from the Control Panel, Windows 95 asks if you want to remove the old printer drivers, too. (Click on the <u>Y</u>es button, unless you think that you'll be adding that printer back on in the near future.)

Sound and Multimedia

The term *multimedia* means mixing two or more mediums — usually combining sound and pictures. A plain old television, for example, could be called a *multimedia tool,* especially if you're trying to impress somebody.

Printer ports and configuration nonsense

Windows 95 shoots information to printers through ports (little metal outlets on the computer's rump). Most printers connect to a port called *LPT1:,* or the first *line printer port.*

Always select this option first. If it works, skip the rest of this technical chatter. You've already found success!

Some people, however, insist on plugging printers into a second printer port, or *LPT2:.* (If you meet one of these people, ask them why.) Still other people buy *serial* printers, which plug into *serial ports* (also known as *COM ports*).

Different brands of printers work with Windows 95 in different ways, but here are a few tips. To connect a printer to a different port, click on the printer's icon with your right mouse button and choose P*r*operties from the pop-up menu. Click on the tab marked Details,

and you can select the port you want. Look to see what port you're plugging the printer into, and select that port from the menu. (Computer ports are rarely labeled, so you'll probably have to bribe a computer guru to help you out. Start tossing Cheetos around your chair and desk; computer gurus are attracted by the smell.)

If you're connecting a printer to a serial port, you need to do one more little chore: Configure the serial port. Click on the P*o*rt Settings box and make sure that the following numbers and characters appear, in this order: `9600`, `8, N, 1, Xon/Xoff`.

The printer should be all set. If not, call over a computer guru. At least you only have to go through all this printer hassle once — unless you buy another printer.

Windows 95 can mix sound and pictures if you have a *sound card:* a gizmo costing about $100 that slips inside the computer and hooks up to a pair of speakers or a stereo.

Macintosh computers have had sound for years. And for years, Mac owners have been able to *assign sounds to system events.* In lay language, that means having the computer make a professional baseball player's spitting sound when it ejects a floppy disk.

Sounds

In Windows 95, you can't assign sounds to the floppy drives, but you can assign noises to other *events* by double-clicking on the Control Panel's Sounds icon.

The Sounds dialog box appears (see Figure 10-11). Windows 95 automatically plays sounds for several system events. An event can be anything as simple as when a menu pops up or when Windows 95 first starts up in the morning.

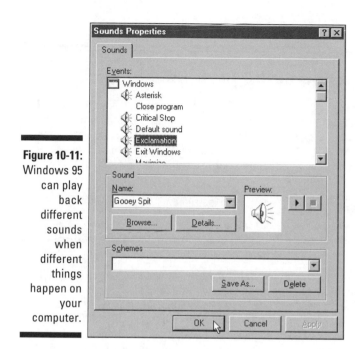

Figure 10-11:
Windows 95
can play
back
different
sounds
when
different
things
happen on
your
computer.

Windows 95 lists the events on the top of the box and lists the possible sounds directly below them in the box called Name. To assign a sound, click on the event first and then click on the sound you want to hear for that event. In Figure 10-11, for example, Windows 95 is set up to make a spitting sound whenever it sends out an urgent dialog box with an exclamation point in it.

✔ Are you satisfied with your new choices of sounds? Click in the box marked Save As, and change the words Windows Default to something else, like My Sound Settings. That way you can still change back to the more polite Windows Default sounds when you don't want houseguests to hear your computer spit. (You can change back to My Sound Effects after they've left.)

✔ To take advantage of this multimedia feature, you have to buy and install a sound card. Then you have to tell Windows 95 about your new card by clicking on the Control Panel's Add New Hardware icon, described later in this chapter.

✔ To hear a sound before you assign it, click on its name and then click on the Preview button (the little black triangle next to the speaker).

✔ You can record your own sounds through most sound cards. You can probably pick up a cheap microphone at Radio Shack; many sound cards don't include one.

Multimedia setup problems

Multimedia gadgetry inevitably brings a multitude of setup problems. There are simply too many file formats and program settings for an easy ride. Although Windows 95 does an excellent job of setting up your computer's hardware automatically, the Control Panel's Multimedia icon lets techno-fiddlers change some of the settings. Because different computers use different parts, the settings listed under the Multimedia icon vary, but here's a general look at what they can do:

Audio: This page controls your sound card's volume settings as well as its recording quality. The better the quality of the recording, the more hard disk space your recordings consume. A quicker way to adjust the volume is to simply click on the little speaker in the corner of the taskbar. (If you don't see that taskbar's little speaker control, click on the Multimedia icon's <u>S</u>how volume control on the taskbar option.)

Video: This option lets you select the size of your videos. You can force them to play back full-screen, for example, or to consume smaller sizes. (**Hint:** Your best bet is to select Original size from the <u>W</u>indow option.)

MIDI: Musicians can tell Windows 95 about new MIDI instruments on this page.

CD Music: Mostly useful for adjusting the volume of headphones that plug into a CD-ROM's headphone jack.

Advanced: Here Windows 95 lists all the multimedia devices attached to your computer (as well as a few devices you may want to add to your computer in the future). By clicking on a device and clicking on the Properties button near the bottom, you can turn a device on or off. If your computer has a game port (found on most sound cards), come here to calibrate your joystick for Windows 95 games.

✔ Be forewarned: Sound consumes a *lot* of disk space, so stick with short recordings — short and sweet B. B. King guitar riffs, for example, or the sound of a doorbell ringing.

✔ Sound card not working right? You may have to muddle through the Multimedia icon, described in the dreary technical sidebar "Multimedia setup problems."

Adding New Hardware

When you wolf down a sandwich for lunch, you know what you ate. After all, you picked it out at the deli counter, chewed it, swallowed it, and wiped the bread crumbs away from the corner of your mouth.

But when you add a new part to your computer, it's turned off — Windows 95 is asleep. And when you turn the computer back on and Windows 95 returns to life, it probably won't notice the new part.

Here's the good news, however: If you simply tell Windows 95 to *look* for the new part, it will probably find it. In fact, Windows 95 will not only spot the new part, but it will introduce itself and start a warm and friendly working relationship using the right settings.

Add New
Hardware

The Control Panel's Add New Hardware icon handles the process of introducing Windows 95 to anything you've recently attached to your computer.

Here's how to tell Windows 95 to look for any new computer parts you may have stuffed inside or plugged into your computer:

1. **Double-click on the Control Panel's Add New Hardware icon.**

   The Windows 95 Hardware Installation Wizard pops out of a hat, ready to introduce Windows 95 to whatever part you've stuffed inside your computer.

2. **Click on the Next button.**

   Windows 95 presents a list of computer parts on-screen.

3. **If you know what type of computer part you've installed, click on its name from the list; otherwise, select Automatically detect installed hardware. Then click on the Next button.**

   Usually you'll have an inkling as to what you've installed: a new video card or modem, for example, or perhaps a sound card or CD-ROM drive. If so, click on the gadget's name from the box; otherwise, leave the program set on automatic.

Here's where things start getting a little different. If you choose Automatically detect installed hardware, Windows 95 looks inside your computer, sniffing out new parts. If it finds anything that looks new, it lists it. Did it guess right? Then click on the Finish button and follow the instructions. If it didn't find anything, though, you need to contact the manufacturer of your new part and ask for a *Windows 95 driver.*

If you didn't select Automatically detect installed hardware but clicked on the name of your device instead, Windows 95 shows you a list of manufacturers. Click on the manufacturer that made your particular part, and Windows 95 shows you a list of models that manufacturer makes. See yours listed? Click on the Finish button and follow the instructions. If it's not listed, you need to contact the company that made your new part and ask them for a *Windows 95 driver.*

✔ Adding a new modem? Then Windows 95 will want to know your current country and area code, as well as whether you dial a special number (such as a 9) to reach an outside line. If you want to change this stuff later, double-click on the Control Panel's Modem icon — that brings you to the same page that the Add New Hardware icon does.

✔ Windows 95 is pretty good about identifying various gadgets that people have stuffed inside it, especially if your computer is Plug and Play compatible and you're installing a Plug and Play part. You can find more information about Plug and Play in Chapter 4.

✔ If you're not sure what type of part you've installed, but you know the company that made it, select Unknown hardware, the choice at the bottom of the Install specific hardware list. Then, when Windows 95 lists a bunch of companies, click on the company that made your part. Windows 95 lists all that company's parts it can recognize.

✔ In Windows 3.1, you had to know where you were going in order to get something done. Windows 95 is much more forgiving, and lots of the icons' functions are overlapping. If you install a new modem, for example, you can use the Add New Hardware icon or the Modem icon to introduce it to Windows 95. Adding a new printer? Use either the Add New Hardware icon or the Printer icon; both take you to the same place — the spot where you tell Windows 95 about your new printer.

Adding and Removing Programs

Add/Remove Programs

By adding an Add/Remove Programs icon to the Control Panel, Windows 95 is trying to trick you into thinking that it's easier than ever to install a program. Nope.

Here's how the installation programs work if you're lucky. When you get a new program, look for a disk marked Install or Installation, and stick the disk into any disk drive that it fits. If the program came on a compact disc, put the disc into your compact disc drive.

Next, double-click on the Control Panel's Add/Remove Programs icon, click on the Install button, and click on Next from the next screen. Windows 95 searches all your disk drives for a disk containing an installation program; if it finds an installation program, it runs it, effectively installing the program. If it doesn't find one, it just gives up.

✔ Most programs you buy at software stores come with installation programs, so Windows 95 can install them without too much trouble. Some of the smaller shareware programs found on online services don't come with installation programs, unfortunately, so you'll have to install them yourself.

✔ Are you forced to install a DOS or Windows program yourself? Make a new folder somewhere on your hard drive and copy all the files from the program's disk to the new folder. Then to load the program, double-click on the program's icon from within that folder. Chapter 11 is filled with tips on creating folders, copying files, and sticking new programs on the Start menu.

✔ The Add/Remove Programs icon can *uninstall* programs, but only if those programs have been designed with the *uninstall* feature in mind. That limitation means that you won't find very many — if any — of your programs listed on the *uninstall* menu. (Microsoft is starting to list many of its programs on the uninstall menu.)

✔ Until the built-in uninstall feature of Windows 95 catches on, the easiest way to remove old or unwanted Windows programs is to buy a third-party *uninstaller* program, such as the Quarterdeck Cleansweep or the Microhelp Uninstaller.

✔ The Setup tab at the top of the Add/Remove Programs screen lets you add or remove some of the programs that came with Windows 95: programs for laptop users, extra wallpaper and sounds, network utilities, games, The Microsoft Network online service, and a few other goodies. To add one of the programs, click in its check box. To remove one you've installed, click in its check box. (Its check mark disappears, as does the program, when you click on the Apply button.)

✔ For safety's sake, make a StartUp Disk — a disk that can still start up your computer if something dreadful happens. Put a blank floppy — or a floppy with destructible information — in drive A and click on the StartUp Disk tab from the top of the Add/Remove Programs program. Click on the <u>C</u>reate Disk button and follow the instructions.

Finding Out Which Icons to Avoid

Unless you have a very pressing reason, avoid these icons in the Control Panel: Network, Regional Settings, Keyboard, System, Microsoft Exchange Profiles, Microsoft Mail Post Office, and Passwords.

✔ The Network icon controls how Windows 95 talks to other computers through your office's network — those cables meandering from PC to PC. Talk to your network administrator before playing with this icon "just to see what it does."

✔ The Regional Settings icon changes the keyboard layout to the one used by people in other countries. It doesn't make the Windows 95 dialog boxes appear in German (although you can order the German version of Windows 95 from Microsoft). Instead, a foreign keyboard layout makes certain keys produce foreign characters. It also changes the way currency appears and stuff like that. You can easily leave the keyboard set for Taiwan by accident, and then you wonder why the time and date look funny.

✔ The Keyboard icon doesn't do any major damage, but it doesn't do any major good, either. It controls how fast a key repeats if you hold it down. Big deal. If the keyboard isn't mmmaking characters repeat, don't messssss with it. In case you're into the Dvorak keyboard layout, it is listed here as well.

✔ The information listed in the System icon turns on network hounds and techno-nerds. It's out of the realm of this book. Ditto for the Mail, Fax, and Microsoft Mail Post Office (although you can find a little online stuff covered in Chapter 13).

✔ Finally, the Passwords icon is kind of like the switch in the new Ford Explorer that can remember different seat- and mirror-adjustment settings for up to four different drivers. By assigning different passwords to different computer users, Windows 95 can switch to a customized desktop setting for each person who logs in.

Part III

Using Windows 95 Applications (And Running DOS, Should the Mood Strike)

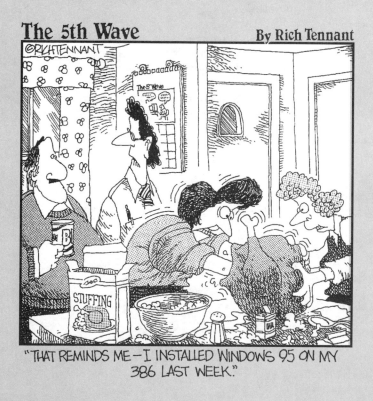

The 5th Wave   By Rich Tennant

"THAT REMINDS ME—I INSTALLED WINDOWS 95 ON MY 386 LAST WEEK."

In this part . . .

Did you know that

- Rubber bands last longer when refrigerated?

- A human's eyelashes generally fall off after 5 months?

- Windows 95 comes with a bunch of free programs that aren't even mentioned on the outside of the box?

This part takes a look at all the stuff you're getting for nothing. Well, for the price on your sales receipt, anyway.

Chapter 11

The Windows 95 Desktop, Start Button, and Taskbar

● ●

In This Chapter

▶ Using the desktop

▶ Making shortcuts

▶ Deleting files, folders, programs, and icons

▶ Retrieving deleted items from the Recycle Bin

▶ Discovering the Start button's reason to live

▶ Putting programs on the Start button menu

▶ Making programs start automatically with Windows

▶ Using the taskbar

● ●

*I*n the old days of computing, pale technoweenies typed disgustingly long strings of code words into computers to make the computers do something — anything.

Windows 95 brings computers to the age of modern convenience. To start a program, simply click on a button. There's a slight complication, however: The buttons no longer *look* like buttons. In fact, some of the buttons are hidden, revealed only by the push of yet another button (if you're lucky enough to stumble upon the right place to push).

This chapter covers the three main Windows 95 buttonmongers: the desktop, the taskbar, and that mother of all buttons — the Start button.

Rolling Objects along the Windows 95 Desktop

Normally, nobody would think of mounting a desktop sideways. Keeping the pencils from rolling off a normal desk is hard enough.

But in Windows 95, your computer monitor's screen is known as the Windows *desktop,* and it's the area where all your work takes place. When working with Windows 95, you'll be creating files and folders right on your new electronic desktop and scattering those files and folders across the screen.

For example, do you need to write a letter asking the neighbor to return the circular saw she borrowed? Here's how to put the desktop's functions to immediate use.

Point at just about any Windows 95 item and click your right mouse button to see a menu listing the things you're allowed to do with that item.

1. **Click on the desktop with your right mouse button.**

   A menu pops up, as shown in Figure 11-1.

2. **Point at the word <u>N</u>ew and click on WordPad Document from the menu that appears.**

   Because you're creating something new — a new letter — you should point at the word <u>N</u>ew. Windows 95 lists the new things you can create on the desktop. Choose WordPad Document, shown in Figure 11-2.

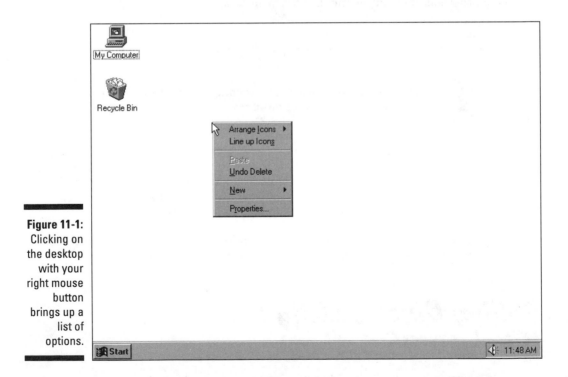

Figure 11-1:
Clicking on
the desktop
with your
right mouse
button
brings up a
list of
options.

Figure 11-2:
Point at the
word <u>N</u>ew
and choose
WordPad
Document
from the
menu.

3. Type a title for your letter and press Enter.

When an icon for a WordPad document appears on the desktop, Windows 95 doesn't want you to lose it. So the first step is to give it a name of up to 255 characters. As soon as you start typing, your new title replaces the old name of New WordPad Document, as shown in Figure 11-3. (If Windows 95 hassles you about your choice of name, skip ahead to Chapter 12.)

Figure 11-3:
Start typing
to create
the icon's
new name.

4. Double-click on your new icon, write your letter, save it, and print it.

Double-clicking on the new icon calls up WordPad, the word processor, so you can write the letter requesting the return of your circular saw. Are you done writing? Then move on to Step 5.

5. Click on <u>S</u>ave from the WordPad <u>F</u>ile menu to save the letter.

6. Head back to the WordPad <u>F</u>ile menu and choose <u>P</u>rint to send the letter to the printer.

7. To store the file, drag the icon to a folder. Or to delete it, drag the file to the Recycle Bin.

After you've finished writing and printing the letter, you need to decide what to do with the file. You can simply leave its icon on your desk, but that clutters things up. If you want to save the letter in a folder, click on the desktop with your right mouse button and choose <u>F</u>older from the <u>N</u>ew menu. Windows 95 tosses a new folder onto your desktop, ready for you to drag your letter into.

Or, if you want to delete the letter, drag the icon to your Recycle Bin (described in the next section).

✔ Windows 95 is designed for you to work right on top of the desktop. From the desktop, you can create new things like files, folders, sounds, and graphics — just about anything. After working with your new file or folder, you can store it or delete it.

✔ You can store your favorite files and folders right on the desktop. Or, to be more organized, you can drag your files and folders into the folders listed in the My Computer window. (The My Computer program gets a lot more coverage in Chapter 12.)

✔ Are you confused about what something is supposed to do? Click on it with your right mouse button. Windows 95 tosses up a menu listing just about everything you can do with that particular object. This trick works on the desktop or just about any icon you'll come across.

✔ Is your desktop looking rather cluttered? Make Windows 95 line up the icons in orderly rows: Click on the desktop with the right mouse button, point at the Arrange Icons option, and choose by Name from the menu.

Using the Recycle Bin

The Recycle Bin, that little wastebasket with green arrows in the upper-left corner of the desktop, is supposed to work like a *real* Recycle Bin — something you can fish the Sunday paper out of if somebody pitched the comics section before you had a chance to read it.

Terribly boring desktop trivia

That's right — Windows 95 considers the desktop to be a mammoth folder. That mammoth folder opens across your screen when you start Windows 95, and it closes up when you shut down Windows 95 with the Start button's Shut Down command.

And because the desktop's a folder, it's actually a subdirectory, too. Windows 95 normally hides it from view, but if you choose Options from the Windows Explorer View menu to display *hidden* files, you see the Desktop folder resting casually in the Windows 95 directory.

Have you made new folders on the desktop? Those folders are really just subdirectories of the Desktop directory.

Recycle Bin

If you want to get rid of something in Windows 95 — a file or folder, for example — simply drag it to the Recycle Bin. Point at the file or folder's icon with the mouse and, while holding down the left mouse button, point at the Recycle Bin. Let go of the mouse button, and your detritus disappears. Windows 95 stuffs it into the Recycle Bin.

But if you want to bypass that cute metaphor, there's another way to delete stuff: Click on your unwanted file or folder's icon with the right mouse button and choose <u>D</u>elete from the menu that pops up. Whoosh! Windows 95 asks cautiously if you're *sure* that you want to delete the icon. If you click on the <u>Y</u>es button, Windows 95 dumps the icon into the Recycle Bin, just as if you'd dragged it there.

So if you like to "drag and drop," feel free to drag your garbage to the Recycle bin and let go. If you prefer the menus, click with your right mouse button and choose <u>D</u>elete. Or if you like alternative lifestyles, click on the unwanted icon with your left button and push your keyboard's Delete key. All three methods toss the file into the Recycle Bin, where it can be salvaged later or, eventually, purged for good.

✔ Want to retrieve something you've deleted? Double-click on the Recycle Bin icon, and a window appears, listing deleted items. See the name of your accidentally deleted icon? Then drag it to the desktop. Point at the icon's name and, while holding down the left mouse button, point at the desktop. Let go of the mouse button, and the Recycle Bin coughs up the deleted item, good as new.

✔ Sometimes the Recycle Bin can get pretty full. If you're searching fruitlessly for a file you've recently deleted, tell the Recycle Bin to sort the filenames in the order in which they were deleted. Click on <u>V</u>iew, point at Arrange <u>I</u>cons, and choose by <u>D</u>elete Date from the menu that pops out. Instead of listing the deleted files in alphabetical order, Recycle Bin now lists the most recently deleted files at the bottom.

✔ The Recycle Bin icon changes from an empty wastepaper basket to a full one as soon as it's holding a deleted file. You may have to squint a little to notice the pieces of paper sticking out the trash can's top.

✔ A Recycle Bin can eat up 10 percent (or more) of your hard disk space. To free up some space, cut down on the amount of room it reserves for saving your deleted files. Click on the Recycle Bin with your right mouse button and choose <u>P</u>roperties from its menu. Normally, Recycle Bin waits until your deleted files consume 10 percent of your hard drive before it begins purging your oldest deleted files. If you want the Recycle Bin to hang on to more deleted files, increase the percentage. If you're a sure-fingered clicker who never makes mistakes, decrease the percentage.

Making a shortcut

Some people like to organize their desktop, putting a pencil sharpener on one corner and a box of Kleenex on the other corner. Other people like their Kleenex box in the top desk drawer. Microsoft knew that one desktop design could never please everybody, so Windows 95 lets people customize their desktops to suit individual tastes and needs.

For example, you may find yourself frequently copying files to a floppy disk in drive A. Normally, to perform that operation, you open the My Computer icon and drag your files to the drive A icon living in there. But there's a quicker way, and it's called a Windows 95 *shortcut*. A shortcut is simply a push button — an icon — that stands for something else.

For example, here's how to put a shortcut for drive A on your desktop:

1. **Double-click on the desktop's My Computer icon.**

   The My Computer folder opens up, showing the icons for your disk drives as well as folders for your Control Panel and Printer. (My Computer gets more coverage in Chapter 12.)

2. **With your right mouse button, drag the drive A icon's shortcut to the desktop.**

   Point at the drive A icon and, while holding down your right mouse button, point at the desktop, shown in Figure 11-4. Let go of your mouse button.

Figure 11-4: Dragging the drive A icon to the desktop creates a shortcut.

3. **Choose Create Shortcut(s) Here from the menu.**

Windows 95 puts an icon for drive A on your desktop, but it looks a little different from the drive A icon you dragged. Because it's only a shortcut — not the original icon — it has a little arrow in its corner, shown in Figure 11-5.

Figure 11-5:
The icon on the left is a shortcut that stands for the icon on the right.

That's it. Now you won't need to root through the My Computer or Explorer folders and programs to access drive A. The drive A shortcut on your desktop works just as well as the *real* drive A icon found in My Computer and Explorer.

✔ A shortcut is the equivalent of an icon in Windows 3.1 Program Manager — a push button that starts a program or loads a file. A shortcut for a disk drive is just like the disk drive icons along the top of Windows 3.1 File Manager, too.

✔ Feel free to create desktop shortcuts for your most commonly accessed programs, files, or disk drives. Shortcuts are a quick way to make Windows 95 easier to use.

✔ If your newly dragged icon doesn't have an arrow in its bottom corner, don't let go of the mouse! You're not making a shortcut. Instead, you've dragged the *real* program to your desktop, and other programs may not be able to find it. Drag the icon back to where it was and try again. (You probably mistakenly held down the *left* mouse button instead of the correct button — the *right* button.)

✔ Have you grown tired of a shortcut? Feel free to delete it. Deleting a shortcut has no effect on the original file, folder, or program that it represents.

✔ You can make as many shortcuts as you'd like. You can even make several shortcuts for the same thing. For example, you can put a shortcut for drive A in *all* of your folders.

✔ Windows 95 shortcuts aren't very good at keeping track of moving files. If you create a shortcut to a file or program and then move the file or program to a different spot on your hard drive, the shortcut won't be able to find that file or program anymore.

Uh, what's the difference between a shortcut and an icon?

An icon for a file, folder, or program looks pretty much like a shortcut, except the shortcut has an arrow wedged in its lower reaches. And double-clicking on a shortcut and double-clicking on an icon do pretty much the same thing: start a program or load a file or folder.

But a shortcut is only a servant of sorts. When you double-click on the shortcut, it runs over to the program, file, or folder that the shortcut represents and kick starts that program, file, or folder into action.

You could do the same thing yourself by rummaging through your computer's folders, finding the program, file, or folder you're after, and personally double-clicking on its icon to bring it to life. But it's often more convenient to create a shortcut so that you don't have to rummage so much.

> ✔ If you delete a shortcut — the icon with the little arrow — you're not doing any real harm. You're just firing the servant that fetched things for you, probably creating more work for yourself in the process.

> ✔ If you accidentally delete a shortcut, you can pull it out of the Recycle Bin, just like anything else that's deleted in Windows 95.

The Start Button's Reason to Live

The Start button lives on your taskbar, and it's always ready for action. By using the Start button, you can start programs, adjust the Windows 95 settings, find help for sticky situations, or, thankfully, shut down Windows 95 and get away from the computer for a while.

The little Start button is so eager to please, in fact, that it starts shooting out menus full of options as soon as you click on it. Just click on the button once, and the first layer of menus pops out, as shown in Figure 11-6.

Figure 11-6:
Click on the taskbar's Start button to see a list of options.

The explosive Table 11-1 shows what the different parts of the Start button do when you point at them.

Table 11-1	The Start Button
This Part	*Does This When You Point at It*
Programs ▶	Probably the most used spot. Point here, and a second menu appears, listing available programs and folders containing related programs.
Documents ▶	Point here to see the names of the last 15 files you've played with. Spot one you want to open again? Click on its name to reopen it.
Settings ▶	Allows access to the Control Panel and Printer settings, as well as ways to customize the Start button menus and taskbar.
Find ▶	Lost a program or file? Head here to make Windows 95 search for it.
Help	Clicking here does the same thing as pressing F1 — it brings up the Windows 95 Help menu.
Run...	Used mostly by old-school, "stick-shift" computer users, it lets you start a program by typing the program's name and *path*.
Shut Down...	Click here to either shut down and restart Windows, close all programs and log on as a different user, or shut it down for the day.
Start	Clicking on the Start button makes the Start menu shoot out of the button's head.

✔ Microsoft boiled down Windows 3.1 Program Manager and came up with the Start button. The Start button can handle just about everything Program Manager does. Those folders listed on the Start button's Programs menu would be program groups in Program Manager. Imagine!

✔ The Start button menu changes as you add programs to your computer. That change means that the Start button on your friend's computer probably offers slightly different menus than the ones on your own computer.

✔ See the little arrows on the menu next to the words Programs, Documents, Settings, and Find? The arrows mean that when you point at those words, another menu pops up, offering more-detailed options.

✔ Need to open a file yet another time? Before you spend time clicking your way through folders, see if it's listed under the Start button's <u>D</u>ocuments area. You can find your past 15 documents listed there, ready to be opened with a click.

Starting a program from the Start button

This one's easy. Click on the Start button and when the menu pops out of the button's head, point at the word <u>P</u>rograms. Yet another menu pops up, this one listing the names of programs or folders full of programs.

If you see your program listed, click on the name. Wham! Windows 95 kicks that program to the screen. If you don't see your program listed, try pointing at the folders listed on the menu. New menus fly out of those folders, listing even more programs.

When you spot your program's name, just click on it. In fact, you don't have to click until you see the program's name: The Start button opens and closes all the menus automatically, depending on where the mouse arrow is pointing at the time.

✔ Still don't see your program listed by name? Then head for Chapter 8 and find the "Finding Lost Files and Folders" section. You can tell Windows 95 to find your program for you.

✔ There's another way to load a program that's not listed — if you know where the program's living on your hard drive. Choose <u>R</u>un from the Start button menu, type the program's name, and press Enter. If Windows 95 finds the program, it runs it. If it can't find the program, though, click on the <u>B</u>rowse button. Shazam! Yet another box appears, this time listing programs by name. Pick your way through the dialog box until you see your program; then double-click on its name and click on the OK button to load it.

✔ If you don't know how to *pick your way through* this particular dialog box, head to the section of Chapter 6 on opening a file. (This particular dialog box rears its head every time you load or save a file or open a program.)

Adding a program to the Start button

The Windows 95 Start button works great — until you're hankering for something that's not listed on the menu. How do you add things to the Start button's menu?

If you're installing a Windows program that comes with its own installation program, breathe a sigh of relief. Those programs automatically put themselves on the Start button menu. But what if your program comes from a simpler household and doesn't have an installation program? Well, it means more work for you, as described here:

1. **Copy the program to your hard drive.**

   Create a new folder somewhere on your hard drive and copy your new program and its files to that folder. (And turn to Chapter 12 if you're a little sketchy about creating folders and copying files.)

2. **Click on the Start button and then point at Settings.**

   A menu shoots out from the right side of the Start menu.

3. **Click on Taskbar and then click on the Start Menu Programs tab.**

   The tab lurks along the top, on the right side.

4. **Click on the Add button and then click on Browse.**

   A new box pops up, as shown in Figure 11-7.

Is Run a *real* DOS command line?

For the most part, Windows 95 treats the Start button's Run command just like a regular ol' DOS command line. When you type in the name of a Windows or DOS program, Windows 95 tries to run it. Windows 95 first searches the current directory and then it looks along the path. If Windows 95 can't find the program, it sends out a message of complaint. (Just click on the OK button and start over.)

If Windows 95 doesn't find the program, you have to type the path name along with the program's name. For example, to load WordPerfect for Windows Version 6, you type something like this:

```
C:\WPWIN60\WPWIN.EXE
```

The Start button's Run command line differs from the DOS command line in one key area: It can't handle DOS commands like DIR and TYPE.

If you're salivating at the thought of a command line, you probably shouldn't be running Windows 95. If you're looking for a quick, menuless way to call up a program, though, you may want to give the Run command an occasional shot.

Figure 11-7:
Click on a folder, and the Browse box lists the programs inside that folder.

Click on the folder to which you copied the program and its files.

Hint: If you can't find that folder, click on the icon of the little folder with the arrow inside, up near the top. That click tells Windows 95 to work its way up the folder listings, eventually showing you a list of your computer's disk drives.

5. **Double-click on the icon of the program you want to add.**

   The program's filename appears in the Command line box. (By double-clicking on the program's name, you were able to avoid typing the name yourself.)

6. **Click on the Next button and then double-click on the folder where you want your program to appear on the Start menu.**

   For example, if you want your new program to appear under the Programs heading, simply click on the Programs folder. In fact, Windows 95 automatically highlights the Programs folder, assuming that you want to install your new program there.

7. **Type the name that you want to see on the menu for that program and then click on the Finish button.**

   Most people just type the program's name. (Just as many people have nicknames, most program's filenames are different from their *real* names. For example, you'd probably want to change WP — the filename — to WordPerfect — the program's real name.)

8. **Click on the OK button at the bottom of the box.**

   That click gets rid of the Taskbar Properties box and *really* finishes the job. Now, when you click on the Start button, you see your new program listed on the menu.

A quicker but dirtier way to add programs to the Start menu

There's a quicker way to add a program to the Start menu, but it's not as versatile. The steps listed let you add a program's icon anyplace on the menu. But if you simply want the program's icon on the menu *now,* and you don't care about location, try this:

Open the My Computer or Explorer program and find the folder to which you've copied your program. Then drag the program's icon over to the Start button and let go. Point at the program and, while holding down the mouse button, point at the Start button. When the icon hovers over the Start button, let go of the mouse button.

Now, when you click on the Start button, you see your newly installed program's icon at the very top.

✔ These steps can put both Windows and DOS programs on your Start menu. (If your DOS program doesn't work, head for Chapter 14, which is full of ways to doctor your DOS programs into health under Windows 95. Plus, it shows how to change the program's icon.)

✔ Windows 95 lets you add programs to the Start menu in several ways. The one I just listed is probably the easiest one to follow step by step.

✔ To get rid of unwanted menu items, follow these steps but click on the Remove button rather than the Add button in Step 4.

✔ Just like your Windows 95 desktop, the Start menu is really just a plain old folder. The folder is a directory called Start Menu, and it lives in the folder where Windows 95 is installed, usually Windows on your C drive. Any program shortcuts that you put in the Start Menu folder appear as items on the Start menu. Also, to rearrange the items on the menu, rearrange the folders in the Start Menu folder.

Shutting down Windows 95

Although the big argument used to be about whether pasta is fattening, today's generation has found a new source of disagreement: Should a computer be left on all the time or turned off at the end of the day? Both camps have decent arguments, and there's no real answer (except that you should always turn off your monitor when you won't be using it for a half hour or so).

However, if you want to turn off your computer, don't just head for the off switch. First, you need to tell Windows 95 about your plans.

To do that, click on the Shut Down command from the Start menu and then click on the Shut down the computer button from the box that appears. Finally, click on the Yes button; that click tells Windows 95 to put away all your programs and to make sure that you've saved all your important files.

After Windows 95 has prepared the computer to be turned off, you see a message on the screen saying that it's okay to reach for the big red switch.

✔ If Windows 95 is acting weird — or if Windows 95 tells you to shut down and restart your computer — click on the Shut Down command from the Start menu. However, choose the Restart the computer option from the box. Windows 95 saves all your files, shuts itself down, and comes back to life, ready for more work.

✔ Don't turn off your computer unless you've first used the Shut Down command from the Start button. Windows 95 needs to prepare itself for the shutdown, or it may accidentally eat some of your important information.

The Taskbar

Put a second or third window onto the Windows 95 desktop, and you'll immediately see the Big Problem: Windows and programs tend to cover each other up, making them difficult to locate.

The solution is the taskbar. Shown in Figure 11-8, the taskbar is that little bar running along the bottom edge of your screen.

The taskbar keeps track of all the open folders and currently running programs by listing their names. And, luckily, the taskbar is almost always visible, no matter how cluttered your desktop becomes.

✔ When you want to bring a program, file, or folder to the forefront of the screen, click on its name on the taskbar.

Figure 11-8:
The taskbar lists the names of all your currently running programs and open folders.

| Start | FreeCell Game #10184 | CD Player | CompuServe - HyperTermina | 9:48 PM |

✔ If the taskbar *does* manage to disappear, press Ctrl+Esc; that action usually brings it to the surface.

✔ If you can only see part of the taskbar — it's hanging off the edge of the screen, for example — point at the edge you can see. When the mouse pointer turns into a two-headed arrow, hold down your mouse button and move the mouse to drag the taskbar back into view.

✔ If the taskbar looks too bloated, try the same trick. Point at its edge until the mouse pointer turns into a two-headed arrow and then drag the taskbar's edge inward until it's the right size.

The taskbar works somewhat like the minimized icons Windows 3.1 loads along the bottom of your screen. There are a few key differences, however: Windows 3.1 only displays icons of *minimized* programs; the taskbar displays icons for any currently running program. Also, Windows 3.1 lets you drag and drop files onto minimized icons — you can hear a WAV file by dragging and dropping it onto a minimized Media Player icon, for example. But you can't drag and drop anything onto the taskbar's program icons; you can only drag and drop files onto open windows.

Clicking on the taskbar's sensitive areas

Like a crafty card player, the taskbar comes with a few tips and tricks. For one thing, it has the Start button. With a click on the Start button, you can launch programs, change settings, find programs, get help, and order pizza. (Well, you can't order pizza, but you can do all the things mentioned in the Start button section earlier in this chapter.)

But the Start button is only one of the taskbar's tricks; some others are listed in Figure 11-9.

Figure 11-9: Clicking or double-clicking in these areas on the taskbar performs these tasks.

Click here to see the Start menu, which lets you start programs, load files, change settings, find files, or just find help.

Click on a blank area with your mouse button and choose Properties to change the taskbar's settings.

Click here to change the sound volume; double-click to adjust the sound card's mixer.

Rest the pointer over the time, and you'll see the current day and date. Double-click, and you can reset the time and date.

Clicking on any program listed down here brings it to the top of the screen.

Double-click here for information about your current modem session.

Clicking on the Start button brings up the Start menu, described earlier in this chapter. Also, hold the mouse pointer over the clock, and Windows 95 shows the current day and date. Or if you want to change the time or date, a double-click on the clock summons the Windows 95 time/date change program.

If you have a sound card, a click on the little speaker brings up the volume control, shown in Figure 11-10. Slide the volume knob up for louder sound; slide it down for peace and quiet. (Or click on the Mute box to turn the sound off completely.)

Figure 11-10: Clicking on the little speaker lets you adjust the sound card's volume.

Double-click on the little speaker to bring up a more advanced mixer program, shown in Figure 11-11, if your sound card offers that feature. Mixers let you adjust volume levels for your microphone, line inputs, CD players, and other features.

Figure 11-11: Double-clicking on the little speaker brings up a mixer program for the sound card.

If you're running a modem, a little picture of a modem appears next to the clock, as shown in Figure 11-12. Double-click on the modem to see statistics on the amount of data your modem is pushing and pulling over the phone lines.

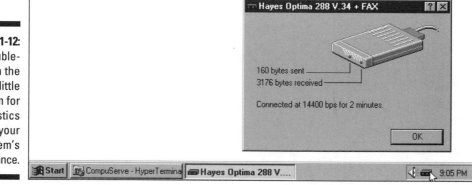

Figure 11-12:
Double-click on the little modem for statistics on your modem's performance.

✔ Other icons often appear next to the clock, depending on what Windows 95 is up to. If you're printing, for example, you see a little printer down there. Laptops sometimes show a battery monitor. As with all the other icons, a double-click on the printer or battery monitor brings up information about the printer's or battery's status.

✔ Want to minimize all your desktop's open windows in a hurry? Click on a blank part of the taskbar with your right mouse button and choose the <u>M</u>inimize All Windows option from the pop-up menu. All the programs keep running, but they're now minimized to icons along the taskbar. To bring them back to the screen, just click on their names from the taskbar.

✔ To organize your open windows, click on a blank part of the taskbar with your right mouse button and choose one of the tile commands. Windows 95 scoops up all your open windows and lays them back down in neat, orderly squares.

Customizing the taskbar

Although Windows 95 starts the taskbar along the bottom of the screen, it doesn't have to stay there. If you prefer that your taskbar hang from the top of your screen like a bat, just drag it there. Point at a blank spot of the taskbar and, while holding down your mouse button, point at the top of the screen. Let go of the mouse button, and the taskbar dangles from the roof, as shown in Figure 11-13.

| Start | FreeCell Game #10184 | CompuServe - HyperTermina | | 10:05 PM |

My Computer

Recycle Bin

Figure 11-13:
You can
move the
taskbar to
any side of
the screen
by dragging
it there.

Do you prefer the taskbar along one side? Drag it there, as shown in Figure 11-14. (The buttons become more difficult to read, however.)

If the taskbar is starting to look too crowded, you can make it wider by dragging its edges outward, as shown in Figure 11-15.

✔ To change other taskbar options, click on a bare taskbar area with your right mouse button and choose Properties from the pop-up menu. From there, you can make the taskbar always stay on top of the current pile of windows, make the taskbar automatically hide itself, hide the clock, and shrink the Start menu icons. Whenever you click on an option button, a handy on-screen picture previews the change. If the change looks good, click on the OK button to save it.

✔ Feel free to experiment with the taskbar, changing its size and position until it looks right for you. It won't break.

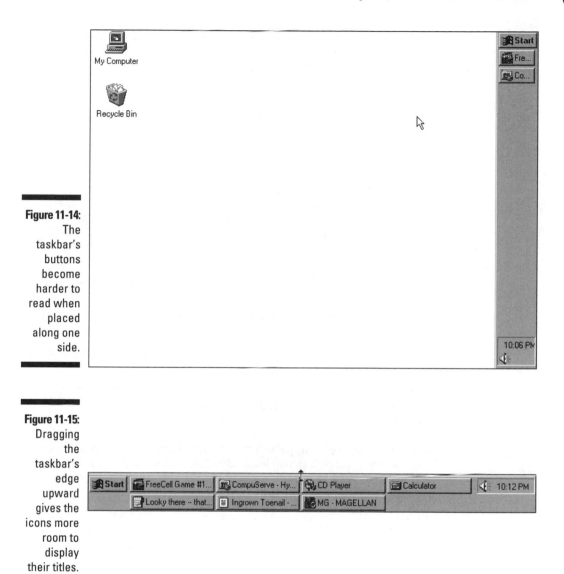

Figure 11-14:
The taskbar's buttons become harder to read when placed along one side.

Figure 11-15:
Dragging the taskbar's edge upward gives the icons more room to display their titles.

Making Windows Start Programs Automatically

Many people sit down at a computer, turn it on, and go through the same mechanical process of loading their oft-used programs. Believe it or not, Windows 95 can automate this computerized task.

The solution is the StartUp folder, found lurking in the Start button's Programs menu. When Windows 95 wakes up, it peeks inside that StartUp folder. If it finds a shortcut lurking, it grabs that shortcut's program and tosses it onto the screen.

Here's how to determine which programs wake up along with Windows 95 and which ones get to sleep in a little.

1. **First, click on the Start button with your *right* mouse button and choose the Open option.**

   Feel free to choose the Explore option if you prefer using Windows Explorer; either program does the trick. Your chosen file manager — My Computer or Windows Explorer — comes to the screen and displays part of the goodies in your Start menu.

2. **Double-click on the folder named Programs.**

   You see shortcuts and folders for all the programs currently listed in your Start button's Programs area.

3. **Double-click on the folder named StartUp to open it onto your screen.**

4. **Drag and drop any programs you want to start automatically into the StartUp window.**

   Windows 95 automatically turns the program's icons into shortcuts. And whenever you start Windows 95 from scratch, those programs load up right along with it.

✔ Do you find yourself using the StartUp area a lot? Make a Shortcut that points straight toward it and leave the Shortcut on your desktop. A drag and a drop onto your StartUp shortcut puts an oft-used program into the Start menu's automatic StartUp area.

✔ You decide which programs start up when Windows 95 does by dragging and dropping files and shortcuts in and out of the StartUp folder.

Chapter 12

Those Scary Windows Explorer and My Computer Programs

*T*he Windows Explorer program is where people wake up from the Windows dream, clutching a pillow in horror. These people bought Windows to make their computers easier to use, to lift them from the old DOS psychobabble of folder levels and application extensions and hidden files.

But open Windows 95 Explorer, and those ugly DOS terms leer up at you. You not only have to juggle that painfully technical DOS stuff, but you have to do it while bouncing from button to button. The My Computer program isn't quite as painful, but it's still awkward enough to leave a few bruises.

This chapter explains how to use the Windows Explorer and My Computer programs, and along the way it dishes out a big enough dose of DOS for you to get your work done. But, if you're really into file management (heaven knows why), consider picking up this book's forefather, *DOS For Dummies*, published by IDG Books Worldwide, Inc. It goes into just enough detail (yet keeps the dirge level gratefully low).

Why Is Windows Explorer So Scary?

Windows Explorer is an awkward mixture of two wildly different computing worlds: DOS and Windows. It's as if somebody tried to combine an automobile with a bathtub. Everybody's confused when the door opens and water pours out.

To join in the confusion, click on a folder with your right mouse button and, when the little menu pops out, choose the Explore option.

Everybody organizes his or her computer differently. Some people don't organize their computers at all. So your Windows Explorer window probably looks a little different from the one shown in Figure 12-1.

Like Windows Explorer, the My Computer program, shown in Figure 12-2, lets you sling files around but in a slightly different way. The My Computer program is a big panel of buttons — sort of an extension of your desktop — and Windows Explorer is a big panel of filenames. In fact, some people like the Windows Explorer *text-based* system of names better than the My Computer *picture-based* system. (It's that right-brained versus left-brained stuff.)

Figure 12-1: You use the Windows Explorer to print, copy, move, rename, and delete files.

Figure 12-2:
The My
Computer
program
performs
the same
tasks as
Windows
Explorer,
but in
slightly
different
ways.

The icons in Windows 3.1 Program Manager are just buttons that stand for your programs. Deleting them doesn't harm the actual program. That's not true with the Windows 95 My Computer program. Unless the icon you're deleting has a little arrow lodged in its lower-left side, that icon is an actual program or file. Make sure that you're deleting the icon you want. (And if you goof and delete the wrong one, fish it back out of the Recycle Bin as soon as possible.)

✔ Although they both end in the word Explorer, the *Windows Explorer* program is completely different from the *Internet Explorer* program. Windows Explorer lets you fiddle with the files stored inside your computer. Internet Explorer, on the other hand, lets you connect to other computers through the phone lines, swapping information through the Internet and World Wide Web.

✔ In a way, learning how to deal with files is like learning how to play the piano: Neither is intuitively obvious, and you hit some bad notes with both. Don't be frustrated if you don't seem to be getting the hang of it. Liberace would have hated file management at first, too.

✔ Tired of using a menu to load Windows Explorer? Press the Shift key while double-clicking any folder you want to explore. The Windows Explorer program pops up, showing you the contents of the current folder.

Getting the Lowdown on Folders

This stuff is really boring, but if you don't read it, you'll be just as lost as your files.

A *folder* is a workplace on a disk. Hard drives are divided into many folders to separate your many projects. You can work with a spreadsheet, for example, without having all the word-processing files get in the way.

Any disk can have folders, but hard drives need them the most because they need a way to organize their thousands of files. By dividing a hard drive into little folder compartments, you can more easily see where everything sits.

The Windows Explorer and My Computer programs enable you to move around to different folders and peek at the files you've stuffed inside each one. It's a pretty good organizational scheme, actually. Socks never fall behind a folder and jam the drawer.

Folders used to be called *directories* and *subdirectories*. But some people were getting used to that, so the industry switched to the term *folders*.

- Folders can be inside folders to add a deeper level of organization, like adding drawer partitions to sort your socks by color. Each sock color partition is a smaller, organizing folder of the larger sock-drawer folder.

- Of course, you can ignore folders and keep all your files right on the Windows 95 desktop. That's like tossing everything into the back seat of the car and pawing around to find your tissue box a month later. Stuff you organized is a lot easier to find.

- If you're eager to create a folder or two (and it's pretty easy), page ahead to this chapter's "Creating a Folder" section.

- Windows created several folders when it installed itself on your computer. It created a Windows folder to hold most of its programs and a bunch of folders inside that to hold its internal engine parts.

- Just as manila folders come from trees, computer folders use a *tree metaphor,* shown in Figure 12-3, as they branch out from one main folder to several smaller folders.

Figure 12-3: The structure of folders inside your computer is treelike, with main folders branching out to smaller folders.

```
Rock (C:)
    Dos
    Program Files
    Util
    Utils
    Windows
        Command
        Config
        Fonts
        Golf
            Sounds
        Help
        Media
        SendTo
        Start Menu
        System
        Temp
```

What's all this path stuff?

Sometimes Windows 95 can't find a file, even if it's sitting right there on the hard disk. You have to tell Windows where the file is sitting — a process called *browsing* — and to do that, you need to know that file's *path*.

A path is like the file's address. When heading for your house, a letter moves to your country, state, city, street, and finally, hopefully, your apartment or house number. A computer path does the same thing. It starts with the letter of the disk drive and ends with the name of the file. In between, the path lists all the folders the computer must travel through to reach the file.

For example, look at the Sounds folder in Figure 12-3. For Windows 95 to find a file stored there, it starts from the C:\ folder, travels through the Windows folder, and then goes through the Golf folder. Only then does it reach the Sounds folder.

Take a deep breath. Exhale. Quack like a duck, if you like. Now, the *C* in C:\ stands for disk drive C. (In the path, a disk drive letter is always followed by a colon.) The disk drive letter and colon make up the first part of the path. All the other folders are inside the big C: folder, so they're listed after the C: part. DOS separates these nested folders with something called a backslash, or \ . The name of the actual file — let's say GRUNT.WAV — comes last.

C:\WINDOWS\GOLF\SOUNDS\GRUNT.WAV is what you get when you put it all together, and that's the official path of the GRUNT.WAV file in the Sounds folder.

This stuff can be tricky, so here it is again: The letter for the drive comes first, followed by a colon and a backslash. Then come the names of all the folders, separated by backslashes. Last comes the name of the file (with no backslash after it).

When you click on folders, Windows 95 puts together the path for you. Thankfully.

Peering into Your Drives and Folders

Knowing all this folder stuff can impress the people at the computer store. But what counts is knowing how to use the Windows Explorer and My Computer programs to get to a file you want. Never fear. Just read on.

Seeing the files on a disk drive

Like everything else in Windows 95, disk drives are represented by buttons, or icons:

3½ Floppy (A:)   5¼ Floppy (B:)   Rock (C:)   121mb (D:)   (E:)

Those disk drive buttons live in both the Windows Explorer and My Computer programs (although the ones in Windows Explorer are usually smaller). See the little disks above the icons labeled *Floppy?* Those are pictures of the types of floppy disks that fit into those drives. You see a compact disc floating above drive E: Double-clicking on that compact disc icon shows you what's currently in your compact disc drive. Hard drives don't have anything hovering over them except a nagging suspicion that they'll fail horribly at the worst moment.

✔ If you're kinda sketchy on those disk drive things, you probably skipped Chapter 2. Trot back there for a refresher course.

✔ Double-click on a drive icon in My Computer, and a window comes up to display the drive's contents. For example, put a disk in drive A and double-click on My Computer's drive A icon. A new window leaps up, showing what files and folders live on the disk in drive A.

✔ Click on a drive icon in Windows Explorer, and you see the drive contents on the right side of the window.

✔ A second window comes in handy when you want to move or copy files from one folder or drive to another, as discussed in the "Copying or Moving a File" section.

✔ The first two icons stand for the floppy drives, drive A and drive B. If you click on a floppy drive icon when no disk is in the drive, Windows 95 stops you gently, suggesting that you insert a disk before proceeding further.

✔ Spot an icon called Network Neighborhood? That's a little doorway for peering into other computers linked to your computer — if there are any. You find more network stuff near the end of this chapter.

Seeing what's inside folders

Because folders are really little storage compartments, Windows 95 uses a picture of a little folder to stand for each separate place for storing files.

To see what's inside a folder, in My Computer or on the desktop, just double-click on the picture. A new window pops up, showing that folder's contents.

Folder-opening works differently in Windows Explorer. In Windows Explorer, folders line up along the left side of a window. One folder, the one you're currently exploring, has a little box around its name.

The files living inside that particular folder appear on the right side of the window. The arrangement looks somewhat like Figure 12-4.

Figure 12-4:
When you click on a folder on the left side of Windows Explorer, that folder's contents appear on the right side of the window.

To peek inside a folder while in Windows Explorer, click on its name on the left side of the window. You see two things: That folder's next level of folders (if it has any) appear beneath it on the left side of the window, and that folder's filenames spill out into the right side of the window.

✔ As you keep climbing farther out on a branch and more folders appear, you're moving toward further levels of organization. If you climb back inward, you reach files and folders that have less in common.

✔ Yeah, this stuff is really confusing, but keep one thing in mind: Don't be afraid to double-click, or even single-click, on a folder just to see what happens. Clicking on folders just changes your viewpoint; nothing dreadful happens, and no tax receipts fall onto the floor. You're just opening and closing file cabinet drawers, peeking into folders along the way.

✔ To climb farther out on the branches of folders, keep double-clicking on new folders as they appear.

✔ To move back up the branches in Windows Explorer, double-click on a folder closer to the left side of the window. Any folders beneath that folder are now hidden from view.

✔ Sometimes a folder contains too many files to fit in the window. To see more files, click on that window's scroll bars. What's a scroll bar? Time to whip out your field guide, Chapter 6.

While in Windows Explorer, move the mouse pointer over the bar separating a folder on the left from its filenames on the right. When the pointer turns into a mutant two-headed arrow, hold down the mouse button. Then move the bar to the left to give the filenames more room, or to the right to give the folders on the right more room. Let go of the mouse when the split is adjusted correctly, and the window reshapes itself to the new dimensions.

Can't find a file or folder? Instead of rummaging through folders, check out the Find command described in Chapter 8. It's the fastest way to find files and folders that were "there just a moment ago."

Loading a Program or File

A *file* is a collection of information on a disk. Files come in two basic types: program files and data files.

Program files contain instructions that tell the computer to do something: balance the national budget or ferret out a fax number.

Data files contain information created with a program, as opposed to computer instructions. If you write a letter to the grocer complaining about his soggy apricots, you're creating a data file.

To open either kind of file in Windows 95, double-click on its name. A double-click on a program file's name brings the program to the screen, whether you found the filename listed in My Computer, Windows Explorer, or even the Find program. If you double-click on a data file, Windows 95 loads the file *and* the program that created it. Then it brings both the file and the program to the screen at the same time.

✔ Windows 95 sticks little icons next to filenames so that you know whether they're program or data files. In fact, even folders get their own icons so that you won't confuse them with files. Chapter 25, at the tail-end of the book, provides a handy reference for figuring out which icon is which. (The tail-end of the book is easier to find than this chapter.)

✔ Because of some bizarre New School of Computing mandate, any data file that Windows recognizes is called a *document.* A document doesn't have to contain words; it can have pictures of worms or sounds of hungry animals.

If the program or folder you're after is already highlighted, just give the Enter key a satisfying little pound with your index finger. That not only keeps your computer from getting out of line, but it shows you how many different ways Windows 95 lets you do things (which means that you don't need to worry about knowing them all).

Don't bother reading this hidden technical stuff

Sometimes programs store information in a data file. They may need to store information about the way the computer is set up, for example. To keep people from thinking that those files are trash and deleting them, the program hides those files.

You can view the names of these hidden files and folders, however, if you want to play voyeur. Choose View from the menu bar and then choose Options from the pull-down menu. Select the Show all files button and then click on the OK button.

The formerly hidden files appear alongside the other filenames. Be sure not to delete them, however: The programs that created them will gag, possibly damaging other files.

Deleting and Undeleting Files and Folders

Sooner or later, you'll want to delete a file that's not important anymore — yesterday's lottery picks, for example, or something you've stumbled on that's too embarrassing to save any longer. But then, hey, suddenly you realize that you've made a mistake and deleted the wrong file. Not to worry: The Windows 95 Recycle Bin can probably resurrect that deleted file if you're quick enough — and your file wasn't on a floppy disk.

Getting rid of a file or folder

To permanently remove a file from the hard drive, click on its name. Then press Delete. This surprisingly simple trick works for files, programs, and even folders.

The Delete key deletes entire folders, as well as any folders inside them. Make sure that you've selected the right file before you press Delete.

✔ When you press Delete, Windows tosses a box in your face, asking whether you're sure. If you are, click on the Yes button.

✔ Be extra sure that you know what you're doing when deleting any file that has an exclamation point in its icon. These files are sometimes hidden files, and the computer wants you to leave them alone. (Other than that, they're not particularly exciting, despite the exclamation point.)

✔ As soon as you find out how to delete files, you'll want to read the very next section, "How to undelete a file."

Deleting a shortcut from the desktop, My Computer, or Windows Explorer just deletes a button that loads a program. You can always put the button back on. Deleting an icon that doesn't have the little shortcut arrow removes that *file* from the hard disk and puts it into the Recycle Bin, where it eventually disappears.

How to undelete a file

Sooner or later, your finger will push the Delete key at the wrong time, and you'll delete the wrong file. A slip of the finger, the wrong nudge of a mouse, or, if you're in southern California, a small earthquake at the wrong time can make a file disappear. Zap!

Scream! When the tremors subside, double-click on the Recycle Bin, and the Recycle Bin box drops down from the heavens, as shown in Figure 12-5.

Figure 12-5:
The Recycle Bin drops down from the heavens to save the day.

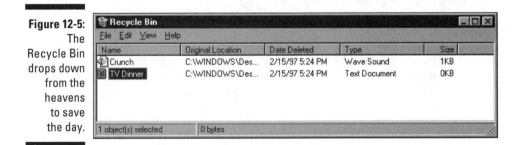

The files listed in the Recycle Bin can be brought back to life simply by dragging them out of the Recycle Bin box: Use the mouse to point at the name of the file you want to retrieve and, while holding down the mouse button, point at the desktop. Then let go of the mouse. Windows 95 moves the once-deleted file out of the Recycle Bin and places the newly revived file onto your desktop.

✔ After the file's on your desktop, it's as good as new. Feel free to store it in any other file for safekeeping.

✔ Unfortunately, the Recycle Bin only holds Windows 95 programs. Don't expect to find any deleted DOS or Windows 3.1 programs in the Recycle Bin.

✔ Don't expect to find programs deleted from your floppy disks, either. (You can find other programs for undeleting files from disks at the software store, fortunately.)

✔ The Recycle Bin normally holds about 10 percent of your hard disk's space. For example, if your hard drive is 200MB, the Recycle Bin holds on to 20MB of deleted files. When it reaches that limit, it starts deleting the oldest files to make room for the incoming deleted files. (And the old ones are gone for good, too.)

Copying or Moving a File

To copy or move files to different folders on your hard drive, use your mouse to *drag* them there. For example, here's how to move a file to a different folder on your hard drive:

1. **Move the mouse pointer until it hovers over the file you want to move and then press and hold down the mouse button.**

2. **While holding down the mouse button, use the mouse to point at the folder to which you'd like to move the file.**

   The trick is to hold down the mouse button the whole time. When you move the mouse, its arrow drags the file along with it. For example, Figure 12-6 shows how Windows Explorer looks when I drag the ZIGZAG.BMP file from my Windows folder on the right to my Junk folder on the left.

Figure 12-6:
The ZigZag file is being dragged to the Junk folder on the left side of the window in order to move it there.

3. **Release the mouse button.**

   When the mouse arrow hovers over the place to which you want to move the file, take your finger off the mouse button.

Moving a file by dragging its name is pretty easy, actually. The hard part often comes when you try to put the file and its destination on-screen at the same time. You often need to use both Windows Explorer and My Computer to put two windows on-screen. When you can see the file and its destination, start dragging.

Both Windows Explorer and My Computer do something awfully dumb to confuse people, however: When you drag a file from one folder to another on the same drive, you *move* the file. When you drag a file from one folder to another on a different drive, you *copy* that file.

I swear I didn't make up these rules. And the process gets more complicated: You can click on the file and hold down Shift to reverse the rules. Table 12-1 can help you keep these oafish oddities from getting too far out of control.

Table 12-1	Moving Files Around
To Do This	*Do This*
Copy a file to another location on the same disk drive	Hold down Ctrl and drag it there.
Copy a file to a different disk drive	Drag it there.
Move a file to another location on the same disk drive	Drag it there.
Move a file to a different disk drive	Hold down Shift and drag it there.
Make a shortcut while dragging a file	Hold down Ctrl+Shift and drag it there.
Remember these *obtuse* commands	Refer to the handy Cheat Sheet at the front of this book.

Here's an easy way to remember this stuff when the book's not handy: Always drag icons while holding down the *right* mouse button. Windows 95 is then gracious enough to give you a menu of options when you position the icon, and you can choose among moving, copying, or creating a shortcut.

✔ To copy or move files to a floppy disk, drag those files to the icon for that floppy disk, which you should find along the top of the Windows Explorer window.

✔ When you drag a file someplace in Windows 95, look at the icon attached to the mouse pointer. If the document icon has a *plus sign* in it, you're *copying* the file. If the document icon is *blank,* you're *moving* the file. Depending on where you are dragging the file, pressing Ctrl or Shift toggles the plus sign on or off, making it easier to see whether you're currently copying or moving the file.

✔ After you run a program's installation program to put the program on your hard drive, don't move the program around. An installation program often wedges a program into Windows pretty handily; if you move the program, it may not work anymore and you'll have to reinstall it.

Selecting More Than One File or Folder

Windows 95 lets you grab an armful of files and folders at one swipe; you don't always have to piddle around, dragging one item at a time.

To pluck several files and folders from a list, hold down Ctrl when you click on the names. Each name stays highlighted when you click on the next.

To gather several files or folders sitting next to each other, click on the first one. Then hold down the Shift key as you click on the last one. Those two items are highlighted, along with every file and folder between them.

Windows 95 lets you *lasso* files and folders as well. Point slightly above the first file or folder you want; then, while holding down the mouse button, point at the last file or folder. The mouse creates a lasso to surround your files. Let go of the mouse button, and the lasso disappears, leaving all the surrounded files highlighted.

✔ You can drag these armfuls of files in the same way as you drag one.

✔ You can delete these armfuls, too.

✔ You can't rename an armful of files all at once. To rename them, you have to go back to piddling around with one file at a time.

Renaming a File or Folder

If you're a he-man stuck with a name like Pink Gardenia, you can petition the courts to change it to Blue Gardenia. Changing a filename requires less effort: Click on the file or folder's name to select it, wait a second, and click on the file's name (its title running beneath or next to it).

The old filename gets highlighted and then disappears when you start typing the file or folder's new name. Press Enter or click on the desktop when you're through, and you're off.

✔ If you rename a file, only its name changes. The contents are still the same, it's still the same size, and it's still in the same place.

✔ You can't rename groups of files this way. The programs spit in your face if you even try.

✔ You can rename folders this way, too. (Renaming a folder can confuse Windows, however, which grows accustomed to folders the way they're first set up.)

Sometimes it's tricky clicking on filenames to rename them. If you're having trouble, just click on the file or folder with your right mouse button and choose Rename from the menu that pops up. Handy button, that right mouse button.

Using Legal Folder Names and Filenames

DOS is pretty picky about what you can and can't name a file or folder, so Windows 95 plays along. If you stick to plain old letters and numbers, you're fine. But don't try to stick any of the following characters in there:

```
: / \ * | < > ? "
```

If you use any of those characters, Windows 95 bounces an error message to the screen, and you have to try again.

These names are illegal:

```
1/2 of my Homework
JOB:2
ONE<TWO
He's no "Gentleman"
```

These names are legal:

```
Half a Term Paper
JOB2
Two is Bigger than One
A #@$%) Scoundrel
```

✔ As long as you remember the characters you can and can't use for naming files, you'll probably be okay.

✔ Like Windows 3.1, Windows 95 programs *brand* files with their own three-letter extension so that Windows 95 knows what program created what file. Normally, Windows 95 hides the extensions so that they're not confusing. But if you happen to spot filenames like SAVVY.DOC, README.TXT, and NUDE.BMP across the hard disk, you'll know that the extensions have been added by the Windows 95 programs WordPad, Notepad, and Paint, respectively. In Windows 3.1, you know what program created what file by looking at the file's extension; with Windows 95, you just look at the file's icon for heritage clues.

If you really want to see a filename's extension, Choose Options from the folder's View menu and then click on the tab marked View. Finally, click on the little box that says Display the full MS-DOS path in the title bar. The extensions then show up in that particular folder. (Click on the box again to remove the extensions.)

You may see a filename with a weird tilde thing in it, such as WIGWAM~1.TXT. That's the special way that Windows 95 deals with long filenames. Most older programs expect files to have only eight characters; Windows 95 whittles long filenames down so that those older programs can use them. (Windows 95 remembers the long filename for itself.)

Copying a Complete Floppy Disk

To copy files from one disk to another, drag 'em over there, as described a few pages back. To copy an entire disk, however, use the Copy Disk command.

What's the difference? When you're copying files, you're dragging specific filenames. But, when you're copying a disk, the Copy Disk command duplicates the disk exactly: It even copies the empty parts! (That's why it takes longer than just dragging the files over.)

The Copy Disk command has two main limitations:

- ✔ It can copy only floppy disks that are the same *size* or *capacity*. Just as you can't pour a full can of beer into a shot glass, you can't copy one disk's information onto another disk unless they hold the same amount of data.

- ✔ It can't copy the hard drive or a RAM drive. Luckily, you really have no reason to copy them, even if you know what a RAM drive is.

Here's how to make a copy of a floppy disk:

1. **Put your floppy disk in your disk drive.**

2. **Double-click the My Computer icon.**

3. **Click on your floppy disk's icon with your right mouse button.**

4. **Choose Copy Disk from the pop-up menu.**

   A box appears, letting you confirm which disk and disk drive you want to use for your copy.

5. **Click on the Start button to begin making the copy.**

But my version of Windows 95 doesn't have the Copy Disk command!

Don't see the Copy Disk command listed in your disk drive icon's pop-up menu? You probably have an early, prerelease version of Windows 95. That version didn't come with the Copy Disk command, so you're stuck with the following archaic DOS version. Here's what to do:

1. **Put your floppy disk in your disk drive.**

2. **Click on the Start button and click on Run from the menu that pops up.**

3. **Type the following information:**

   If you're copying the disk in drive A, type this and press the Enter key:

DISKCOPY A: A:

That's the word DISKCOPY, a space, the letter A followed by a colon, another space, and the letter A followed by a colon.

If you're copying the disk in drive B, type this and press the Enter key:

DISKCOPY B: B:

Everything's the same as before, except you substitute the letter B for the letter A.

4. **Follow the instructions on the screen.**

> ✔ All this *capacity* and *size* stuff about disks and drives is slowly digested in Chapter 2.

> ✔ The Copy Disk command can be handy for making backup copies of your favorite programs.

> ✔ In fact, you should always use the Copy Disk command when making backup copies of programs. Sometimes programs hide secret files onto their floppies; by making a complete copy of the disk with the Copy Disk command, you can be sure that the entire disk gets copied, hidden files and all.

Creating a Folder

To store new information in a file cabinet, you grab a manila folder, scrawl a name across the top, and start stuffing it with information.

To store new information in Windows 95 — a new program, for example — you create a new folder, think up a name for the new folder, and start moving or copying files into it.

New, more organized folders make finding information easier, too. For example, you can clean up a crowded Letters folder by dividing it into two folders: Business and Personal.

Here's how to use Windows Explorer to create a new folder — a folder called Business — that lives in your Letters folder:

1. **On the left side of the Windows Explorer window, click in the area in which you want the new folder to appear.**

   If you want a new Games folder in your Windows folder, for example, you click on the Windows folder on the left side of Windows Explorer. In the Letters example, you click on the Letters folder, shown in Figure 12-7, because you want the Business folder to appear in the Letters folder.

Figure 12-7:
You can organize the Letters folder by creating new folders, one each for business and personal letters.

   Click on the Letters folder, and its current contents spill out into the right side of Windows Explorer.

2. **Click on the right side of Windows Explorer with your right mouse button and choose New; when the menu appears, choose Folder.**

   The My Computer window lets you create a folder when you right-click in any window; Windows Explorer lets you create a folder only when you right-click within its right-hand side. A box pops up and asks you to think of a name for your new folder.

3. Type the new folder's name and press Enter.

Windows 95 can sometimes be picky about names you give to folders and files. For the rules, check out the "Using Legal Folder Names and Filenames" section earlier in this chapter.

After you type the folder's name and press Enter, the new Business folder is complete, ready for you to start moving your business letter files there. For impeccable organization, follow the same steps to create a Personal folder and move your personal files there, using the "dragging" process shown in Figure 12-8 (and explained in the "Copying or Moving a File" section in this chapter).

✔ Want to install a new Windows program that doesn't come with an installation program? Create a new folder for it and copy its files there. Then head to Chapter 11 to see how to put the new program's name in the Start menu for easy clicking.

Figure 12-8:
You can drag files into the new Business and Personal folders to organize your work.

✔ To move files into a new folder, drag them there. Just follow the directions in the "Copying or Moving a File" section.

✔ When copying or moving lots of files, select them all at the same time before dragging them. You can chew on this stuff in the "Selecting More Than One File or Folder" section.

✔ Just as with naming files, you can use only certain characters when naming folders. (Stick with plain old letters and numbers, and you'll be fine.)

Seeing More Information about Files and Folders

Whenever you create a file or folder, Windows 95 scrawls a bunch of secret hidden information on it: its size, the date you created it, and even more trivial stuff. To see what Windows 95 is calling the files and folders behind your back, select <u>V</u>iew from the menu bar and then choose <u>D</u>etails from the menu.

In fact, you can simply click on the right-most button on the toolbar, which lives atop the My Computer and Windows Explorer windows. Each of the four buttons on the right arranges the icons in a different way, as shown in Figure 12-9, showing different amounts of information. (And clicking on those buttons simply changes the way Windows 95 displays the icons — it doesn't hurt anything.)

Figure 12-9: Click on these buttons in the toolbar to change the way Windows 95 displays icons in the window.

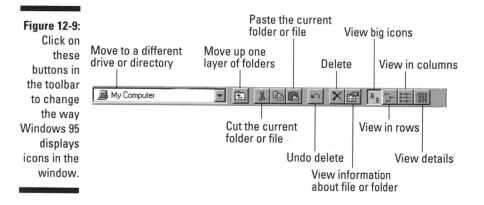

✔ Is the toolbar not living on top of your window? Put it there by choosing <u>T</u>oolbar from the <u>V</u>iew menu. That little bar of buttons now appears atop your window like a mantel over a fireplace.

✔ If you can't remember what those little toolbar buttons do, rest your mouse pointer over them and make it look lost. Windows 95 displays a helpful box summing up the button's mission, and a further explanation often appears along the window's bottom.

✔ Although some of the additional file information is handy, it can consume a lot of space, limiting the number of files you can see in the window. Displaying only the filename is often a better idea. Then, if you want to see more information about a file or folder, try the following tip.

✔ Hold down Alt and double-click on a file or folder to see its size, date, and other information.

✔ With the Alt+double-click trick (described in the preceding paragraph), you can change a file's attributes as well. Attributes are too boring to be discussed further, so duck beneath the technical stuff coming up in the sidebar "Who cares about this stuff, anyway?"

At first, Windows 95 displays filenames sorted alphabetically by name in its Windows Explorer and My Computer windows. But, by right-clicking in a folder and choosing the different sorting methods in the Arrange Icons menu, you display them in a different order. Windows puts the biggest ones at the top of the list, for example, when you choose sort by Size. Or you can choose sort by Type to keep files created by the same application next to each other. Or you can choose sort by Date to keep the most recent files at the top of the list.

Dragging, Dropping, and Running

You can drag files around in Windows 95 to move them or copy them. But there's more: You can drag them outside of the Windows Explorer or My Computer window and drop them into other windows to load them into other files and programs, as shown in Figure 12-10.

Figure 12-10: The mouse pointer changes shape as you drag the Egyptian Stone file into the Paint window.

For example, drag the Egyptian Stone file into the Paint window and let go of the mouse button. Paint loads the Egyptian Stone file, just as if you'd double-clicked on it in the first place.

This feature brings up all sorts of fun ideas. If you have a sound card, you can listen to sounds by dropping sound files into the Media Player or Sound Recorder windows. You can drop text files into Notepad to load them quickly. Or you can drop WordPad files into WordPad.

✔ Okay, the first thing everybody wants to know is what happens if you drag a sound file into WordPad? Or a WordPad file into Notepad? Or any other combination of files that don't match? Well, Windows 95 either embeds one file into the other — a process described in Chapter 9 — or sends you a box saying that it got indigestion. Just click on the OK button, and things return to normal. No harm done, either way.

✔ The second question everybody asks is why bother? You can just double-click on a file's name to load it. That's true. But this way is more fun and occasionally faster.

✔ You've never dragged and dropped before? Chapter 4 contains complete instructions.

✔ Old-time Windows users will want to know if they can load files by dropping them onto taskbar icons along the screen's bottom. Not any more — Windows 95 lets you drop things only into *open* windows. But if you drag the object over to the taskbar icon that you're interested in and let the mouse pointer hover over it for a while, the icon blossoms into an open window, ready to receive the object. (Yep, there's a lot of mouse-pointer hovering in Windows 95.)

Who cares about this stuff, anyway?

Windows 95 gives each file four special switches called *attributes*. The computer looks at the way those switches are set before it fiddles with a file.

Read Only: Choosing this attribute allows the file to be read but not deleted or changed in any way.

Archive: The computer sets this attribute when a file has changed since the last time it was backed up with the special DOS or Windows 95 BACKUP command.

Hidden: Setting this attribute makes the file invisible during normal operations.

System: Files required by a computer's operating system have this attribute set.

The Properties box makes it easy — perhaps too easy — to change these attributes. In most cases, you should leave them alone. They're just mentioned here so that you'll know what computer nerds mean when they tell cranky people, "Boy, somebody must have set *your* attribute wrong when you got out of bed this morning."

How Do I Make the Network Work?

Windows 95 can connect to bunches of other computers through an office network and, luckily, that makes it pretty easy to grab files from other people's computers. At least it's pretty easy if somebody else has already set up the network. But after the network's running, you'll be running right alongside it. There isn't much new to learn.

Network

See the Network Neighborhood icon on your computer's desktop (and shown in the margin)? That icon is the key to all the computers currently connected to your computer.

Double-click on that icon and a window appears, as shown in Figure 12-11. Your windows naturally differ because you have different computers. (And the computers probably have different names, too.)

Figure 12-11: Double-click on the Network Neighborhood icon to see which computers on the network you can access, and then double-click on the one you want to peek inside.

Double-click on the icon of the computer you want to peek inside and a new window appears, as shown in Figure 12-12, showing that computer's contents.

✔ From here, everything works just like the normal Windows Explorer window. Feel free to point and click in the other computer's folders. To copy files back and forth, just drag and drop them to and from your computer's window to the other computer's window.

Figure 12-12:
You can
work with
another
computer's
files
through a
network
using your
Windows
Explorer
program.

✔ You can only access the computers that your network administrator has given you access to. Don't get carried away; you're not really getting away with anything.

✔ Networks can be set up in dozens of different ways; sometimes another computer's program will work on your computer, and other times the program won't. Again, your network administrator should be your guide.

Making My Computer and Windows Explorer List Missing Files

Sometimes Windows 95 snoozes and doesn't keep track of what's *really* on the disk. Oh, it does pretty well with the hard drive, and it works pretty well if you're just running Windows programs. But it can't tell when you stick in a new floppy disk. Also, if you create a file from within a DOS program, Windows 95 may not know that the new file is there.

If you think that the Windows Explorer or My Computer window is holding out on you, tell it to *refresh,* or take a second look at what's on the floppy disk or hard drive. You can click on <u>V</u>iew from the menu bar and choose <u>R</u>efresh from the pull-down menu, but a quicker way is to press the F5 key. (It's a function key along the top or left side of the keyboard.) Either way, the programs take a second look at what they're supposed to be showing and update their lists if necessary.

Press the F5 key whenever you stick in a different floppy disk and want to see what files are stored on it. Windows 95 then updates the screen to show that *new* floppy's files, not the files from the first disk.

Formatting a New Floppy Disk

New floppy disks don't work straight out of the box; your computer burps out an error message if you even try to use them fresh. Floppy disks must be formatted, and unless you paid extra for a box of *preformatted* floppy disks, you must format them yourself. The My Computer program handles this particularly boring chore quite easily. It's still boring, though, as you'll discover when repeating the process 12 times — once for each disk in the box.

Here's the procedure:

1. **Place the new disk into drive A or drive B and close the latch.**

2. **In either Windows Explorer or the My Computer window, click on the drive's icon with your right mouse button and choose For<u>m</u>at from the menu.**

3. **If you're formatting a *high-capacity* disk in drive A, select the <u>F</u>ull setting under Format type and select <u>S</u>tart in the top-right corner.**

   Your disk drives whir for several minutes, and then Windows 95 asks whether you want to format another.

   Then remove the floppy disk and return to Step 1 until you've formatted the entire box.

4. **Click on the Close button when Windows 95 is through.**

   ✔ You can format disks in your drive B by clicking on the drive B icon with your right mouse button. Likewise, you can change a disk's capacity by clicking on the little arrow in the <u>C</u>apacity box. You don't know the capacity of your disks? Head for the handy chart in Chapter 2.

   ✔ Don't get your hopes up: The <u>Q</u>uick (Erase) option won't speed things up unless your disk has already been formatted once before.

   ✔ If you want to be able to boot your computer from a disk, check the Copy s<u>y</u>stem files option. These System Disks can come in handy if your hard drive ever goes on vacation.

   ✔ In fact, if Windows 95 ever goes on vacation, you should have an emergency disk. The Add/Remove Programs icon in the Windows 95 Control Panel makes one for you. (Chapter 10 explains how to create a startup disk.)

Chapter 13

The *Free* Programs!

• •

• •

*W*indows 95 comes with a lot of free programs, but it doesn't install them all onto your hard drive automatically; some of them stay on the installation disks. If you installed Windows 95 over Windows 3.1, some of your older programs are still kicking around, too. What's the point? You probably won't see all this chapter's programs on your particular computer.

These little programs won't work wonders, though. Microsoft programmers squirm a little in their chairs if you even call them *programs*. No, Microsoft calls these things *applets* — mini programs designed to demonstrate what a *real* Windows program could do if you head back to the software store and buy one. If your needs are simple, these simple programs may fill them. But when your needs start growing, your software budget will probably have to grow as well.

Oh, yeah — and if you want information on the latest Internet and World Wide Web doodads now packaged with Windows 95, head for Chapter 15.

Word Processing with WordPad

Wordpad

You can find most of the little programs that come with Windows 95 listed under the Accessories section of the <u>P</u>rograms menu (which lurks in the menu that leaps up from the Start button). The icon for WordPad looks pretty fancy — a distinguished-looking fountain pen, like the ones that get ink on your hands.

Although the icon is fancy, WordPad isn't quite as fancy as some of the more expensive word processors on the market. You can't create multiple columns, for example, like the ones in newspapers or newsletters, nor can you double-space your reports. But WordPad works fine for letters, simple reports, and other basic documents. You can change the fonts around to get reasonably fancy, too, as shown in Figure 13-1.

WordPad can also handle the Windows *TrueType fonts* — that font technology that shapes how characters appear on-screen. You can create an elegant document by using some fancy TrueType fonts and mail it on a disk to somebody else. That person can view it in WordPad, just as you did. (Before TrueType, people could see only the fonts they had laboriously installed on their own computers.)

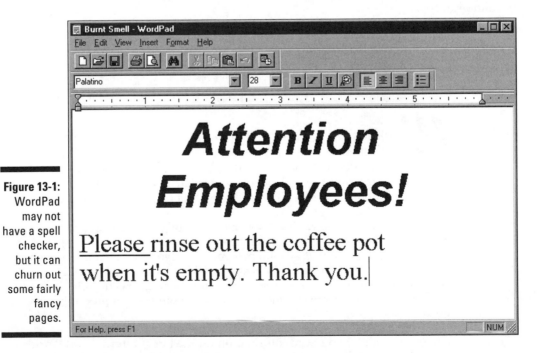

Figure 13-1:
WordPad
may not
have a spell
checker,
but it can
churn out
some fairly
fancy
pages.

Plus, WordPad can handle all that embedding and linking stuff talked about in Chapter 9.

- ✔ WordPad works well for most word-processing needs: writing letters, reports, or term papers on somber philosophers with weird last names. Unless you're a lousy speller, you'll find WordPad easy to use, and you'll like its excellent price.

- ✔ If you're ditching your typewriter for Windows, remember this: On an electric typewriter, you have to press the Return key at the end of each line or else you start typing off the edge of the paper. Computers, in contrast, are smart enough to sense when words are about to run off the end of the screen. They automatically drop down a line and continue the sentence. (Hip computer nerds call this phenomenon *word wrap*.)

  Press Enter only when you're finished typing a paragraph and want to start a new one. Press Enter twice to leave a blank line between paragraphs.

- ✔ WordPad replaces the old Write word processor from Windows 3.1, and it does almost everything Write could do. You won't find any way to add headers or footers, however; nor will WordPad let you double-space your documents. Finally, none of the new applications that come with Windows 95 let you search for funny characters, such as Tabs or Paragraph marks.

Opening and saving a file

In a refreshing change of pace, all Windows 95 programs enable you to open and save a file in exactly the same way: Choose File at the top of the program's window, and a menu tumbles down. Choose Open or Save, depending on your whim. A box pops up, listing the files in the current folder. Select the name of the file you want to open (click on it) or type the name of a new file. Then click on OK. That's it.

- ✔ If you want to open a file you spot listed in Windows Explorer or the My Computer window, double-click on the file's name. Windows 95 yanks the file into the right program and brings both the program and the file to the screen.

- ✔ You can find more explicit instructions on opening a file in Chapter 6.

- ✔ Folders and equally mind-numbing concepts are browbeaten in Chapter 12.

- ✔ When you save a file for the first time, you have to choose a name for it, as well as a folder to put it in. WordPad subsequently remembers the file's name and folder, so you don't have to keep typing them each time you save your current progress.

- WordPad can create files in three formats: a plain text file known as *ASCII,* a Word 6 file, or a *Rich Text Format.* All three formats are covered in the next section.

- Sometimes you open a file, change it, and want to save it with a different name or in a different folder. Choose Save As, not Save; WordPad then treats your work as if you were saving it for the first time — it asks you to type in a new name and a location.

- Although you can make up filenames on the fly in WordPad, you can't use WordPad to create new folders. That duty falls to Windows Explorer or My Computer, discussed in Chapter 12.

Saving a WordPad file in different formats

Just as you can't drop a Ford engine into a Volvo, you can't drop a WordPad file into another company's word processor. All brands of word processors save their information in different ways in order to confuse the competition.

WordPad can read and write in three file formats. As soon as you try to create a new file, WordPad forces you choose between three formats: a Word 6 Document, a Rich Text Document, and a Text Only Document. Each format meets different needs.

- **Word 6 Document:** This format creates files that can be read by Microsoft's *real* (and expensive) word processor, Microsoft Word. Many of the most popular competing word processors can read Word 6 files, too. You'll probably be safe with this format.

- **Rich Text Document:** These files can also be read by a wide variety of word processors. Like the Word 6 documents, Rich Text documents can store **boldfaced** and *italicized* words, as well as other special formatting. These files can be *huge,* however. Don't choose this format unless it's the only format your friend's word processor accepts.

- **Text Only Document:** Almost all brands of word processors can read plain old text, making Text Only Document the safest format if you plan on exchanging files with friends. The Text Only document can't have any boldface type, italic type, columns, or any other fancy stuff, however. ***Nerdly note:*** Text Only files are also called *ASCII* files (pronounced *ASK-ee*).

If somebody asks you to save a WordPad file in a different format, choose Save As from the File menu. Click on the arrow next to the Save file as type box and choose the new format from the drop-down list. Type a new name for the file into the File name box and press Enter. *Voilà!* You've saved your file in the new format.

✔ The other word processor that comes with Windows 95, Notepad, can't handle anything but Text Only files. Notepad can't load WordPad's Word 6 files, and if it opens the Rich Text documents, the files look really weird. (WordPad can easily read Notepad's files, though.) Notepad gets its due later in this chapter.

✔ Although most word processors can read and write ASCII files, problems still occur. You lose any formatting, such as italicized words, special indents, or embedded pictures of apples.

✔ ASCII stands for American Standard Code for Information Interchange. A bunch of technoids created it when they got tired of other technoids saving their information in different ways. Today, most programs grudgingly read or write information using the ASCII format. In fact, ASCII files can even be exchanged with computers from different home planets, such as Apple Macintosh and UNIX workstations, with only minor technical glitches.

Other WordPad stuff

✔ WordPad is always in Insert mode: When you add something in the middle of a sentence, all the words move to the right to make room for the incoming stuff. WordPad doesn't support the Overwrite mode, where the incoming letters are written right over the old stuff. The Insert key on the keyboard won't do anything, even if you push it really hard.

✔ A faster way to open a file is to press and release Alt and then press F and then O. If you memorize the keyboard commands, you won't have to trudge through all the menus with the mouse. If you don't remember the key commands, check out the handy chart in Table 13-1. You can find other time-savers listed, as well.

✔ To open a file, feel free to "drag" its name from the Windows Explorer or My Computer window and drop the name directly into WordPad's open window. Whoosh! WordPad immediately sucks the file's contents into the open window.

✔ Want to change your page margins? Choose File and choose Page setup when the menu drops down. The Page Layout dialog box lets you specify top, bottom, and side margins.

✔ Saved a file in WordPad, but now you want to delete it? Head for Windows Explorer or My Computer and delete it there. WordPad is an overly sensitive program; it can only *create* files, not destroy them.

Table 13-1	WordPad Shortcut Keys
To Do This	*Do This*
Open a file	Press Alt, F, and O.
Save a file	Press Alt, F, and S.
Save a file under a new name	Press Alt, F, and A.
Print a file	Press Alt, F, and P.
Select the entire document	Click rapidly three times in the left margin.
Select one word	Double-click on it.
Add *italics* to selected text	Hold down Ctrl and press the letter I (press Ctrl+I).
Add **boldface** to selected text	Hold down Ctrl and press the letter B (press Ctrl+B).
Add <u>underline</u> to selected text	Hold down Ctrl and press the letter U (press Ctrl+U).

Drawing Pictures with Paint

Paint

Do you love the smell of paint and a fresh canvas? Then you'll hate Paint. After working with real fibers and pigments, you'll find the computerized painting program that comes with Windows 95, Paint, to be a little sterile. But at least there's no mess. Paint creates pictures and graphics to stick into other programs. The icon for Paint is a picture of a palette, found in the Accessories menu (which leaps out from the Start menu's Programs menu).

Paint offers more than just a paintbrush. It has a can of spray paint for that *airbrushed* look, several pencils of different widths, a paint roller for gobbing on a bunch of paint, and an eraser for when things get out of hand. Figure 13-2 was drawn with Paint.

In addition to capturing your artistic flair, Paint can team up with a digital camera or scanner to touch up pictures in your PC. You can create a flashy letterhead to stick into letters in WordPad. You can even create maps to paste into your party fliers.

✔ Drawings and pictures can be copied from Paint and pasted into just about any other Windows 95 program.

Figure 13-2:
Paint can create exotic art, like this picture my mother drew.

✔ Remember that *cut and paste* stuff from Chapter 9? Well, you can cut out or copy chunks of art from the Paint screen using the *select* or *free-form select* tools described later in this section. The art goes onto the Windows 95 Clipboard, where you can grab it and paste it into any other Windows program. (Paint doesn't support "Scraps," also covered in Chapter 9.)

✔ Paint enables you to add text and numbers to graphics, so you can add street names to maps, put labels inside drawings, or add the vintage year to your wine labels.

Paint replaces Paintbrush from Windows 3.1. In fact, if you installed Windows 95 over Windows 3.1, the Paint icon is labeled *Pbrush* rather than Paint. Unlike Paintbrush, the Paint program no longer saves files in PCX format. If you used PCX files, you may want to copy your old version of Paintbrush back onto your hard drive. (The old version can also do a few other things that Paint can't, such as erasing in straight lines when you hold down the Shift key.)

Figuring out how to draw something

Paint comes with a row of drawing tools along the left side of the window. Not even Jeane Dixon can figure out what they do, so Table 13-2 explains them. Remember this, though: If you hold the mouse pointer over a mysterious-looking tool, a box pops up listing the tool's name, and a description of the tool appears along the bottom of the Paint window.

Below the drawing tools panel lies the *palette bar,* which is shown in Figure 13-3. *Palette* is a fancy name for the colors you can dab onto your drawing.

Table 13-2	Paint Tools
What It Looks Like	*What It's Called and What It Does*
	Free-Form Select: Grabs irregular chunks of the screen for cutting or copying to the Clipboard and pasting elsewhere.
	Select: Grabs a rectangular chunk of the screen for cutting or copying to the Clipboard and pasting elsewhere.
	Eraser: Rubs out everything, leaving nothing showing but the current background color.
	Fill With Color: Pours color into an area, filling it up to its boundaries.
	Pick Color: Picks up a color from the current picture.
	Magnifier: Enlarges a portion of the picture for easier viewing of details.
	Pencil: Just like it sounds, this pencil draws freehand. Very hard to use.
	Brush: Works more like a felt pen with an adjustable tip.
	Airbrush: Adds spray paint on the drawing. It's good for touching up pictures of bus stop benches.
	Text: Enables you to add text, along with standard effects like bold and italics.
	Line: Draws a straight line between two points. (Hold down Shift to make vertical or horizontal lines.)
	Curve: Draws a line and then lets you bend it, twice—truly weird.
	Rectangle, Polygon, Ellipsis, and Rounded Rectangle: Click on these tools to create shapes that look just like the icons.

Figure 13-3:
You use the
palette bar
to choose
different
colors.

Colors to choose from

Currently selected color

Currently selected background color

The key to using Paint is to realize that you're always working with *two* colors: the color of the background and the color you're dabbing on top of it. Paint starts out with the drab combination of black lines on a white background.

To change the color of the *foreground* — the color you use to draw things — click on one of the colors in the palette with the *left* mouse button. To change the color of the *background* — the color you're drawing *on* — click on that color in the palette with the *right* mouse button. You see your new background color when you start a new drawing.

Some of the tools have adjustable tips. When you click on the tool, look in the box beneath the toolbar. If a variety of tips appears, you can click on those tips to change the size and shape of your tool. (The best way to figure them out is to just click and play.)

After you select colors, click on the tool you're after in the toolbar and then start slapping paint around. Here are a few tips to help you with some of the tools' less-than-self-explanatory features:

✔ **Eraser:** This eraser doesn't really erase colors so much as it changes them to a different color. Because the background color is usually white, moving the eraser over your drawing usually leaves white splotches. To leave *different colored* splotches, click on a different color in the palette using the right mouse button.

The Eraser can also erase specific colors, ignoring the other colors. For example, if you don't like the yellow in a drawing, click on the Eraser tool and then click on yellow in the palette along the bottom. Then click on the preferred color in the palette — say, purple — with the right mouse button. When you hold down the right mouse button and move the pointer over the drawing, all the yellow parts magically change to purple.

✔ **Pencil:** Although Paint puts this tool in your hand when it is first loaded, the pencil is probably the most difficult tool to use. Use the other tools to create shapes and then click on the pencil for minor touch-ups.

- ✔ **Cutting/Moving pieces:** When you cut pieces out of a drawing, some- times you leave white holes; other times the holes are a different color. What's the trick? Holes take on the shade of the currently selected *background* color.

- ✔ **Pasting:** You can paste anything you want into Paint, and Paint is most accommodating. In fact, if you're trying to paste something that's bigger than the size of the current Paint window, Paint respectfully asks whether it should make the window bigger so that everything fits. (The version in Windows 3.1 wasn't that nice.)

Making new wallpaper in Paint

Anything you make in Paint can be turned into wallpaper and used as a backdrop. Just save your fun new file in the Windows folder. When you head for the Control Panel's Display area, the new file is listed with the other potential wallpaper files. Or you can bypass that step by saving the file and choosing the Set as Wallpaper (Tiled) or Set as Wallpaper (Centered) options from the Paint program's File menu.

Save your file before you try to choose either of the "Set as Wallpaper" options, however, or Paint yells at you. Finally, if you don't have a color monitor and a mouse, you may find Paint unwieldy. More detailed wallpaper installation information awaits in Chapter 10.

Calling Other Computers with HyperTerminal

The old modem program that came with Windows, Terminal, could handle the basics of logging onto a BBS and grabbing files, but it wasn't fancy enough for today's more-sophisticated Internet surfers. Neither is its replacement, HyperTerminal, so you probably won't be using it much.

- ✔ Modems are computer gizmos that can translate the computer's digital information into sound and squirt it over the phone lines to other modems. They come in two types: internal and external. *Internal modems* plug into the nether reaches of the computer, and *external modems* have a cable that plugs into a serial port on the computer's rump. Both types do the same thing, but the external ones have little lights on them that blink as the sound flows back and forth.

✔ HyperTerminal works only with *text-based* online services that are disappearing, such as CompuServe, GEnie, MCI Mail, and computer bulletin boards. It doesn't work with graphics-based bulletin boards, such as America Online and some portions of CompuServe, like its weather maps. And no, you can't use HyperTerminal for looking at cool pictures on the World Wide Web.

Don't pick up the phone while the modem is using it to transmit information. Just picking up the handset can garble the signal and possibly break the connection.

After HyperTerminal is finally up, running, and downloading a file, you'll spot a little modem icon next to the clock along the bottom of the taskbar. Double-click on the little modem, and HyperTerminal displays statistics on how fast your modem is slinging data.

You can find an entire chapter devoted to HyperTerminal in this book's more advanced sequel, *MORE Windows 95 For Dummies,* published by IDG Books Worldwide Inc.

Dialing Phones Automatically with Phone Dialer

The Windows 95 Phone Dialer spiffs up your desktop telephone, even if it's a really cheap one. First, it lets you assign your most frequently dialed phone numbers to push buttons: Just click on the button, and Phone Dialer dials the number. In addition, Phone Dialer keeps track of calls you make using the program. Can't remember whether you made that important call yesterday morning? Choose Show Log from the Tools menu, and you see a list of the phone numbers you've dialed, when you dialed them, and how long the conversation lasted.

If Windows 95 has already been introduced to your modem, you won't see the window shown in Figure 13-4 the first time you load Phone Dialer from the Start menu. If you're setting the program up for the first time, you need to tell Windows 95 four things: your country, your area code, whether you need to dial a number (such as "9") to get an outside line, and whether your phone is touch-tone. (You only need to fill this stuff out once.)

Here's how to store your favorite radio station or pizza delivery service (or whatever) into the Phone Dialer.

1. **Click on one of the buttons along the program's right side, shown in Figure 13-5.**

   The box on the top is probably handiest. A box appears, ready for you to type the name and phone number of the place you're calling.

Figure 13-4:
The Phone
Dialer
needs to
know some
basic
information
about your
modem and
phone
before it
will work.

Figure 13-5:
Click on one
of the
buttons
along the
program's
right side.

2. **Type the name of the place you're calling into the Name box; then press Tab and type the place's phone number into the Number to dial box.**

Start typing the place's name, and the letters appear in the top box. Press Tab to move the cursor to the second box, where you can type the phone number, as shown in Figure 13-6. You can use the numbers on your keyboard's numeric keypad or the ones along the top of your keyboard, whichever you prefer. (The Function keys won't work, however.)

3. **Click on the Save button.**

Figure 13-6:
Type the
name and
phone
number into
the boxes.

The Phone Dialer reappears, showing its newly configured dial button, shown in Figure 13-7. To dial the number, click on the button.

Figure 13-7:
Click on the
button to
dial that
particular
number.

✔ The Phone Dialer can be handy for making those complicated long-distance calls with too many digits to remember.

✔ The Phone Dialer can dial using a Calling Card number, turn Call Waiting on and off, and dial extra numbers to reach outside lines. Whoopee!

✔ Are you using Phone Dialer on your laptop in the hotel room? Phone Dialer automatically sets up your call for dozens of countries, from Albania to Zambia (and Afghanistan and Zimbabwe, too) — lots of international stuff in Windows 95.

The Techie Programs

Windows 95 comes with several technical programs designed to make the nerd feel at home. The Windows 95 installation program doesn't automatically install all of these programs, however. If you want to go back and add them, grab your Windows 95 installation disks (or compact disc) and head for Chapter 18. That chapter explains how to use the Control Panel's Add/Remove Programs feature to make Windows 95 toss a few more goodies onto your hard drive.

Meanwhile, the next few sections describe some of the more technical programs in Windows 95.

The Disk Defragmenter

What it does: When a computer reads and writes files to and from a hard disk, it's working like a liquor store stock clerk after a Labor Day weekend. It has to reorganize the store, moving all the misplaced beer cans out of the wine aisles. The same disorganization happens with computer files. When the computer moves files around, it tends to break the files into chunks and spread them across your hard drive. The computer can still find all the pieces, but it takes more time. A Disk Defragmenter reorganizes the hard drive, making sure that all the files' pieces are next to each other.

What it looks like: The Disk Defragmenter, shown in Figure 13-8, can sometimes speed up your hard drive.

Figure 13-8:
Defragment your hard drive if your computer's been acting more sluggish than usual.

Why bother with it: Your hard drive can grab files more quickly if all the files' pieces are stored next to each other. The Disk Defragmenter organizes the files, speeding up access times.

Where it lives: Click on the Start button and then choose Programs⇨ Accessories⇨System Tools⇨Disk Defragmenter.

How to use it: When the program pops up, click on the drive you want defragmented. The program looks at the drive and says whether the drive needs any work. Take the program's advice. (You probably won't have to use the program more than every couple of months, depending on how often you're using your computer.)

ScanDisk

What it does: Sometimes a computer goofs and loses track of where it has stored information on a hard disk. ScanDisk examines a hard disk for any errors and, if it finds anything suspicious, offers to fix the problem.

What it looks like: ScanDisk, shown in Figure 13-9, can sometimes repair errors on your hard disk.

Why bother with it: ScanDisk not only finds hard disk errors, but if you click in the Automatically fix errors box, it fixes them.

Where it lives: Click on the Start button and then choose Programs⇨ Accessories⇨System Tools⇨ScanDisk.

How to use it: After loading the program, click on the drive you want to check. Then click on the Automatically fix errors box until a check mark appears and click on the Start button. If you still have problems, rerun the program, but select the Thorough option to make ScanDisk work a little harder. (The Thorough option takes an extra five or ten minutes.)

Figure 13-9:
If Windows 95 sends error messages complaining about your hard disk, give ScanDisk a try.

ScanDisk - 202mb (C:)

Select the drive(s) you want to check for errors:

- 5¼ Floppy (B:)
- 202mb (C:)
- 121mb (D:)

Type of test

- ⦿ Standard
  (checks files and folders for errors)
- ○ Thorough
  (performs Standard test and scans disk surface for errors) Options...

☐ Automatically fix errors

Start   Close   Advanced...

The Smaller or Optional Programs

Not all Windows 95 programs are cartwheelers. Some of them are small, innocuous doodads. In fact, Windows 95 doesn't automatically install *all* its possible freebie programs. If you followed the normal installation, you probably won't find many of the following programs listed on any menus. The next few sections tell you which programs you're missing — as well as how to install them.

My version of Windows 95 doesn't have the right programs!

Depending on the buttons you punched when you installed Windows 95, you find different varieties of programs installed on your hard drive. Very few people get all the programs installed. If you feel left out and want some of the optional programs mentioned in this chapter, follow these steps:

1. **Double-click on the Control Panel's Add/Remove Programs icon.**

   You can load the Control Panel by clicking on Settings in the Start menu.

2. **Click on the Windows Setup tab.**

   It's the tab in the middle of the three along the top; a box appears showing the various components of Windows 95, as well as the amount of space they need to nestle onto your computer's hard drive.

3. **Click in the little box by the programs or accessories you want to add.**

   A check mark appears in the box of the items you select. To select part of a category — a portion of the accessories, for example — click on the category's name and click on the Details button. Windows 95 lists the items available in that category so that you can select the ones you want. If you clicked on the Details button, click on the OK button to continue back at the main categories list.

4. **Click on the OK button and insert your installation disks when asked.**

   Windows 95 copies the necessary files from your installation disks onto your hard drive. You can remove Windows 95 accessories the same way, but by *removing* the check mark from the box next to their name.

CD Player

Adding a CD-ROM drive to a computer doesn't always add multimedia as much as it adds Bachman Turner Overdrive to the lunch hour. It's a well-known fact that most multimedia computer owners pop a musical CD into their computer's disk drive now and then.

The Windows 3.1 Media Player can play music CDs, but Windows 95 comes with a full-fledged CD Player, shown in Figure 13-10.

Figure 13-10:
The Windows 95 CD Player lets you keep track of your songs.

The CD Player lets you add song titles to the menu, as well as create your own play lists. If you're feeling random, choose the Random Order setting under Options to make Windows 95 act like a juke box. Now, if it just came with a pool table.

✔ Music too loud? Just click on the little speaker in the corner of the taskbar. An easy-to-use sliding bar lets you lower the volume — no more frantic searching to save your ears.

✔ Don't remember what some of those buttons do? Just rest your mouse pointer over them, and Windows 95 sends a message to the screen to help you out. In Figure 13-10, for example, the CD Player says those two triangles let you jump to the previous track on the CD.

✔ Looking for a certain song, but can't remember which one it is? Choose the Intro Play option under Options. The CD Player automatically plays the first few seconds of every song on the CD until you recognize the one you're after.

✔ As soon as you insert an audio CD, Windows 95 begins playing it — as long as your CD-ROM drive supports that feature. To stop Windows 95 from immediately playing the CD, hold down Shift while inserting the CD into the CD-ROM drive.

The online services

Most people have heard about *online services,* where you can hook your computer up to the phone lines and, under the pretense of making direct deposit payments through your checking account, swap pictures of your cat wearing a beret with newfound friends on the Cat User Group.

Smelling money, Microsoft started its own online service to compete with CompuServe, America Online, GEnie, the Internet, and the plethora of other online services that hatch each day.

Windows 95 comes with software that's itching to access *The Microsoft Network.* Shown in Figure 13-11, The Microsoft Network looks more like a Windows program than an online service. It uses the same folders and format used by Windows 95. (It also uses the Internet's World Wide Web, just like all the other Web pages you'll come across, but that's another story.)

- ✔ Don't bother searching through the Windows 95 box for mail-in forms in order to subscribe to The Microsoft Network. Instead, you can find the sign-up form right on the Start button menu, listed under <u>P</u>rograms. Point and click, and Windows 95 starts dialing. (That convenience is why all the other online services are a little bit worried about the competition.)

- ✔ In fact, they were so worried, they did some wheeling and dealing and now you can find icons for CompuServe, America Online, and AT&T's online services. (They're in a folder near the Start button, and they're covered in Chapter 15.)

- ✔ Just as you can place pictures, sounds, and charts in a Windows word processor file, you can place pictures, sounds, and charts in messages swapped over The Microsoft Network. For example, you can easily paste a picture of yourself (or your cat) into a message to a friend.

- ✔ The Microsoft Network offers the standard online fare: electronic mail, bulletin boards, chat rooms, file libraries, and Internet newsgroups. Because Microsoft is running the show, you are able to find lots of technical support for Microsoft products online, as well.

FreeCell

The Windows 3.1 favorite time-waster, Solitaire, has been passed up by a new contestant: FreeCell. FreeCell has been a real card game for years; it entered the Microsoft world with Windows NT (an earlier, big version of Windows that didn't excite very many people).

Figure 13-11:
By dialing
The
Microsoft
Network
with your
modem, you
can read
magazines,
swap
messages
with
people, and
find help
with your
computer
problems.

Microsoft has tossed FreeCell to the masses in Windows 95. Although
FreeCell looks a lot like Solitaire, it plays a lot differently. Shown in Figure
13-12, FreeCell works with double-clicks: Instead of making you drag the
cards around, FreeCell simply jumps them into place.

Figure 13-12:
Aces along
the top
edge of
FreeCell
make for a
rough
game.

The object is pretty simple: Sort the cards in order by suit and number from Ace to King on the four right-hand squares. While moving the cards up there, you can move other cards temporarily to the four *free cells* — temporary card-storage areas — on the left-hand side.

- ✔ FreeCell comes with 32,000 different games. So far, none of them has been proven unbeatable.

- ✔ If you're looking for a challenge, try game numbers 285; 27,006; or 31,465. In fact, you may find one or two other difficult ones, as well.

- ✔ Moved the wrong card? Quick, press F10. That's the Undo button, but only if you press it before clicking on another card.

- ✔ After you've won 65,535 games, FreeCell resets your winning streak statistics to zero. Be forewarned.

Hearts

Windows 95 has no shortage of card games, that's for sure. If you're tired of Solitaire and FreeCell, you might give Hearts a try. Shown in Figure 13-13, it's the same version of Hearts that came with Windows for Workgroups.

The game works just like *real* Hearts. One person tosses a card onto the table, everybody else tosses down a card of the same suit, and the person with the highest card grabs the pile. What's the tricky part? You want the *lowest* score — any card with a heart is one point, and the queen of spades is worth 13 points.

Figure 13-13: Windows 95 comes with Hearts, the same version that came in Windows for Workgroups.

✔ There's a catch. If one player grabs all the hearts and the queen of spades, that player doesn't get any points, and all the other players are penalized 26 points.

✔ If nobody is around at the office network, the computer fills in for the other three players, and you can still play. You don't need a network to play Hearts.

✔ _**Cheat alert:**_ The computer automatically sorts your cards by suit at the screen's bottom. However, it doesn't sort the cards that represent the other players' hands — the cards around the edges. Therefore, you can't get an idea of what cards the other players have by watching the position of their cards.

✔ If you migrated from Windows for Workgroups, you're probably already used to playing Hearts over the network. Windows 95 keeps Hearts in the mix of games, along with Solitaire.

Backup

Everybody knows that you're supposed to make backup copies of your computer's information. The problem is finding the time to do it.

The Microsoft Backup program, shown in Figure 13-14, isn't anything special except in one key area: It can handle long filenames. Because the old-school, DOS-based backup programs can only handle eight-character filenames, they can't make reliable backups in Windows 95.

Figure 13-14:
Windows
95 comes
with a
backup
program
that can
handle long
filenames.

To keep Windows 95 users from treading dangerously, Microsoft tossed a backup program in with Windows 95 until all the other companies update their backup programs. After you tell the backup program which programs to save, it copies them to floppy disks or a tape backup unit.

It you haven't bought a tape backup unit yet, now may be a good time to put one on your shopping list. They've come way down in price, and copying huge hard drives onto hundreds of floppies is a bore, even if Windows 95 *does* let you play FreeCell while you're doing it.

Briefcase

Do you want to move files between your laptop and desktop — and still come up with the right file when you need it? Briefcase lets you connect two computers with a serial or parallel cable and shoot files between them. Best yet, Briefcase can tell which one is most up to date, so you'll always be keeping the current copy.

Of course, if you want a more full-featured version, stick with LapLink from Traveling Software. That program has been doing the same thing for years (and it comes with the cables you need, too).

Notepad

Windows comes with two word processors, WordPad and Notepad. WordPad is for the letters you're sprucing up for other people to see. Notepad is for stuff you're going to keep for yourself.

Notepad is quicker than WordPad. Double-click on its icon, and it leaps to the screen more quickly than you can reach for a notepad in your back pocket. You can type some quick words and save them on the fly.

Understanding Notepad's limitations

Notepad's speed comes at a price, however. Notepad stores only words and numbers. It doesn't store any special formatting, such as italicized letters, and you can't paste any pictures into it, as you can with WordPad. Notepad is a quick, throw-together program for your quick, throw-together thoughts.

✔ Notepad tosses you into instant confusion: All the sentences head right off the edge of the screen. To turn one-line, runaway sentences into normal paragraphs, turn on the *word wrap* feature by choosing <u>W</u>ord Wrap from the <u>E</u>dit menu. (You have to turn this feature on each time you start Notepad, strangely enough.)

✓ Notepad prints kind of funny, too: It prints the file's name at the top of every page. To combat this nonsense, choose File and then choose Page Setup. A box appears, with a funny code word in the Header box. Delete the word and click on the OK button. If you want to get rid of the automatic page numbering, clear out the Footer box as well.

✓ Here's another printing problem: Notepad doesn't print exactly what you see on-screen. Instead, it prints according to the margins you set in Page Setup under the File menu. This quirk can lead to unpredictable results.

Turning Notepad into a logbook

Although Notepad leans toward simplicity, it has one fancy feature that not even WordPad can match. Notepad can automatically stamp the current time and date at the bottom of a file whenever you open it. Just type **.LOG** in the very top left-hand corner of a file and save the file. Then whenever you open that file again, you can jot down some current notes and have Notepad stamp it with the time and date. The result looks similar to what is shown in Figure 13-15.

✓ Don't try the .LOG trick by using lowercase letters and don't omit the period. It doesn't work.

✓ To stick in the date and time manually, press F5. The time and date appear, just as they do in the .LOG trick.

Figure 13-15: Add the word .LOG to the top of the file, and Notepad stamps it with the time and date whenever you open it.

```
Journal - Notepad                    _ □ ✕
File  Edit  Search  Help
.LOG

8:32 PM 9/22/94

Dreamt last night that Stacy had
brought an oryx into the office.
Or perhaps it was a gnu or a yak.
We immediately started playing
Scrabble in the lunch room.

6:34 AM 2/18/95

Slept, awoke, slept, awoke.
Despair. Kafka was right.

5:34 PM 2/22/95

The rental video jammed in the
VCR; so did the envelope
opener, and Tina's orange.
```

Calculator

Calculator is, well, a calculator. It looks simple enough, and it really is — unless you mistakenly set it for Scientific mode and see some nightmarish logarithmic stuff. To bring the calculator back to normal, choose <u>V</u>iew and choose <u>S</u>tandard.

To punch in numbers and equations, click on the little buttons, just as if it were a normal calculator. When you press the equal sign (=), the answer appears at the top. For an extra measure of handiness, you can copy the answers to the Clipboard by pressing Ctrl+C (holding down the Ctrl key while pressing C). Then click in the window where you want the answer to appear and press Ctrl+V. That method is easier than retyping a number like 2.449489742783.

- ✔ Unlike in other Windows programs, you can't copy the Calculator's answer by running the mouse pointer over the numbers. You have to press Ctrl+C or choose <u>E</u>dit➪<u>C</u>opy.

- ✔ If the mouse action is too slow, press the Num Lock key and punch in numbers with the numeric keypad.

- ✔ In Windows 95, Calculator fixes the subtraction and decimal point problems found in the Windows 3.1 version. It has been verified to be at least as accurate as the *Star Trek* key chain calculators.

Adding the à in voilà (Character Map)

To add weird foreign characters, such as *à*, *Ł*, or even *Đ*, choose Start➪<u>P</u>rograms➪Accessories➪Character Map. A box like the one shown in Figure 13-16 appears, listing every available character and symbol.

Figure 13-16:
You can use the Character Map to find foreign characters and stick them in your work.

Character Map window showing Font: Times New Roman, Characters to Copy: à, a grid of available characters with buttons Close, Select, Copy, Help. Table of available characters in the selected font. Keystroke: Alt+0224

Follow these steps to put a foreign character in your work:

1. **Make sure that the current font — the name for the style of the characters on the page — shows in the Font box.**

   If the current font is not showing, click on the down arrow and click on the font when it appears in the drop-down list.

2. **Scan the Character Map box until you see the symbol you're after; then pounce on that character with a double-click.**

   The symbol appears in the Characters to Copy box.

3. **Click on Copy to send the character to the Clipboard.**

4. **Click on the Close button to close the Character Map.**

5. **Click in the document where you want the new symbol or character to appear.**

6. **Press Ctrl+V, and the new character pops right in there.**

   (Give it a second. Sometimes it's slow.)

The symbols in the Character Map box are easier to see if you hold down the mouse button and move the pointer over them.

That weird Alt+0208 stuff is too trivial to bother with

In the bottom right-hand corner, Character Map flashes numbers after the words Keystroke: Alt+. Those numbers hail back to the stone-tablet days of adding foreign characters when word processing. Back then, people had to look up a character's code number in the back of a boring manual.

If you remember the code numbers for your favorite symbols, however, you can bypass Character Map and add them directly to documents. For example, the code number listed in the bottom corner for é is 0233.

Here's the trick: Press and release Num Lock, hold down Alt and type **0233** with the numeric keypad. Let go of the Alt key, and the é symbol appears.

If you constantly use one special character, this method may be faster than using Character Map. (Press and release Num Lock after you're finished.)

✔ When working with foreign words, keep the Character Map handy as an icon, ready for consultation.

✔ For some fun symbols like ✎, 🖮, ✍, ✒, ⚥, ☺, or ✐ switch to the Wingdings font. It's full of little doodads to spice up your work.

✔ You can grab several characters at a time by double-clicking on each of them and then copying them into your work as a chunk. You don't have to keep returning to the Character Map for each one.

Sound Recorder and Media Player

If you've bought and installed a sound card for your computer, you can play and record sounds with Sound Recorder. It looks and works pretty much like a tape recorder. One warning, however: Don't get carried away when recording particularly long sounds. They take a *lot* of space on the hard drive.

Media Player can't record, but it can play from a wide variety of devices. It can play sounds from a sound card, as well as connect to MIDI keyboards. It can access CD-ROM drives for both sound and data. It even plays videodiscs.

✔ Windows 95 comes ready to run with some of the most popular sound cards. Other sound cards or CD-ROM drives come with special drivers on a floppy disk that is boxed with the package.

✔ Chapter 2 covers sound cards and CD-ROM drives.

✔ *MORE Windows For Dummies,* a "next-step-up" Dummies book, shows you how to use Sound Recorder and Media Player to play and record sounds, listen to compact discs, and even watch movies.

✔ Or if you're *really* entranced by flashing lights and screaming sounds, check out *Multimedia & CD-ROMs For Dummies.* This book shows you how to buy, set up, and use all those cool multimedia gizmos everybody's talking about.

Solitaire

Windows 95 Solitaire works just like the card game, so here are just a few pointers for the computerized version:

✔ When the boss comes by, click on the minimize button, that underscore-looking thing in a box in the upper-right corner. If you can't move the mouse quickly enough, hold down Alt and press the spacebar, followed by the letter N. In either case, Solitaire turns into an icon at the bottom of the screen. Double-click on the icon to resume play when the boss passes.

✔ Using Windows isn't easy on a laptop, and Solitaire can be a nightmare. You can play Solitaire with a keyboard by using an awkward combination of Tab, Enter, and the arrow keys. And older laptops with black-and-white screens make it difficult to tell when a card is being placed on the right color.

✔ Sharp-eyed players will notice some background fun: The bats flap their wings, the sun sticks out its tongue, and a card slides in and out of a dealer's sleeve. These shenanigans only occur when you play in *timed* mode. To start the fun, choose Options from the Game menu and make sure that you put an X in the Timed Game box.

Minesweeper

Despite the name, Minesweeper does not cause any explosions, even if you accidentally uncover a mine. And it works better on laptops than Solitaire does. Minesweeper is more of a math game than anything else—no jumping little men here.

Start by clicking on a random square. If you click on a hidden mine, you lose on the first click; otherwise, some numbers appear in one or more of the little squares. The number says how many mines are hidden in the squares surrounding that square.

Each square is surrounded by eight other squares. (Unless it's on the edge; then there are only five. And only three squares surround corner squares.) If, through the process of elimination, you're sure that a mine exists beneath a certain square, click on it with the right mouse button to put a little flag there.

Eventually, through logical deduction (or just mindless pointing and clicking), you either accidentally click on a mine and are blown up, or mark all the mine squares with flags and win the game.

The object of the game is to win as fast as you can.

How Did Windows 3.1 Hold Up?

Like an evolving creature, Windows 95 has changed Windows 3.1 fairly drastically. To see whether your favorite programs have been improved, removed, or destroyed, check out Table 13-3; it lists Windows 3.1 programs and their Windows 95 replacements. (Chapter 16 contains even more information to help Windows 3.1 users make their move.)

Table 13-3	Windows 3.1 Programs and Their Windows 95 Replacements
The Windows 3.1 Program	**Its Windows 95 Equivalent**
Program Manager	Start button. (Program Manager is still included, in case you prefer to stick with it.)
File Manager	Windows Explorer and My Computer programs. (File Manager is still included, in case you like it better.)
Write	WordPad; both adds and removes features.
Paintbrush	Paint; both adds and removes features.
Cardfile, Calendar	Gone with no replacements, although Windows 95 leaves the Windows 3.1 versions on the hard disk in case you've upgraded.
Character Map, Calculator, Notepad, Media Player, Sound Recorder, MS-DOS Prompt, Solitaire, ClipBook Viewer, Hearts	Still the same in Windows 95. (Sometimes ClipBook Viewer is called Clipboard Viewer.)
Terminal	Replaced with HyperTerminal, a telecommunications program with many more features.
Control Panel	Replaced by Control Panel window, a similar collection of icons.
PIF Editor	Replaced by Properties sheet: Click on a DOS program's icon with the right mouse button and choose Properties from the menu to tweak the program's settings.
Clock	Replaced by a permanent clock on the taskbar.

Chapter 14

Uh, How Do I Run My Old DOS Programs?

In This Chapter

▶ Running DOS programs under Windows 95

▶ Making your own PIFs for DOS programs

▶ Changing fonts in a DOS window

▶ Halting runaway DOS programs

*W*indows 95 programs are used to a communal lifestyle where they all eat from the same granola trough. They can share the computer's memory without bickering. DOS programs, however, hail from a different computing era. Windows 95 must nurse DOS programs along, or the DOS programs won't run.

In fact, Windows keeps a special chart called a *PIF* (an acronym for *program information file*) for each problem-causing DOS program. A PIF (rhymes with *sniff*) contains the care and feeding instructions that Windows needs to make a particular DOS program happy.

The information in these PIFs can include some pretty meaty stuff. This chapter chops it into easily digestible chunks, but you may want to keep a napkin around, just in case.

Running DOS Programs Under Windows

Some DOS programs are easy to run under Windows 95. Just head for the Start menu (or Windows Explorer or the My Computer window), double-click on that program's icon, and stand back while it heads for the screen. Sometimes the DOS program fills the entire screen while Windows waits in the background. Other times, the program runs happily in its own window, oblivious to everything around it.

But some DOS programs refuse to run under Windows 95 at all. They were designed to use *all* of a computer's resources, so they balk if they think that Windows 95 is just tossing them a few scraps.

To trick these DOS programs into feeling at home, Windows 95 gives each problem-causing DOS program its own PIF containing the special instructions needed to trick that program into running in Windows.

For example, a PIF may tell Windows 95 to put the DOS program in a window or to make the program fill the entire screen. PIFs tell Windows 95 the type of memory that the DOS program craves and how much of that memory it wants. Other settings are cosmetic, such as specifying what type of font to use.

Windows 95 can automatically create PIFs for the most popular DOS programs. In fact, when you're double-clicking on a DOS program's icon, you're probably double-clicking on that program's PIF. Windows 95 consults the PIF and then runs the program accordingly.

✔ When Windows 95 installs itself, it searches to see what programs you've already installed on the computer. When it finds a troublesome DOS program that it recognizes, it tosses a PIF for that program into the computer and puts an icon for that PIF on the Start menu and in the My Computer and Windows Explorer programs. The PIF also serves as a shortcut, telling Windows 95 where the DOS program lives on the computer.

✔ If you've installed a new DOS program and want to run it under Windows 95, check out the section in Chapter 11 about putting a favorite program into the Start menu. If Windows 95 recognizes that new DOS program, it creates a PIF and everything is hunky-dory.

✔ Some DOS programs come with their own Windows PIFs. When you install such a program, it tosses its PIF onto the hard drive. PIF names usually start with the program's filename and end in the letters PIF. When Windows 95 installs itself, it searches the hard drive looking for PIFs. If it finds any, it updates them and uses them as shortcuts for the DOS program.

✔ If you double-click on a DOS program that doesn't have a PIF, Windows 95 uses general-purpose settings that allow almost any DOS program to run without a problem. If there is a problem, you'll have to make your own PIF, a process described in the very next section.

Getting Your Own PIFs for DOS Programs

If a DOS program isn't working under Windows 95, call the company that made it and tell the company that you need its PIF for Windows 95. If the company doesn't have one, call your computer dealer or bribe a computer guru to make one for you.

Until then, choose the Shut down command from the Start menu and choose the Restart the computer in MS-DOS mode from the box that pops up. Windows leaves the screen, and a DOS prompt appears, ready for you to run your DOS program.

When you're ready to go back to Windows 95, exit your DOS program and type **EXIT** at the C:\> thing to get your windows back on-screen.

Don't bother trying to make your own PIF. This process is heavy stuff, meant for advanced users who *enjoy* piddling with PIFs. Besides, some DOS programs won't run under Windows 95 no matter how much PIF coddling they get. Until you become a PIF manufacturer, you're better off sticking with Windows 95 programs when running Windows 95. Most companies are writing Windows 95 versions of their DOS programs, so there's less need to run a DOS program in Windows 95 anyway.

Figuring Out the DOS Window's Buttons

When a DOS program fills the whole screen, it looks like a general, run-of-the-mill DOS program. But when it runs in a window, you'll notice little buttons along the program's top edge. Those buttons are the toolbar. (And if you don't see them, click on the icon in the window's uppermost-left corner and choose Toolbar from the menu that dangles down.) See Figure 14-1 for a

Figure 14-1: Clicking on the buttons above a DOS program's window performs these tasks.

Copy selected information to the Clipboard

Let the program run in the background

Choose a new font for the current session

Switch to full-screen

Select information for copying

Adjust program's settings (PIF)

Choose a new font for the current session and future sessions

Paste the information that's on the Clipboard

look at the toolbar.

Figure 14-1 shows what each button is supposed to do. If you don't want to remember all that, just remember this:

Rest your mouse pointer over almost any confusing button in Windows 95 or one of its programs, and a window pops up to explain that button's reason or living.

✔ First question: What's the difference between the two Font buttons? Well, they both change the size and style of the font in the current window, but the button on the left changes the font for the *current* session; the one on the right does that, too, but it also remembers your choice for that program's *future* sessions.

✔ Clicking on the little button with the outward-pointing arrows makes the DOS program run in full-screen mode. To cram the program back into a window, press Alt+Enter.

The Background button lets your DOS program work in the background — sorting a database, calculating a spreadsheet, or downloading a file — even when the program's not running on the top of the pile. If the program needs to be able to run in the background, click on that button. Otherwise, clicking on the Background button only slows things down.

Changing Fonts in a DOS Window

DOS programs are used to roaming free and wild, but Windows 95 can force them to run inside a window, just like any Windows 95 program. A DOS window functions pretty much like any other window: You can move it around, tug on its borders to change its size, or shrink it into an icon if it's getting in the way.

If the DOS program normally fills the whole screen under Windows 95, try this to run it inside a window: Hold Alt and press Enter. The DOS program hops into a window on-screen.

Unfortunately, a DOS window sometimes won't fit comfortably on the screen. To fix that oversight, change the size of the font used by the window. That action makes the letters larger or smaller so that the information fits better on the screen. Follow these steps to change the font size for a DOS window:

1. **Click on the button with the capital A on it, shown in Figure 14-1.**

   It's that button along the top, toward the right. The dialog box shown in Figure 14-2 then appears. The little numbers on the right side of the dialog box, which start with 2 x 4, are the sizes of the available fonts.

2. **Click on the different numbers and look in the preview boxes to see how the words on the DOS program window will look in that font size.**

   The window's total size in relation to the desktop appears in the Window preview box; the size of the letters appears in the Font preview box. Figure 14-2, for example, shows the font size 8 x 12 selected; the

Figure 14-2:
Change a
DOS
window's
font size to
change the
entire
window's
size.

Window preview box shows that a window of that size would cover almost the entire desktop.

Smaller font-size numbers make for smaller words and a smaller DOS

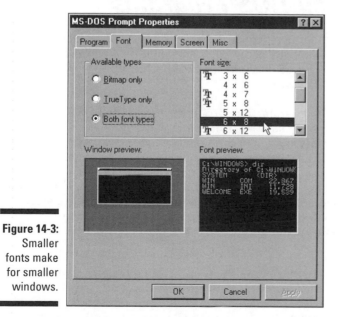

Figure 14-3:
Smaller
fonts make
for smaller
windows.

window. For example, the 6 x 8 font shrinks the DOS window to the more manageable size shown in Figure 14-3.

You can make the fonts larger, too, so that they're easier to read. If you're using a laptop on a plane, try some of the larger fonts so that the passenger sitting next to you won't have to strain so hard to see what you're doing.

✔ The changing-fonts trick works only with DOS programs that display mostly text — such as spreadsheets and word processors. DOS programs that use graphics don't work too well in windows. Their displays don't completely fit in a window, and the colors almost always look weird.

✔ You can change a DOS window's size by dragging the borders, but that's pointless. A DOS program's display doesn't shrink or grow in size like a Windows 95 program does. If you drag the border in, you just cover up your view of the program.

✔ If you want to cut or paste anything from a DOS program in a window, head back to Chapter 9 for information about the DOS window versions of cut, copy, and paste.

Although TrueType fonts usually look better than Bitmap fonts in Windows programs, that doesn't hold true as often with DOS programs. Test both Bitmap and TrueType fonts before making a final selection.

Halting Runaway DOS Programs

Like startled Arkansas farmers who wake up in the belly of a spaceship, some DOS programs simply freak out when they find themselves running under Windows 95. For example, some freeze up solid, stubbornly beeping each time you press a key.

To halt a runaway DOS program, first look at the top of the DOS window. If the first word along the top says Mark or Select, Windows 95 thinks that you're trying to copy information from the DOS window. Press Esc to restore order. If you really were trying to copy something, head for Chapter 9.

If pressing Esc doesn't work, try holding Alt and pressing Enter. That action tells Windows 95 to let the temperamental program have the entire screen. For example, if a program suddenly switches from text to graphics in a window, Windows 95 sometimes freezes the program until you use the Alt+Enter trick.

That trick didn't work, either? Then things are getting serious. If the confused DOS program is in a window, follow these steps:

1. **Press Ctrl+Alt+Delete.**

2. **When the list of currently running programs appears, click on your runaway program's name.**

3. **Click on the ominous-looking End Task button.**

4. **When Windows 95 asks whether you're sure, click on the Yes button.**

Hopefully, these steps will rip the DOS program from the computer's memory; use these steps pretty much as a last resort.

If the frozen DOS program is running full-screen, hold Ctrl, press and hold Alt, and then press Delete (Ctrl+Alt+Delete). When Windows 95 asks whether you're sure that you want to close the program, press End Task.

If you click on the End Task button or press the Ctrl+Alt+Delete combination, you lose any unsaved work in the DOS program.

- ✔ Only use the End Task or Ctrl+Alt+Delete method as a last resort. If at all possible, quit the DOS program in an orderly fashion. For some programs, you hold down Alt and press X; in others, you press F10 or Esc. Almost all programs are different. (That's one reason why people are switching to Windows 95; its commands are more predictable.)

- ✔ After you use End Task or Ctrl+Alt+Delete, save any work in the other windows. Then exit Windows 95 and start it up again. That DOS program may have sabotaged things on its way out.

Chapter 15

Cruising the World Wide Web

● ●

In This Chapter

▶ Understanding the Internet and World Wide Web

▶ Understanding differences between the Internet and online services

▶ Knowing how to access the World Wide Web

▶ Using the Microsoft Internet Explorer Web Browser

▶ Navigating the World Wide Web

● ●

*I*n the late 1960s, the U.S. government worried that enemies could drop bombs on its main cluster of Department of Defense computers, quickly turning circuits into slosh. So, the scientists moved the computers away from each other, connecting them globally with high-speed phone lines and a unique system of information forwarding.

If a computer in Hawaii blew up, for example, the data chain from surrounding computers wouldn't simply stop there. The other computers would automatically reroute their information to other computers in the network, and everybody would still have e-mail waiting the next morning (except for the folks in Hawaii, of course).

With this sprawling chain of new networks running automatically in the background, enemies no longer have a single target to destroy. The system has proven quite durable, and thousands of other networks have hopped on for a ride. Many academic institutions climbed aboard as well, helping the system grow to gigantic proportions. Now known as the *Internet,* the information chain's built-in independence keeps it difficult to use, completely uncensored, and rampantly random in quality.

Anybody can use the Internet and its trendy World Wide Web to sample the information strewn about the globe. And best yet, Windows 95 now includes most of the tools you need to jump aboard and start "surfing" the Web that everybody's been talking about.

This chapter tackles the untamed world of the Internet, where nobody's in charge, very few people are making much money, yet many people still manage to have fun.

Who Uses the Internet and World Wide Web?

Universities, corporations, government entities and millions of plain ol' normal folk use the Internet every day. Many simply send messages back and forth — *electronic mail* or *e-mail*. Other users swap programs, pictures, or sounds — anything that can be stored as data inside a computer.

The government loves the Internet. The FBI posts pictures of its ten most wanted criminals (`http://www.fbi.gov/mostwant/tenlist.htm`) for public viewing, for example, and the Internal Revenue Service (`http://www.irs.ustreas.gov`) lets Internet users make free copies of tax forms 24 hours a day.

Universities, too, love the network. Departments can file grant forms more quickly than ever. Worried about the goo coagulating in the center of your bromeliads? The Internet's famed botanical directory (`http://herb.biol.uregina.ca/liu/bio/idb.shtml`) allows researchers to move quickly from Aarhus University's Biological Sciences department to the Zoosporic Fungi database.

Many computer companies support their products on the Internet. Callers correspond with repairmen, hopefully figuring out why their latest computer doodads aren't working. After posting messages back and forth, callers can often download a software cure or patch to fix the problem.

Spotting a new way to advertise, businesses have also jumped aboard. Some vintage guitar dealers (`http://www.choiceguitar.com/guitars.html`), for example, display photos of their classic guitars, like the one shown in Figure 15-1, hoping to snag potential buyers. Some sites even let you click a picture to hear the howl of a '67 Stratocaster.

Curious about the new V6 engines in Volkswagen's camper vans? Head for Volkswagen's special spot (`http://www.vw.com/cars/`), shown in Figure 15-2, to flip the pages of its latest "point and clickable" brochure.

- ✔ The Internet is a rapidly growing collection of computers linked around the globe. More than 20 million people use the Internet for swapping information with other computers.

- ✔ The World Wide Web (also called the *Web*) is software that runs on the Internet. The Web looks like a kiosk in a hotel or airport lobby. There, you push different areas of the screen to find the right rental car. The World Wide Web tosses similar menus on your computer screen; the menus are called Web pages. You point and click the on-screen buttons to view things like museums, beach cameras, pizza menus, guitar shops, city maps, and three more subjects since you began reading this paragraph.

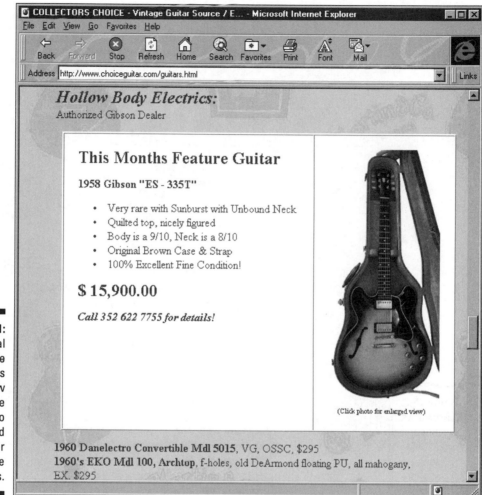

Figure 15-1:
Several World Wide Web sites allow prospective buyers to see and hear vintage guitars.

✔ Just as television's channel surfers flip from channel to channel sampling the wares, Web surfers move from page to page, sampling the esoteric piles of information.

✔ An area created on the World Wide Web for you to view is called a *Web site,* which usually contains a bunch of Web pages for perusing. Just about anybody can set up a Web site, but doing so involves some programming skills using languages called *HTML* (hypertext markup language) and Java. Surfing across the pages is much easier than building the wave itself. That's why most people remain Web surfers.

✔ Because setting up a Web site on the Internet is fairly easy for programmers, plenty of more frivolous sites exist, too. One guy displays continuously updated photographs of the beach at Zandvoort in the

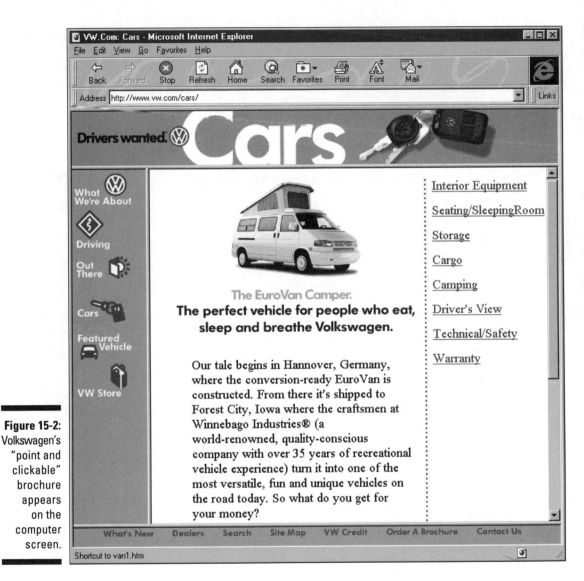

Figure 15-2:
Volkswagen's "point and clickable" brochure appears on the computer screen.

Netherlands (http://www.csd.uu.se/~s96fst/), for example. Another fellow displays a puzzle game involving that wondrous can of mystery flesh, Spam (http://www.rowan.edu/~hess/spam.html).

✔ You surf the Web by doing business with an *Internet Service Provider* or *ISP.* You pay the ISP for a password and phone number to call. When your computer dials the number and connects to your ISP's network, you type your password and grab your surfboard: You've entered the Web.

✔ If you're computer-inclined, some ISPs provide hard disk space on their computers so you can create *your* own Web pages for other Internet members to visit. Show the world pictures of your kids and cats! Share favorite recipes! Talk about your favorite car waxes! Swap tips on constructing fishing flies!

✔ Some ISPs charge for each minute you're connected; others provide a flat fee for unlimited service. The going rate seems to be stabilizing at around $20 a month for unlimited service. Make sure that you find out your rate before hopping aboard, or you may be surprised at the end of the month.

How Does an Online Service Differ from the Internet?

Big corporations started following the government's lead on computer networks years ago. H&R Block, eager to get some use out of its huge computer network when it wasn't tax time, set up an online service company called CompuServe. People still pay hourly fees to dial CompuServe and swap information, join discussion forums with people of similar interests, and download free software — all within the CompuServe community of networked computers.

As computers and modems grew more popular, other online services grew, too. America Online, Prodigy, Sierra Online, and other companies set up networks for people to call.

But as the World Wide Web grew in popularity, online services dwindled, mainly because they were too self-contained. The Web simply offered more information, and in most cases, at a better price.

✔ Today, most online services offer access to the Internet to keep their customers from leaving. Other online services, like CompuServe, are converting to a more Weblike structure. The transition makes the service easier for Web surfers to navigate.

✔ Most online services also expanded their e-mail systems, letting their members send and receive mail through the Internet.

✔ In addition to a modem and Internet account, the World Wide Web requires special software to view it. Called a *Web browser,* this software makes your monitor look more like a television screen, with areas where people can click to see more information. (Web browsers get their own section later in this chapter.) Online services that allow access to the Internet come with a Web browser. Or, you can use Internet Explorer, the Web browser that comes with Windows 95.

What Online Services Does Windows 95 Come With?

The latest version of Windows 95 comes with icons that access a bundle of online services and networks. You can point and click your way to The Microsoft Network, CompuServe, America Online, and AT&T WorldNet. Here's a look at what's what.

The Microsoft Network

Set Up The Microsoft Network

When Microsoft, always smelling cash, saw people making money through online services, it started an online service of its own. Microsoft called it The Microsoft Network, and made the service outrageously easy to use: Anytime Windows 95 was installed on a computer, a Microsoft Network icon appeared on the desktop, just a click away.

Talk about free advertising! A curious Windows 95 user merely clicked the MSN icon, and the program took over, slyly grabbing its prey by the arms and telling the user exactly how to install the system and begin enjoying the pleasures of online life.

Needless to say, competing online services were outraged and headed for the courts, claiming unfair competition. Microsoft, eager to keep things from getting *too* ugly, struck a deal: It would put icons for the other online services on a desktop folder, too.

But because proprietary online services — The Microsoft Network included — are dying compared to the Internet, Microsoft has converted The Microsoft Network into a huge Web site, instead. (And, of course, it still costs money to join.)

CompuServe

Setup CompuServe 3.0

One of the earliest and most expensive online services, CompuServe earned a reputation as one of the more cost-effective services, as well. Because the service cost so much, forum messages were short, to the point, and mature. Beavis-and-Butthead types simply couldn't afford to post.

The Internet is grabbing the CompuServe audience today, though. CompuServe launched a family-oriented, easy-to-use, flat-fee online service called Wow!, but pulled out a few months later.

✔ CompuServe still attracts about a million users.

✔ Some versions of Windows 95 come with a Wow! icon in their online folder. Feel free to delete it, because Wow! died.

✔ Realizing its need to widen its network, CompuServe now allows its members to surf the Web, as well as send e-mail to and from Internet members.

America Online, or AOL

AOL & Internet FREE Trial!

Entering the market long after CompuServe, America Online used splashy graphics, easy-to-use buttons, and a huge marketing campaign to quickly boost its subscription past 5 million people. Unfortunately, many people simply take advantage of its "30-day trial offer," discover the AOL passageway to the Internet, and bail.

Still, if you're looking for an easy way to try out online services and still have access to the Internet and World Wide Web, America Online may be your best bet.

✔ America Online recently switched to a $20 flat fee providing unlimited access to the Internet.

✔ Be sure and save those America Online trial offer disks. They can be reformatted, as explained in Chapter 12, allowing you to store your own files on them.

✔ America Online can be a great way to start experiencing online life. It provides a free trial period, and it lets you probe both the advantages of the America Online built-in forums and passageway to the Internet. Because the service has grown so popular, however, many users are complaining of excessive busy signals.

AT&T WorldNet

AT&T WorldNet Signup

One of the newest entrants to the online service business, AT&T set a new pricing standard when it muscled its way into the Internet Service Provider ring in March 1996. Whereas most companies charged people an hourly rate for Web surfing, AT&T let its long-distance customers access the Internet all they wanted for a flat fee of $19.95.

Everybody else started offering the same deal, so AT&T extended its flat-fee offer to *everyone* — not just its long-distance customers.

✔ AT&T WorldNet Service comes with its own Web site offering standard fare: news, weather, entertainment, and convenient passageways to other Internet areas.

- ✔ CompuServe and America Online are *online services,* offering information only available through their own service in addition to Internet fare available to any Internet member. The messages on the CompuServe Chess Forum, for example, can only be read through CompuServe.

- ✔ Online services harbor hordes of Internet users who share their favorite sites, define weird Internet terms, and trade tips to novice users.

- ✔ AT&T WorldNet Service, by contrast, is an Internet provider, not an online service. The only chess information it contains can be found on any other Internet provider.

What Do I Need to Access the World Wide Web?

In addition to a little luck and ambition, you need a computer, a modem, and software to access the World Wide Web. You probably have the computer. The modem, described in Chapter 2, connects your computer to the phone lines for dialing other computers.

Plenty of companies offer World Wide Web software, usually called a *Web browser.* For this reason, Web browsers get their own section next. (Best yet, it's usually free, and comes free with new copies of Windows 95.)

Finally, you need an *Internet Service Provider* or ISP — a company that works like your gas and electric company, supplying you with a service and taking your money because of it. They give you a number for your computer to call and a password for you to type. You can find an ISP listed in your community's Yellow Pages under *Computers — Online Services & Internet or Telecommunications.* Or, ask your local computer dealer for names and numbers. Also, many computer stores sell software called *Internet in a Box* that contains the software and the phone number you need to begin.

- ✔ Because the government created the Internet, it's often cumbersome to use. Sometimes your computer can slip in as easily as a crooked politician. Other times, you're required to fill out many forms and enter a lot of numbers. Don't be afraid to ask a friend for help when connecting to your ISP for the first time.

- ✔ Don't be afraid to bug your ISP, too. The best ones come with technical support lines, where somebody can talk you through the installation process.

Should I connect to the Web through an ISP or an online service?

Both an online service and an Internet Service Provider let you connect to the Internet with Web browser software and begin pointing and clicking your way around the world. Both have their advantages.

Online services are often easier to use. Icons for CompuServe and America Online both come with Windows 95, making them relatively easy to set up. As an added perk, online services offer their own banks of information, inaccessible to Web users. Only CompuServe members can access CompuServe's many valuable product support forums, for example.

Plus, online services usually offer toll-free phone numbers to call from around the world (or at least around the United States). If you travel a great deal, this feature can be a valuable way to connect to the Internet from hotel rooms.

What are the disadvantages? Online services tend to have slower connections to the Internet, and their phone numbers are often busy.

If you don't travel much and want a fast, steady connection to the Internet, you may be best off going straight through an Internet Service Provider.

✔ Life rolls along much easier once you're aboard the Internet. The Web is *enormous,* but it contains speedy indexes to ferret out your favorite goodies. Type in a subject, and the Web spits out bunches of places to visit.

✔ Because Windows 95 can run so many things in the background, forgetting that you're connected to the Internet is an easy thing to do. If you're being charged by the hour, make sure that you keep a wary eye on your taskbar to see whether you're connected to the Internet or not.

✔ The software package *Internet in a Box* comes with a Web browser called Netscape. That's the Internet software used by 80 percent of the World Wide Web users.

What Is a Web Browser?

Your Web browser is your Internet surfboard — your transportation between the computers strewn along the Web. By pointing and clicking on your Web browser's buttons, you can easily move from one page to another.

Just as every page of a book has a number, each Web page has as an address. Type that specific address into a Web browser, press Enter, and that Web page appears on the screen.

Web browsers allow an even lazier way to flip through the Web's pages. They use *hypertext,* or *Web links*. Web page owners embed addresses of other Web pages into their own Web page. For example, Peeping Tom's Web Page (`http://www.csd.uu.se/~s96fst/`) presents a highlighted list of places where people have special video cameras attached to their computers. Click on Australia, and up comes a current view of Sydney outside Matthew Perkins's bedroom window.

Early Web browsers could only display words on the screen. The links were underlined or boldfaced so users knew where to click and head for the exciting parts. More sophisticated Web browsers began placing buttons and pictures on the screen.

Today's Web browsers come with little add-on bits of software for spicing things up. They can handle animated cartoons, voices, sounds, music, scrolling marquees, and other flashy goodies. If you kind of squint, it looks like your computer's turning more and more into a TV.

- ✔ You don't like that new Web page you just clicked your way into? Click on the big Back button at the top of your Web browser (on the top-left corner of Internet Explorer).Your Web browser immediately scurries back to your last location.

- ✔ Many places set up their own Web sites as simply collections of links to certain hobby areas, such as growing vegetables, weaving, or making bombs.

- ✔ <u>Web sites</u> come with <u>hyper links</u>. Highlighted words or buttons are linked to certain <u>addresses</u> of other computers on the Web. Click on the <u>highlighted</u> word or button, and your Web browser takes you to the Web page with that address.

- ✔ In the item above, the words "Web sites," "hyper links," "addresses," and "highlighted" would all be considered *highlighted*. If you pointed and clicked on one of them in a Web page, your Web browser would take you to a Web page offering more information about that subject.

- ✔ Web site addresses look pretty strange. They usually start with the letters `http://www` and end with something even more weird-looking, like `winespectator.com`. In fact, now you know what all those strange-looking words in parenthesis mean throughout this chapter.

- ✔ Two particular Web browsers attract the most attention. Eighty percent of the Internet crowd use a Web browser called *Netscape Navigator*. Netscape bit into the browser market early, and remains a key player.

- ✔ Microsoft, desperately playing catch-up in what could be as profitable as tomorrow's television, quickly wrote its own browser: *Internet Explorer*. Internet Explorer once came bundled with the Windows 95 extra-charge software, *Microsoft Plus*. Now, Microsoft has gotten more intense with its distribution, and it's giving the software away.

What options should I choose while installing Internet Explorer Version 3?

Installing the latest version of Internet Explorer? Chances are, the program will ask you what portions of itself you'd like to install. Here's the rundown:

Internet Mail: Go for it. This feature allows you to send and receive e-mail with people you meet on the Web.

Internet News: Thousands of people hold discussions on Internet *newsgroups*. For example, people interested in sailboats can join the sailboat newsgroup and swap chatter. The Internet News program lets you search the

discussions for interesting subjects and send your responses. Fun, but time-consuming.

NetMeeting (Windows 95 only): Yawn. Instead of group phone calls, people can type at each other.

Active Movie: Go for it. Because Microsoft is behind it, Active Movie may become a standard for viewing multimedia files – sounds and videos — on the Net.

HTML Layout Control: Save this stuff for people who design their own Web pages; you won't be using it.

✔ Internet Explorer comes free on all new PCs with Windows 95, and it's free for the downloading on the Microsoft Web site (http://www.microsoft.com). Several online services now offer Internet Explorer, and you may even find it bundled with some magazines.

✔ Just about any brand of Web browser works in a pinch, although some of the most groovy animation on the Web only works with Netscape Navigator.

How Do I Use Microsoft Internet Explorer?

After you've chosen and set up your Internet Service Provider — either by choosing The Microsoft Network, CompuServe, America Online, AT&T WorldNet, or somebody *not* included in the Windows 95 Online Services folder — you're ready to cruise the Internet.

Setting up the Internet provider can be a drag — more of a drag than this book can get into, unfortunately. If you're having trouble getting your computer set up for the Internet, a book like *The Internet For Dummies*, 3rd Edition, or *Modems For Dummies* may help (both published by IDG Books Worldwide, Inc.).

After you bring Internet Explorer to the screen, shown in Figure 15-3, you can put it to work. The next few sections show how.

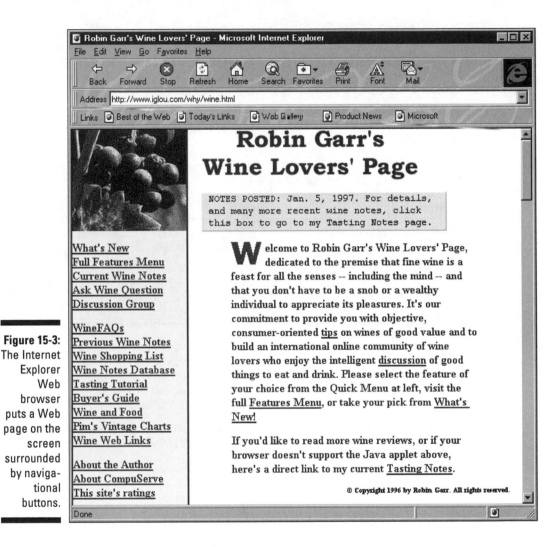

Figure 15-3:
The Internet
Explorer
Web
browser
puts a Web
page on the
screen
surrounded
by naviga-
tional
buttons.

What's a Start page?

Just as your television set always shows some channel when you turn it on,
your Web browser automatically displays a certain portion of the ever-
running Internet when loaded.

This first Web page you see is called your *Start page*. Most Start pages look
like large menus, and work as a base of operations. From there, you can
move around the Internet, searching for topics by looking in indexes or
simply pointing and clicking from topic to topic.

✔ Most Web browsers come with their own home page. When you install Internet Explorer and first log onto the Web, for example, you're whisked away to the Microsoft home page. The competing company's browser, Netscape Navigator, takes you to the Netscape home page.

✔ You can turn any Web site into a home page. While viewing the page you'd like to assign as your new home page, choose Options from the Internet Explorer View menu. Click the Navigation tab. Make sure that the words Start Page are in the Page box, and then click the Use Current button.

✔ To return to your Start page quickly, whenever you're connected to the Internet, click on the Home button along the top of Internet Explorer. (See the button in Figure 15-3, between the Refresh and Search buttons?)

✔ Don't confuse a *Start page* with a *Home page*. A Start page is the first page you see when you load your browser and log on to the Web. A Home page is the first page you see when you log onto a Web site. Figure 15-3 is Robin Garr's Home page, for example; from there, you can move around to other Web pages on his Web site. Figures 15-1, 15-2, and 15-4 are merely Web pages from Web sites; they aren't Home pages, because they're not the first page you see when you log onto those Web sites.

✔ Don't use a competing company's home page as your own. Netscape and Microsoft don't get along, and their products show it. Internet Explorer often chokes when on the Netscape home page, and Netscape Navigator doesn't seem to like the Microsoft home page, either.

How do I move around between Web pages?

Internet Explorer lets you move from page to page in three different ways:

✔ Pointing and clicking on a button or link that automatically whisks you away to another page

✔ Typing a complicated string of code words into the browser's Address box and pressing Enter

✔ Clicking the navigation buttons along a browser's menu

The first way is the easiest. Look for a page's *links* — highlighted words or pictures — and click on them. See the list of topics along the left side of Figure 15-3? Clicking on "Wine Notes Database" takes you to the Web page where Robin Garr shares his wine sampling observations. See how the adjacent text in Figure 15-3 contains underlined words? Those are also links; click on the underlined words to see Web pages with more information about them.

Buttons won't help if a friend gives you a napkin with a cool Web page's address written on it, however. In that case, you need to type the Web site's address yourself. That's fairly easy, as long as you don't misspell anything. See the Web site address for the Wine page along the top of Figure 15-3? I typed http://www.iglou.com/why/wine.html into the address box and pressed Enter; Internet Explorer scooted me to Robin Garr's Wine page. To head for the Volkswagen Web site, type in http://www.vw.com/cars/ and press Enter. That brings you to the site in Figure 15-2.

Finally, you can maneuver through the Internet by clicking on various parts of Internet Explorer itself. Clicking on the Favorites button along the top reveals a folder where you can stash buttons leading to your favorite Web sites. Click Go from the topmost menu for some other navigational menus.

Feel free to explore the Internet by simply clicking on the buttons. You really can't get into any trouble; if you get stuck, you can always click the Home button along the top to move back into safety.

- ✔ The easiest way to start surfing the Internet is to be a button pusher, so remember this bit o' wisdom: Watch how your mouse pointer changes shape as you move it over a Web page. When the pointer changes into a little hand, you're hovering over a button that aches to be pressed.

- ✔ Why the caution? Because Web page manufacturers get mighty creative these days, and it's often hard to tell where to point and click. Some buttons look like sturdy elevator buttons; others look more like fuzzy dice or vegetables. But when you click on a button, the browser takes you to the page relating to that button. Clicking on the fuzzy dice may bring up a betting odds sheet for local casinos, for example.

- ✔ Pointed and clicked yourself into a dead end? Click the Back button along the top, left-hand corner to head for the last Web page you visited.

- ✔ Visited a Web site in the past few weeks, but can't remember which one? Choose History from the Internet Explorer Go menu to see links to all the sites you've visited in the past few weeks.

- ✔ Text can be grabbed, too. Slide your cursor over the text while holding down the mouse button, just as if you were in a word-processing program. When Internet Explorer highlights the text, press Ctrl+C to copy the text to the Clipboard.

How can I revisit my favorite places?

Sooner or later, you'll stumble across a Web page that's indescribably delicious. To make sure that you can visit it later, add it to your favorite places folder. Click on the folder marked Favorites from the top of the Internet Explorer menu and choose the Add to Favorites... option. That effort deposits a link to your current page into the folder.

To return to the page, click on the Favorites folder along the top of the screen again, and click on the name of the link you want to revisit.

What's an Index or Search Engine?

Just as it is nearly impossible to find a book in a library without a card catalog, it is nearly impossible to find a Web site on the Internet without a good index. Luckily, several exist.

To find one, click on the Internet Explorer Search button along the top of the menu. The Internet Explorer Search page appears, as shown in Figure 15-4.

Type the name of the subject you're searching for into the Search box and click the Search button. After a few seconds, Internet Explorer brings up a list of Web sites dealing with that subject.

Figure 15-4: Internet Explorer can search the Web for any subject.

✔ Internet Explorer lets you use close to a dozen different search engines. Each one uses a slightly different index and searches for material in a different way. For example, Figure 15-4 shows ten search engines: infoseek, NetGuideLive, Microsoft, AltaVista, Yahoo!, Lycos, HotBot, Web Crawler, Magellan, and excite.

✔ If you don't like what one index is coming up with, click on another one and try again.

✔ AltaVista is a personal favorite. Microsoft is a least favorite, because it just searches Microsoft's own network.

✔ Searches usually come up with hundreds or even thousands of hits relating to your subject. If you come up with too many, try again but be more specific.

It Doesn't Work!

Don't feel bad. The Internet's been around for a while, but this whole Web thing is pretty darn new, and getting pretty overburdened. It's not supposed to work smoothly. Here are some of the most common problems and some possible solutions.

I can't get it to install!

Installing Internet Explorer isn't all that difficult; the hard part is telling Explorer how to connect to your Internet Service Provider — the company that's providing the phone connection to the Internet. Because the ISPs all use slightly different ways to connect, your best bet is to call the tech support number and ask for help.

Yeah, installation is a pain, but remember — you only have to install the thing once. After Internet Explorer is installed, you can simply click on a button to make it dial up the connection and start surfing.

Secret Book Plug: If you still can't get the thing to install, take a peek at my *MORE Windows 95 For Dummies* (published by IDG Books Worldwide, Inc.) in the bookstores. You don't have to buy it, just peek at the 12-step process at the beginning of Chapter 6.

I keep getting busy signals!

This problem means that your Internet Service Provider is probably offering a great deal — unlimited access to the Internet for one low price. Unfortunately, a bargain means that many people are going to be calling at the same time as you, leading to busy signals.

What's the answer? Reassess your priorities. Are you looking to save money or find a reliable connection to the Internet? You may be able to find a better deal with a different provider.

The Web page says it needs Java!

Computer programmers abandoned their boring old TV sets and turned to their exciting new computers for entertainment. Now, they're trying to turn their computers back into TV sets. They're using a fancy bit of programming called Java that adds animation and other gizmos to the Internet.

If you see things like little raisins dancing across a Web page, you know it's using Java or something similar.

What's the problem? Early versions of Internet Explorer didn't support Java. What's the solution? Upgrade to the latest version. (You can download it from the Microsoft Web page at `http://www.microsoft.com`.)

The Web page says that it's optimized for Netscape, not Explorer!

The vast majority of Web surfers use Netscape Navigator, not Internet Explorer. So, the vast majority of programmers optimize their Web pages for the Navigator program.

Usually, this fact doesn't matter. Internet Explorer is catching up rapidly and can often display the page as well as Netscape Navigator. Other times, the differences won't even be noticeable. You just won't see an animation of a cockroach crawling across the screen, for example.

However, sometimes a Web page simply won't work right with Internet Explorer. What's the solution? Give up. Thousands of pages out there work fine with Internet Explorer. In fact, some pages are optimized for Internet Explorer and don't work as well with Netscape Navigator.

I can't figure any of this stuff out!

The Internet and its World Wide Web can be rough for beginners to figure out — and it's much too complex to be stuffed into a single chapter of this book. To pick up more information on the Internet, head for the bookstore and pick up a copy of *The Internet For Dummies* or *The World Wide Web For Teachers* (published by IDG Books Worldwide, Inc.). (What? Not a teacher? Well, you're certainly not a dummy, either, and you bought this book . . . .)

Part IV

Been There, Done That: Quick References for Moving to Windows 95

The 5th Wave   By Rich Tennant

*Bill Gates dreams...

*Yes, he sleeps with his glasses on.

JUSTICE DEPT.

"THAT'S RIGHT, MS. BINGAMAN, HE'S COLLECTING A ROYALTY FROM EVERYONE ON EARTH, AND THERE'S NOTHING WE CAN DO ABOUT IT."

In this part . . .

Moving from Windows 3.1 to Windows 95 is like moving into a new house and trying to find the bathroom in the dark. Until you get used to the floor plan, you bump into things.

After you discover where things are, that sense of urgency disappears and you can relax. Other people, however, always miss their old place, with its familiar light switches, windows, and plumbing.

This part of the book is for Windows 3.1 owners who've already paid their dues and figured out the old Program Manager and File Manager. Here, you find ways to make Windows 95 work like the old standby, Windows 3.1. Or if you're looking for the quickest way to get the most done, you can find that here as well.

Chapter 16

Make Windows 95 Work Like My *Old* Windows!

● ●

In This Chapter

▶ Bringing back Program Manager

▶ Resurrecting File Manager

▶ Replacing the Task List

▶ Finding Cardfile and Calendar

▶ Finding Paint

● ●

*F*ile Manager and Program Manager may not have been perfect, but hey, at least their faults were *familiar* to the 60 million Windows 3.1 users out there. This chapter shows how to make Windows 95 act like old, faithful, Windows 3.1.

Where Did My Program Manager Go?

Windows 95 dumped Program Manager in favor of the Start menu, which pops up when you click on the famous Windows 95 Start button. And when you scratch your head (and play with the thing for about 15 minutes), the similarities between the Start menu and Program Manager start to appear.

For example, Program Manager lets you organize your programs in separate Program Group windows. The Windows 95 Start menu organizes programs in separate folders branching out from the menu's Programs listing.

But if you prefer the Windows 3.1 Program Manager for starting programs — or you want to use Program Manager until you grow more accustomed to Windows 95 — here's how to bring the ol' Program Manager back to life:

1. Click on the Start button and choose Run from the menu.

A box pops up, asking you to type the name of a program you want to run.

2. Type progman **into the Open box and click on the OK button.**

The box should look like the one in Figure 16-1. When you click on the OK button, Program Manager appears, as shown in Figure 16-2.

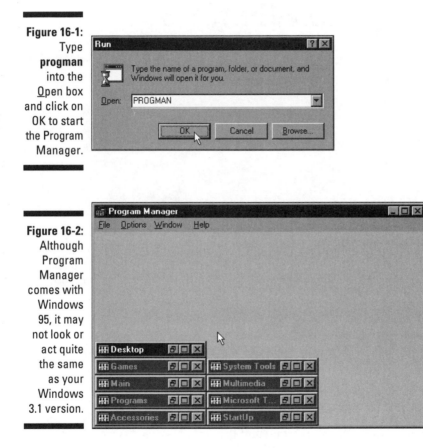

Figure 16-1:
Type **progman** into the Open box and click on OK to start the Program Manager.

Figure 16-2:
Although Program Manager comes with Windows 95, it may not look or act quite the same as your Windows 3.1 version.

Be prepared for a few adjustments, however. Program Manager is wearing Windows 95 clothing, as shown in Figure 16-2. Minimized Program Groups stack themselves along the screen's bottom like cigars in a box, and the tiling and cascading features don't work as well as they do in Windows 3.1.

Resize the windows, and Program Manager looks a little more familiar, as shown in Figure 16-3.

Figure 16-3:
When the icons are turned into windows, Program Manager looks more familiar.

✔ Program Manager still has some limitations. For example, some newly installed programs won't install their icons on Program Manager — they put them on the Start menu instead.

✔ To put a program's icon on Program Manager, just drag the icon there from the My Computer or Windows Explorer program. Windows 95 automatically turns the icon into a shortcut for launching the program. (After all, the Windows 95 fancy shortcuts are almost the same as the icons in the Windows 3.1 Program Manager.)

✔ The new Program Manager makes it much harder to drag and drop icons onto Program Groups that are minimized along the screen's bottom. The minimized group icons are much closer together than they used to be, making it harder to tell where your dropped icon will fall.

✔ Program Manager hails from the older, 16-bit school of programs, so it can't handle long filenames very well. In fact, if you drag a file called Egyptian Stone from My Computer to Program Manager, Program Manager renames the file Egypti˜1. That funny ˜ thing, covered more extensively in Chapter 12, is how Windows 95 abbreviates long filenames so that older programs can still recognize them.

✔ Closing Program Manager no longer shuts down Windows 95. To shut down, you need to click on the Start button and choose Shut Down from the menu.

✔ If you *really* prefer Program Manager over the Start menu, tell Windows 95 to automatically load Program Manager whenever you turn on your computer. The secret is to put the file PROGMAN.EXE in the StartUp folder. (The file's in your Windows folder, and Chapter 11 explains how to add a program to the StartUp folder.)

Where Did File Manager Go?

Nobody really likes the Windows 3.1 File Manager, except perhaps the old-timers who struggled with the Windows 3.0 File Manager.

Although File Manager's replacements — the My Computer and Windows Explorer programs included with Windows 95 — are slightly easier to use, file management will never compete with a hockey game for entertainment.

If you don't want to learn any new tricks, however, feel free to bypass My Computer and Windows Explorer and return to File Manager — it's included with Windows 95. Here's how to bring the File Manager to life:

1. **Click on the Start button and choose Run from the menu.**

   A box pops up, asking you to type the name of a program you want to run.

2. **Type** winfile **into the Open box and click on the OK button.**

   When you click on the OK button, the File Manager appears, as shown in Figure 16-4.

File Manager looks pretty much like the one in Windows for Workgroups. The biggest difference is in the minimized windows. Just as with Program Manager, File Manager's minimized windows look like hot dogs dropped to the window's bottom, as shown in Figure 16-5.

   ✔ You can still copy files by dragging them and dropping them into windows inside File Manager. But it's hard to drop a file onto a minimized drive because those minimized drives are now hot-dog thin. And you can't load documents into programs by dragging and dropping them onto the taskbar's list of programs, either; Windows 95 says that you can only drag and drop files into open windows.

Figure 16-4:
The File Manager included with Windows 95 doesn't look or act quite the same as the Windows 3.0 version.

Figure 16-5:
Minimized
windows lie
like hot
dogs along
the bottom
edge.

✔ The Windows 95 version of File Manager, just like its version of Program Manager, still wears an old-school, 16-bit hat. So File Manager can't recognize the long filenames used by many Windows 95 programs. In fact, when File Manager comes across any filenames longer than 8 characters, it abbreviates them and puts a weird ˜ thing in the name.

✔ File Manager also adds the weird ˜ thing if it comes across any filename with a space in it, like a file named LOST IN or something similar.

✔ When you rest your mouse pointer over an icon in Windows 95, a box usually pops up and explains the icon's purpose in life. You won't find any helpful pop-up boxes in File Manager or Program Manager, however; they're too old to have that trick built in.

✔ In fact, with all its limitations, you probably won't want to spend much time with File Manager. Instead of spending time figuring out File Manager's new limitations, it's probably wiser to spend time figuring out how to use My Computer or Windows Explorer. (They're both covered in Chapter 12.)

Where Did the Task List Go?

The Windows 3.1 Task List — the program that pops up when you double-click on a blank part of your window's wallpaper — is gone for good. Windows 95 has replaced it with the Start menu.

But here's the good news: The Windows 95 Start menu, when combined with the taskbar, can do everything the Task List can do: load programs and switch between them, arrange windows, and quit programs.

Plus, the Windows 95 Start button leaps to life when you press Ctrl+Esc —
the same key combination that started the Windows 3.1 Task List.

Where Are Calendar, Cardfile, and Paintbrush?

The Windows 3.1 Calendar and Cardfile are gone for good. Windows 95
doesn't come with them, and Microsoft figured it didn't need to toss in
replacements, either.

If you install Windows 95 over Windows 3.1, however, your Calendar and
Cardfile programs are still on your computer; they're listed on the Start menu.

A new, improved version of Paintbrush comes with Windows 95, and you
find it listed in the Start menu's Program area under Accessories. It's now
called Paint, and it's described in Chapter 13.

Bringing the Task List back from the dead

To placate the old-timers, Windows 95 still
comes with the Task List program. In fact, the
program has been updated a bit to make
it more interesting. To load Task List, double-
click on Taskman, a program icon in your Windows directory. (Or type **taskman** at the Start
menu's Run command line.)

The Task List leaps to the screen.

The Task List doesn't come with a Help file, so
you need to fiddle with the menus to see what's
listed. But Task List is a fairly powerful program: It lists all the currently running programs
and windows so you can choose among them;
it can tile or cascade open windows across
the screen; and it comes with a command line,
like the Start menu's Run area. Plus, it lets you
minimize *all* the open windows with one command. It even lets you shut down Windows 95.

The program itself can be customized, allowing for large or small buttons. If you're looking
for a handy desktop accessory, check out the
Task List before buying a third-party utility.

Chapter 17

Just Tell Me the *Easy* Way!

● ●

In This Chapter

▶ Copying a file to a floppy disk

▶ Finding the Start button and Start menu

▶ Finding a lost file, folder, or program

▶ Adding programs to the Start menu

▶ Arranging open windows

▶ Opening a new compact disc box

▶ Changing the screen's wallpaper

▶ Installing a new program

● ●

*T*his is it — quick and easy answers to the Windows 95 questions everybody wants to know. Feel free to put sticky notes next to your favorite answers.

How Do I Copy a File to a Floppy Disk (And Vice Versa)?

Want to copy a file from your hard disk to a floppy disk? Double-click on the My Computer icon and open the folder where your file is currently living. Using the right mouse button, click on the file's icon and stand back: A menu pops out. Point at the Send To command, and another menu shoots out. Finally, click on the name of the floppy disk you want to send the file to — drive A or drive B, for example.

Oh, and don't forget to put a floppy disk into the drive.

This method doesn't work for copying files from floppies to a hard drive; the hard drive doesn't appear on the Send To menu. To move the file there, drag its icon from the floppy drive window to the folder on the hard drive. For more information, head to Chapter 12.

Copying a Complete Floppy Disk

To copy files from one disk to another, drag 'em over there, as described in the preceding section. But if you want to make a complete copy of a floppy — a backup of your novel in progress, for example — follow these steps:

1. **Put your floppy disk in your disk drive.**

2. **Double-click the My Computer icon.**

3. **Click your floppy disk's icon with your right mouse button.**

4. **Choose Copy Disk from the pop-up menu.**

   A box appears, letting you confirm which disk and disk drive you want to use for your copy.

5. **Click the Start button to begin making the copy.**

How Do I Find the Start Button and Start Menu?

Normally, you find the Start button lurking on the end of the taskbar — a long, ribbon-like string that covers an edge of the screen. You can't even find the taskbar? Then press Ctrl+Esc. That almost always brings up the Start menu — the menu that pops up when you click on the Start button.

How Do I Start a Program?

Click on the taskbar's Start button and point your mouse at the word Programs on the pop-up menu. When you point at the various folders that pop up, the folders open, revealing more options.

Spot the program you're after? Click on its name, and Windows 95 brings the program to life. If you don't spot the program, head for the "How Do I Find a File, Folder, or Program?" section coming up next.

More taskbar information lurks in Chapter 11.

You can also start programs from the My Computer or Windows Explorer programs. Double-click on a folder to open it; double-click on a program to load it. Double-clicking on a file usually loads the program that created the file, as well as opens the file itself.

How Do I Find a File, Folder, or Program?

Click on the Start button, point at the Find command, and click on the Files or Folders option. Type the name of your program — just the first few letters will do — and click on the Find Now button.

The Find program lists all files, folders, and programs on drive C that begin with the letters you typed. If you spot your program, double-click on it to bring it to life. If you don't spot what you're after, head for Chapter 8 for a more detailed explanation of the Find program.

How Can I Add Programs to the Start Menu?

The congenial Windows 95 allows several ways to add files, folders, and programs to the Start menu, but here's one of the easiest.

Open the My Computer program and find the icon for your program. Point at the program's icon and, while holding down the mouse button, point at the Start button. Then let go of the mouse button. That's all there is to it.

Click on the Start button, and you see your newly added program at the top of the menu.

Hit Chapter 11 for more tips.

How Do I Keep My Icons Neatly Arranged?

When first installed, Windows 95 lines up all your icons neatly in their folders. But if you start changing a folder's size or moving icons around, they quickly lose their orderly arrangement and start overlapping.

The solution? Click on a blank part of the folder with your right mouse button and point at Arrange Icons on the menu. Click on Auto Arrange, and Windows 95 automatically keeps your icons arranged in neat rows.

What's the downside? Lazy Windows 95 makes you repeat this command on *every* window or folder you want to keep arranged automatically. Sigh.

How Do I Organize Open Windows So That They're All Visible?

Too many overlapping windows scattered across your screen? Use one of the tile commands, and Windows 95 gives each window an equal amount of space on your desktop.

1. **Using the right mouse button, click on a blank part of the taskbar.**

   Clicking near the clock usually works well.

2. **Choose Tile <u>H</u>orizontally or Tile <u>V</u>ertically.**

   One command lines up the windows in columns; the other lines them up in rows. Try whichever scheme looks best. Or turn to Chapter 7 for more information.

How Do I Set the Time and Date?

To change the computer's time and date, double-click on the taskbar's clock, usually found at the bottom-right corner of the screen. A calendar and clock pop up, letting you change the date, time, or even the time zone. Hit Chapter 10 for the full scoop.

How Do I Open a New, Plastic-Wrapped Compact Disc Box?

With your teeth, being careful not to scratch your gums. Sometimes a thumbnail works well, or even a letter opener. It's a miracle of technology, but the plastic wrap is often tougher than the plastic case itself.

How Do I Change My Screen's Wallpaper?

Using the right mouse button, click on a blank part of your desktop. Then choose <u>P</u>roperties from the pop-up menu. See the list of names in the second column, under the word <u>W</u>allpaper? Click on one of the names for a quick preview.

More Wallpaper instructions are hanging around in Chapter 10.

How Do I Change the Name of a File or Folder?

Call up My Computer or Explorer and click on the icon of the file or folder you want to rename; that action highlights the icon, making it change color.

Wait a second or two and then click directly on the file or folder's current name. Start typing the new name, which automatically replaces the old name. Press Enter when you're through.

Windows 95 won't let you change every icon's name, however. For example, you're stuck with the names *Recycle Bin* and *3 1/2 Floppy (A:)*, along with a few others.

How Much Room Do I Have on My Hard Drive?

Open the My Computer program and click on your hard drive's icon with your right mouse button. Choose Properties from the menu that appears, and a box appears, listing your hard drive's size (and showing you a pretty graph, too).

How Do I Install a New Program?

Here's the easy way, if everything works the way it's supposed to:

Double-click on the My Computer program and double-click on the Control Panel living inside it.

After the Control Panel hits the screen, double-click on the Add/Remove Programs icon. After the next window pops up, click on the Install button and follow the instructions. (Or flip to Chapter 10 for more detailed instructions; that chapter offers help if the Install button doesn't work, too.)

Part V
Help!

The 5th Wave   By Rich Tennant

"SOFTWARE SUPPORT SAYS WHATEVER WE DO, DON'T ANYONE START TO RUN."

In this part . . .

*W*indows 95 can do hundreds of tasks in dozens of ways. This means that approximately one million things can fail at any given time.

Some problems are easy to fix. For example, one misplaced pair of clicks in the taskbar makes all your programs disappear. Yet one more click in the right place puts them all back.

Other problems are far more complex, requiring teams of computer surgeons to diagnose, remedy, and bill accordingly.

This part helps you separate the big problems from the little ones. You'll know whether you can fix it yourself with a few clicks and a kick. If your situation's worse, you'll know when it's time to call in the surgeons.

Chapter 18

The Case of the Broken Window

In This Chapter

▶ How to recognize the four versions of Windows 95

▶ What to do if you're stuck in Menu Land

▶ How to install a new "driver" for a new computer gizmo

▶ How to install other parts of Windows 95

▶ What to do when you click on the wrong button

▶ What to do when your computer freezes

▶ How to deal with DOS programs that don't look right in a window

▶ What to do when your printer is not working correctly

Sometimes you just have a sense that something's wrong. The computer makes quiet grumbling noises, or Windows 95 starts running more slowly than Congress. Other times something's obviously wrong. Pressing any key just gives you a beeping noise, menus keep shooting at you, or Windows 95 greets you with a cheery error message when you first turn it on.

Many of the biggest-looking problems are solved by the smallest-looking solutions. Hopefully, this chapter points you to the right one.

Uh, Which Version of Windows 95 Am I Really Using?

Unfortunately, four versions of Windows 95 exist, and that can bring four separate versions of problems.

First came the Microsoft preview version of Windows 95. Released in the early summer of 1995, it wasn't the real version of Windows 95. It was a test version, designed to let Microsoft expose Windows 95 to as many different types of computers as possible. That way Microsoft could find out the parts that didn't work right and fix them before the *real* version of Windows 95 came out later in the year.

If you bought a version of Windows 95 for about $30, you may be using the preview version — not the real version of Windows 95. That means that you shouldn't be surprised if it starts acting funny or doesn't behave like the software described in this book. (If a friend gave you a free program that doesn't seem to be working right, this may be the problem, as well.)

Next, on August 24, 1995, Microsoft began selling the version of Windows 95 that just about everybody's using today. That version fixed most of the problems discovered in the preview version. (At least 60 million people are using this second version, and that probably includes you.)

If you bought a copy of Windows 95 after November 1996, you probably have the third version. *That* version comes with a free copy of Internet Explorer for the Web Surfers. (Previously, Microsoft made people buy that software in a package called Microsoft Plus.)

At about the same time, Microsoft began selling a new version of Windows 95 to computer makers. Sold only on new PCs, this fourth version contains mostly mechanical improvements the industry developers have been howling for. And no, you can't simply upgrade your computer with this fourth new version, because it can only be installed on a completely empty hard drive — meaning that it's more trouble than most people are willing to handle.

✔ Never got a copy of Internet Explorer? Find a friend who has access to the World Wide Web and show them Chapter 15; that chapter shows how to access the Microsoft Web page where you can find free copies! (You can find a copy of the latest version on many online services, such as CompuServe, too.)

✔ Many people are still using Windows 3.1 rather than Windows 95. (Although industry statistics are hard to come by, it looks like more people are still using their old copies of Windows 3.1 than upgrading to Windows 95.)

✔ The new fourth version of Windows 95 being shipped on new PCs is pretty boring, actually, unless you enjoy big computer words. It has a new File Allocation Table 32 file system, which lets Windows 95 play better on bigger hard drives (but at a slower speed). It has Crypto APIs, some sort of secret code stuff for developers. It lets Windows take better advantage of PC Cards and share IRQs. It offers PCI bridging and docking and, if you haven't fallen asleep yet, new power management technologies that let parts of your computer rest when they're not being used.

✔ If you're excited about having the latest in Windows 95 technology, you can download some of this gadgetry from the Microsoft Web Page at http://www.microsoft.com. Beware, however: The latest technology invariably brings about the latest in problems.

Making an Emergency StartUp Disk

Unless you grab a spare floppy right now, this information won't do you any good.

See, Windows 95 can make an emergency StartUp Disk. Then, when Windows 95 refuses to load, you can pop the disk into your computer's mouth, push the reset button, and a bare-bones version of Windows 95 comes to the screen. That bare-bones version may be enough to get you started. At the very least, it can make it easier for a computer guru friend to get your computer started.

So grab a floppy disk that's blank or doesn't have important information on it — perhaps one of those America Online Trial offers that come in all the magazines. This procedure erases the disk's contents and there's no turning back.

1. **Double-click on the Control Panel's Add/Remove Programs icon.**

   You can load the Control Panel by clicking on Settings in the Start menu.

2. **Click on the Windows StartUp Disk tab.**

   It's the right-most tab of the three along the top.

3. **Click on the Create Disk button.**

   Windows 95 tells you to insert a disk into drive A. Before pushing the disk into the drive, grab a felt pen and write Emergency StartUp Disk on the floppy disk's label.

4. **Insert a blank disk into drive A when told; then click on the OK button.**

   Windows 95 formats the blank disk and copies special files onto it, allowing it to start your computer in the worst of situations. Put the disk in a safe place and hope you never have to use it.

   • In an emergency, put the disk in drive A and push your computer's reset button. The computer "boots" off the floppy disk; that is, the computer comes to life, even though its hard drive isn't working.

   • When loaded from the floppy disk, Windows 95 comes up in "DOS prompt" mode. It won't look anything like the real Windows 95, but a computer guru may be able to use the DOS prompt as a doorway to fix whatever's gone wrong.

My Mouse Doesn't Work Right

Sometimes the mouse doesn't work at all; other times the mouse pointer hops across the screen like a flea. Here are a few things to look for:

- If no mouse arrow is on the screen when you start Windows, make sure that the mouse's tail is plugged snugly into the computer's rump. Then exit and restart Windows 95.

- If the mouse arrow is on-screen but won't move, Windows may be mistaking your brand of mouse for a different brand. You can make sure that Windows 95 recognizes the correct type of mouse by following the "Adding New Hardware" steps, as described in Chapter 10.

- A mouse pointer can jump around on-screen if it's dirty. First, turn the mouse upside-down and clean off any visible dirt stuck to the bottom. Then turn the little lever until the mouse ball pops out. Wipe off any crud and blow any dust out of the hole. Pull any stray hairs off the little rollers and stick the ball back inside the mouse. If you wear wool sweaters (or have a cat that sleeps on the mouse pad), you may have to clean the ball every week or so.

- If the mouse was working fine and now the buttons seem to be reversed, you've probably changed the right- or left-handed button configuration setting in the Control Panel. Double-click on the Control Panel's Mouse icon and make sure that the configuration is set up to match your needs. (That's covered in Chapter 10, by the way.)

I'm Stuck in Menu Land

If your keystrokes don't appear in your work but instead make a bunch of menus shoot out from the top of the window, you're stuck in Menu Land. Somehow you've pressed and released Alt, an innocent-looking key that's easy to hit accidentally.

When you press and release Alt, Windows turns its attention away from your work and toward the menus along the top of the window.

To get back to work, press and release Alt one more time. Alternatively, press Esc. One or the other is your ticket out of Menu Land.

I'm Supposed to Install a New "Driver"

When you buy a new toy for the computer, it should come with a piece of software called a *driver*. A driver is a sort of translator that lets Windows know how to boss around the new toy. If you buy a new keyboard, sound card, compact disc player, printer, mouse, monitor, or almost any other computer toy, you need to install its driver in Windows. Luckily, it's a fairly painless process covered in the "Adding New Hardware" section of Chapter 10.

✔ Companies constantly update drivers, fixing problems or making the drivers perform better. If the computer device is misbehaving, a newer driver may calm it down. Call the manufacturer and ask for the latest version. Or, if you've entered the world of the Internet, fire up your modem and head for the manufacturer's Web page so that you can make a free copy.

✔ For floppy-disk-insertion etiquette, see Chapter 2.

✔ Not all computer toys work with Windows 95. Check with the store before you buy so that you aren't stuck with something that won't work.

✔ The best place to find drivers for Windows 95 is often the Microsoft Web Page. If you're looking for something hard to find, fire up Internet Explorer, head for `http://www.microsoft.com`, and look for the drivers area.

His Version of Windows 95 Has More Programs Than Mine!

Windows 95 installs itself differently on different types of computers. As it copies itself over to a hard drive from floppy disks or a compact disc, it brings different files with it. If installed on a laptop, for example, Windows 95 brings along programs that help a laptop transfer files and keep track of its battery life.

Computers with smaller hard drives will probably get the minimum files Windows 95 needs to run. Chapter 3 describes some of the programs and accessories Windows 95 comes with; here's how to copy them to your computer if Windows 95 left them off the first time.

1. Double-click on the Control Panel's Add/Remove Programs icon.

You can load the Control Panel by clicking on Settings in the Start menu.

2. **Click on the Windows Setup tab.**

    It's the tab in the middle of the three along the top; a box appears that shows the various components of Windows 95, as well as the amount of space they need to nestle onto your computer's hard drive.

3. **Click in the little box by the programs or accessories you want to add.**

    A check mark appears in the box of the items you've selected. To select part of a category — a portion of the accessories, for example — click on the category's name and click on the Details button. Windows 95 lists the items available in that category, so you can only click on the ones you want. If you clicked on the Details button, click on the OK button to continue back at the main categories list.

4. **Click on the OK button and insert your installation disks when asked.**

    Windows 95 copies the necessary files from your installation disks onto your hard drive. You can remove Windows 95 accessories by *removing* the check mark from the box next to their name.

Windows 95 comes with some pretty weird stuff, so don't get carried away and copy *all* of it over — especially until Microsoft gets it all working right.

I Clicked on the Wrong Button (But Haven't Lifted My Finger Yet)

Clicking the mouse takes two steps: a push and a release. If you click on the wrong button on-screen and haven't lifted your finger yet, slowly slide the mouse pointer off the button on-screen. Then take your finger off the mouse.

The screen button pops back up, and Windows 95 pretends nothing happened. Thankfully.

My Computer Is Frozen Up Solid

Every once in a while, Windows just drops the ball and wanders off somewhere. You're left looking at a computer that just looks back. Panicked clicks don't do anything. Pressing every key on the keyboard doesn't do anything — or worse yet, the computer starts to beep at every key press.

When nothing on-screen moves except the mouse pointer, the computer is frozen up solid. Try the following approaches, in the following order, to correct the problem:

Approach 1: Press Esc twice.

That action usually doesn't work, but give it a shot anyway.

Approach 2: Press Ctrl, Alt, and Delete all at the same time.

If you're lucky, Windows flashes an error message saying that you've discovered an "unresponsive application" and lists the names of currently running programs — including the one that's not responding. Click on the name of the program that's causing the mess and click on the End Task button. You lose any unsaved work in it, of course, but you should be used to that. (If you somehow stumbled onto the Ctrl+Alt+Delete combination by accident, press Esc at the unresponsive-application message to return to Windows.)

If that still doesn't do the trick, try clicking the Shut down button that's next to the End Task button, or pressing Ctrl+Alt+Delete again.

Approach 3: If the preceding approaches don't work, push the computer's reset button.

The screen is cleared, and the computer acts like you turned it off and on again. When the dust settles, Windows 95 should return to life.

Approach 4: If not even the reset button works, turn the computer off, wait 30 seconds, and then turn it back on again.

Don't ever flip the computer off and on again quickly. Doing so can damage its internal organs.

My DOS Program Looks Weird in a Window

DOS programs are *supposed* to look weird when running in a window. Windows 95 forces the computer to contort into different graphics lifestyles. Most DOS programs look different when displayed in these new graphics modes.

You do have a few alternatives, however:

- Click on the DOS program window to highlight it and then hold Alt and press Enter. Windows 95 steps to the background, letting the DOS program have the whole screen. *Then* the DOS program looks normal. Press Alt Enter to put it back in the window. Or hold Alt and press Esc to return to Windows, with the DOS program as an icon listed on the taskbar. (Exit the DOS program normally to automatically return to Windows.)
- Play with the DOS program's fonts as described in Chapter 14.
- Buy the Windows or Windows 95 version of the DOS program.
- Buy a more expensive graphics card that allows for even more graphics modes. Chances are, one of the modes will suit the DOS program a little better.

The Printer Isn't Working Right

If the printer's not working right, start with the simplest solution first: Make sure that it's plugged into the wall and turned on. Surprisingly, this step fixes about half the problems with printers. Next, make sure that the printer cable is snugly nestled in the ports on both the printer and the computer. Then check to make sure that it has enough paper — and that the paper isn't jammed in the mechanism.

Then try printing from different programs, such as WordPad and Notepad, to see whether the problem's with the printer, Windows 95, or a particular Windows program. Try printing the document by using different fonts. All these chores help pinpoint the culprit.

The Windows Help program can also pitch in; click on <u>H</u>elp from the Start menu, click on the Index tab, and type the words **printer problems** into the box. Press Enter, and Windows 95 leads you through a program designed to figure out why the printer's goofing off.

You may have to call the printer's manufacturer and ask for a new Windows driver. When the disk comes in the mail, follow the instructions in the "Fiddling with the Printer" section of Chapter 10.

Chapter 19

Error Messages (What You Did Does Not Compute)

∙ ∙

In This Chapter

▶ Not enough memory

▶ A:\ is not accessible. The device is not ready.

▶ Destination disk drive is full

▶ The file or folder that this shortcut refers to cannot be found

▶ This filename is not valid

▶ There is no viewer capable of viewing Word Pad document files

▶ Deleting this file will make it impossible to run this program

▶ Open with

▶ You must type a filename

▶ Windows 95 was not properly shut down

∙ ∙

*M*ost people don't have any trouble understanding error messages. A car's pleasant beeping tone means that you've left your keys in the ignition. A terrible scratching sound from the stereo means that the cat's jumped on the turntable.

Things are different with Windows 95, however. The error messages in Windows 95 could have been written by a Senate subcommittee, if only they weren't so brief. When Windows 95 tosses an error message your way, it's usually just a single sentence. Windows 95 rarely describes what you did to cause the error. And even worse, Windows 95 hardly ever says how to make the error go away for good.

Here are some of the words that you'll find in the most common error messages Windows 95 throws in your face. This chapter explains what Windows 95 is trying to say, why it's saying it, and just what the heck it expects you to do about it.

Not enough memory

Meaning: Windows 95 is running out of the room it needs to operate.

Probable cause: You have too many windows simultaneously open on the screen.

Solutions: A short-term solution is to close some of the windows. DOS windows often take up a lot of memory, so start by shutting them down. Also, make sure that you're not using any large color pictures of peacocks for wallpaper. It takes much less memory to tile small pictures across the screen (see Chapter 10 for information about tiling windows). If Windows 95 still acts sluggish, click on the Start button, choose Shut down, and choose the Restart the computer option.

For a long-term solution, make sure that you have plenty of empty space on the hard drive so that Windows has room to read and write information. Delete any files or programs you don't use anymore.

Finally, consider buying some more memory. Windows works much better with 8MB of memory than with 4MB of memory. And 12MB or 16MB of memory is better still. Today, people are walking out the door with 32MB of memory in their laptops, and nobody's laughing. In fact, the oldsters are crying because memory costs about one-tenth of what it did five years ago.

 Whenever you cut or copy a large amount of information to the Clipboard, that information stays there, taking up memory — even after you've pasted it into another application. To clear out the Clipboard after a large paste operation, copy a single word to the Clipboard. Doing so replaces the earlier, memory-hogging chunk, freeing some memory for other programs.

A:\ is not accessible. The device is not ready.

Meaning: Windows can't find a floppy disk in Drive A.

Probable cause: No floppy disk is in there.

Solution: Slide a disk in, push down the little lever if it's a 5 ¼-inch drive, and wish all errors were this easy to fix.

Destination disk drive is full

Meaning: Windows 95 has run out of room on a floppy disk or on the hard drive to store something.

Probable cause: Windows 95 tried saving something to a disk file but ran out of space.

Solution: Clear more room on that disk before saving your work. Delete any junk files on the hard disk. BAK (backup) files and TMP (temporary) files often qualify as junk files that can be deleted, but only if their date shows them to be old and forgotten. Also, delete any programs you don't use anymore. (For example, if you use Word for Windows as your word processor now, you probably don't need to keep the DOS version of Word 4.0 on the disk.)

Also, in this era when the Microsoft Monster Truck Madness game consumes 100MB of hard drive space for a rowdy race, it may be time to upgrade to a larger hard drive.

The file or folder that this shortcut refers to cannot be found

Meaning: Windows 95 can't find the program that's supposed to be attached to a Shortcut icon.

Probable cause: One of the programs has moved or deleted a file after a shortcut was attached to it.

Solution: Try using the Windows 95 Find program, described in Chapter 8. If the Find program can't find it, double-click on the Recycle Bin to see if it's in there and can be salvaged.

This filename is not valid

Meaning: Windows 95 refuses to accept your choice of filename.

Probable cause: You've tried to name a file by using one or more of the forbidden characters.

Solution: Turn to the section about renaming a file in Chapter 12 and make sure that you're not naming a file something you shouldn't.

There is no viewer capable of viewing WordPad document files

Meaning: Windows 95 can't show you what's in that file using Quick View.

Probable cause: You're probably trying to view a word processor file using Quick View, and that file probably ends in the hidden letters DOC. Window 95, therefore, thinks that it's about to see a WordPad file and gets confused by another word processor's format.

Solution: Quick View simply can't view this file, unfortunately. To see inside the file, you must load it into its own word processor.

Deleting this file will make it impossible to run this program and may make it impossible for you to edit some documents

Meaning: You're trying to delete a file containing a program.

Probable cause: You're clearing off some hard disk space to make room for incoming programs.

Solution: Just make sure that you know what program you're deleting before you delete it. And make sure you have the program sitting on the shelf so that you can reinstall it if you decide you need it after all.

Open with

Meaning: Windows 95 doesn't know what program created the file you've double-clicked on, so it's asking *you* to figure it out. Windows 95 then sticks a list of programs on the screen and asks you to choose the right one to open the file with. (The Microsoft programmers can get away with ending sentences with prepositions.)

Probable cause: Windows 95 usually sticks secret hidden codes known as file extensions onto the ends of filenames. Notepad, for example, uses the letters TXT. When you double-click on the Notepad icon, Windows 95 spots the secret, hidden TXT letters and uses the Notepad program to open the file.

Solution: This problem's a little rough, so you may have to experiment. First, find the Open With window's box marked Always use this program to open this file and click in the box to turn off that option. Next, try double-clicking on Notepad from the Open With window's vast list of programs. If your screen fills with legible text, you're saved! Close Notepad and double-click on the mischievous file again. This time, however, leave the Always use this program to open this file box checked so that Windows 95 learns that Notepad should automatically open that file.

You must type a filename

Meaning: Windows 95 insists that you type a filename into the box.

Probable cause: You've chosen (accidentally or otherwise) the Rename command from a menu or clicked on an icon's title in *just the right* way.

Solution: Type in a new filename — consisting of mostly numbers and letters — to describe the file, and you'll be fine. Or if you're just trying to get out of the filename box, press Esc, and the Rename box dissipates.

My computer keeps saying "Windows 95 wasn't properly shut down"!

If your computer complains that it wasn't properly shut down when you first turn it on to begin work, that usually means you succumbed to temptation: You just flipped the computer's Off switch when you were done working.

That's a Compu-No-No. Instead, click on the Start button and choose Shut Down from the menu that shoots up. Finally, click the Yes button to shut down the computer. Then, when Windows 95 says it's okay to turn off your computer, it's okay to reach for the Off switch.

Windows 95 needs that extra time to get ready for the nap.

Chapter 20

Help on the Windows 95 Help System

In This Chapter

▶ Finding helpful hints quickly

▶ Using the Windows 95 Help program

▶ Finding help for a particular problem

▶ Moving around in the Help system

▶ Making a master help index

▶ Marking help sections for later reference

*J*ust about everybody's written a bizarre computer command (like Alt+F4) on a stick-on note and slapped it on the side of the monitor.

Windows 95 comes with its *own* set of stick-on notes built right in. You can pop them up on-screen and leave them there for easy access. In a way, they're virtually real stick-on notes because they can never escape from inside the computer. Actually, it's probably better that way: You'll never find a "How to Change Wallpaper" stick-on note on the bottom of your shoe.

This chapter covers the Windows 95 built-in Help system. When you raise your hand in just the right way, Windows 95 walks over and offers you some help.

Get Me Some Help, and Fast!

Don't bother plowing through this whole chapter if you don't need to: Here are the quickest ways to make Windows 95 dish out helpful information when you're stumped. Each tip is explained more fully later in this chapter.

Press F1

When you're confused in Windows 95, press the F1 key. That key *always* stands for "Help!" Most of the time, Windows 95 checks to see what program you're using and fetches some helpful information about that particular program or your current situation. In fact, pressing F1 usually brings up a huge Help program, which gets its own section later in this chapter.

Click the *right* mouse button on the confusing part

Windows 95 tosses many forms in your face. When a particular form, setting, box, or menu item has your creativity stifled, click on it with your right (the opposite of left) mouse button. A <u>W</u>hat's This? box appears, as shown in Figure 20-1, letting you know that Windows 95 can offer help about that particular area. Click on the <u>W</u>hat's This? box, and Windows 95 tosses extra information onto the screen, explaining the confusing area you clicked on.

Figure 20-1:
Click on confusing areas with your right mouse button; if a <u>W</u>hat's This? box appears, click on the box to see more information about the confusing area.

Choose <u>H</u>elp from the main menu

If pressing F1 doesn't get you anywhere, look for the word <u>H</u>elp in the menu along the top of the confusing program. Click on <u>H</u>elp, and a menu drops down, usually listing two words: <u>H</u>elp Topics and <u>A</u>bout. Click on Help

Topics to make the Windows 95 Help program leap to the screen. (Clicking on <u>A</u>bout just brings a version number to the screen, which can be dangerously irritating when you're looking for something a little more helpful.)

Click on the leaping arrows

Sometimes the Windows 95 Help program scores big: It tells you *exactly* how to solve your particular problem. Unfortunately, however, the Help program occasionally says you need to load a *different* program to solve your problem. Don't get grumpy, though: Look for a little leaping arrow, like the one shown in Figure 20-2.

Figure 20-2:
Click on the little leaping arrow, and the Windows 95 Help program automatically takes you to the right place.

Click on the little leaping arrow, and Windows 95 automatically takes you to that other program you need to use. Yep, it's refreshingly helpful.

Consulting the Windows 95 Built-In Computer Guru

Almost every Windows program has the word <u>H</u>elp in its top menu. Click on <u>H</u>elp, and the Windows 95 built-in computer guru rushes to your aid. For example, click on <u>H</u>elp in Paint, and you see the menu shown in Figure 20-3.

To pick the computer guru's brain, click on <u>H</u>elp Topics, and Windows 95 pops up the box shown in Figure 20-4. This box is the table of contents for all the help information Windows 95 can offer on the Paint program.

Figure 20-3:
Click on the
word <u>H</u>elp
when you
mean
"Help!"

Figure 20-4:
<u>H</u>elp Topics
lists a quick
table of
contents of
helpful
subjects.

See any subject covering what you're confused about? Then double-click on
it. For example, if Erasing has you stumped, double-click on the word
Erasing; the Help program then shows what additional help it can offer, as
shown in Figure 20-5.

Want to see more information on erasing small areas? Double-click on that
listed subject, and a new window pops up, as shown in Figure 20-6, bringing
even more detailed information to the screen.

Windows 95 can offer help with any underlined topic. As the mouse pointer
nears an underlined topic, the pointer turns into a little hand. When the
hand points at the phrase that has you stumped, click the mouse button. For
example, click on <u>background color</u> in the Paint Help box, and Windows
95 displays more help on what background colors are supposed to mean, as
shown in Figure 20-7.

Figure 20-5:
Double-click on a topic to see more specific help areas.

Figure 20-6:
By clicking your way from general subjects to specific areas, you can find the help you need.

Figure 20-7:
Click on
underlined
words and
phrases to
see quick
definitions.

The Windows 95 Help system is sometimes a lot of work, forcing you to wade through increasingly detailed menus to find specific information. Still, it can be much faster than paging through the chunky Windows 95 manual. And it's often much faster than tracking down the newly pocket-protected neighbor who's just announced himself to be a "computer expert."

- ✔ The quickest way to find help in any Windows 95 program is to press F1. Windows automatically jumps to the table of contents page for the help information it has for the current program.

- ✔ Windows 95 packs a lot of information into its Help boxes; some of the words usually scroll off the bottom of the window. To see them, click on the scroll bar (described in Chapter 6) or press PgDn.

- ✔ Sometimes you click on the wrong topic and Windows 95 brings up something really dumb. Click on the Contents button at the top of the window, and Windows 95 scoots back to the contents page. From there, click on a different topic to move in a different direction.

- ✔ Underlined phrases and words appear throughout the Windows 95 Help system. Whenever you click on something that's underlined, Windows 95 brings up a definition or jumps to a spot that has information about that subject. Click on the Help Topics button to return to where you jumped from.

- ✔ If you're impressed with a particularly helpful page, send it to the printer: Click on Menu and choose Print Topic from the menu that appears. Windows 95 shoots that page to the printer so you can keep it handy until you lose it.

✔ Actually, to keep from losing that helpful page, read about sticking an electronic bookmark on that page, as described later in this chapter.

✔ If you find a particularly helpful reference in the Help system, shrink the window to an icon on the taskbar. Click on the button with the tiny bar near the window's upper-right corner. Then you can just double-click on the taskbar's Help icon to see that page again.

✔ To grab a help message and stick it in your own work, highlight the text with your mouse and choose Copy from the menu. Windows then lets you highlight the helpful words you want to copy to the Clipboard. I dunno why anybody would *want* to do this, but you *can* do it, just the same.

Sticking Electronic Stick-on Notes on Help Pages

Windows 95 lets you add your *own* notes to its helpful system of stick-on notes. If you make a stunning revelation and want to remember it later, follow these steps to add a paper clip to the current help topic and add your own notes to that help topic:

1. **Click on the word Options at the top of the page.**

   The Options menu appears.

2. **Click on the Annotate option.**

   The Annotate box appears.

3. **Start typing your own notes into the big box.**

   You can type as much as you want. Use the cursor-control keys to move around and the Delete or Backspace key to edit mistakes.

4. **Click on the Save button after you enter your note.**

   Windows paper-clips your words to the current help page; a tiny picture of a paper clip appears to remind you of your additions.

Whenever you see that help page again, click on the paper clip next to the name of the topic, and your words reappear, as shown in Figure 20-8.

If you ever want to delete your paper-clipped note, click on the paper clip and click on the Delete button. Your note disappears.

Figure 20-8:
Click on the little paper clip to see the reminders you added earlier.

Finding Help for Your Problem

If you don't see your problem listed in the particular table of contents page you've accessed, there's another way to find help (although it takes a little more time and effort). Click on the Index tab at the top of any help window; the box shown in Figure 20-9 leaps to the screen. Type a few words describing your problem. When you type them, Windows 95 shows any matches in the box below it.

If Windows matches what you type with an appropriate topic, click on the topic that looks the most pertinent and then click on the button. Windows jumps to the page of information that describes that particular subject the best.

A quicker way to find help is to click on the scroll bar or press PgUp and PgDn to see what subjects Windows is willing to explain. If you see a subject that even remotely resembles what you're confused about, double-click on it. Windows 95 brings up that page of help information.

From there, you can jump around by clicking on underlined words and phrases. Sooner or later, you stumble onto the right page of information. When you do, try to give it a *bookmark,* as described in "Trying to Find the Same Page Again," later in this chapter.

> ✔ Windows searches alphabetically and, unfortunately, isn't very smart. So, if you're looking for help on margins, for example, don't type **adding margins** or **changing margins**. Instead, type **margins** so that Windows jumps to the words beginning with M.

Figure 20-9:
Windows
95 lets you
perform
more
detailed
searches in
the index.

> 🖊 In fact, if you have trouble finding help for your specific problem, use
> the Find command, described in the next section. Instead of forcing you
> to type the right words in the right order, the Find command roots
> through every word in the Help file and brings back every match.

Finding Help on Specific Problems

When you're looking for help on a specific problem, it's sometimes hard to
be a casual pointer and clicker. You want help *now!*

For people who want to make sure that they wring every ounce of help from
the Windows 95 Help system, Microsoft included a special Find index: You
can tell the Help program to make an index of every word it mentions in its
help libraries. That way, you can type the word **PCMCIA,** for example, and
know you'll see every paragraph in the Help system that contains the word
PCMCIA. You won't have that nagging suspicion that Windows 95 didn't give
you help because you didn't type **32-bit PCMCIA** or some other sneaky
computer gibberish.

Why doesn't Windows 95 come with the Find index already set up and ready
to go? Because the Find index can eat up a lot of hard drive space. If you can
afford the space, however, create the Find index by following these steps:

1. **From within any program, press F1 to bring up its Help program and then click on the Find tab.**

   The Find tab is along the top of the window, toward the right side.

2. **Choose between Express or Custom and then click on the Next button.**

   The Express option adds more help files to the index but uses up more space. The Custom option lets you choose which help files to add to the index. The Express option is more foolproof, so go for that one if your computer isn't strapped for hard disk space.

3. **Click on Finish.**

   Twiddle your thumbs for a minute or so while Windows 95 indexes every word, from *a* to *zooming*. You only have to create the index once, thankfully, and then it is yours for the wringing.

   - After you create an index, clicking on the Find tab brings you straight to the search area. Type the word you're looking for, and, if it's mentioned in the Help system, Windows 95 brings up that nugget of helpful information.

   - You must create an index for each Windows 95 program you use. Although this can be inconvenient, it keeps Windows 95 from grabbing huge chunks of hard drive real estate merely to create indexes of programs you never use.

Trying to Find the Same Page Again

The Windows 95 Help system is better than ever, and finding help for a particular trouble is relatively painless. But how do you return to that page a few minutes — or even a few days — later?

After you find that perfect page, look for the word Bookmark listed along the top. If you spot a button marked Bookmark, you're in luck: Click on Bookmark in the menu bar, select Define from the menu, and click on the OK button.

Now, when you access the Help system days or even years later, you can click on the Bookmark menu item. A menu tumbles down, listing the pages you bookmarked. Click on the name of the page you're after, and Windows hops to that screen. Quick and easy.

The problem? Very few of the Help programs included with Windows 95 come with the Bookmark system. Unfortunately, it seems to be a Windows 3.1 remnant. Luckily, you can usually make the Annotation system work in its place.

Part VI
The Part of Tens

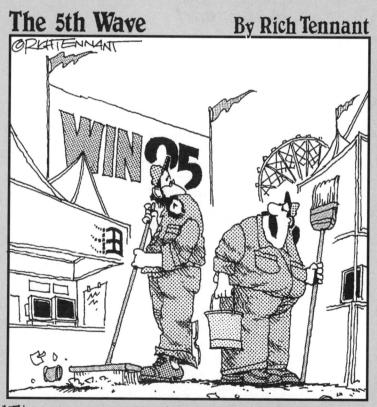

The 5th Wave — By Rich Tennant

"THIS WAS WORSE THAN WOODSTOCK—PEOPLE PASSED OUT ON BAD APPS, AND A BUNCH OF ANALYSTS PUSHED OVER AN ESPRESSO MACHINE SCREAMING 'LATTE TO THE PEOPLE!'"

In this part . . .

*E*verybody likes to read Top Tens in magazines —
especially in the grocery store checkout aisle when
you're stuck behind someone who's just pulled a rubber
band off a thick stack of double coupons and the checker
can't find the right validation stamp.

Unlike the reading material at the grocery store, the
chapters in this part of the book don't list ten new
aerobic bounces or ten ways to stop your kids from
making explosives with kitchen cleansers. Instead, you
find lists of ways to make Windows 95 more efficient — or
at least not as hostile. You find a few tips, tricks, and
explanations of eccentric acronyms like *DLL*.

Some lists have more than ten items; others have fewer.
But who's counting, besides the guy wading through all
those double coupons.

Chapter 21

Ten New Windows 95 Features Worth Checking Out

· ·

In This Chapter

▶ Using the right (not just the left) mouse button

▶ Peeking inside files with Quick View

▶ Using long filenames

▶ Using the Recycle Bin

▶ Highlighting icons with a "lasso"

▶ Using the Windows 95 Wizards

▶ Jumping to the right place in Help

· ·

*L*ike a new car model, Windows 95 adds several improvements over the old Windows 3.1 version. Some of the changes are cosmetic, like the fancy new lime-green, 3-D mouse pointers. Other changes are more useful, like the way you can peek inside files without having to load a program.

Consider this chapter a pamphlet that explains some of the best new features Windows 95 has to offer.

The Right Mouse Button Now Does Something, Too

Although mice have had at least two buttons for the past decade, Windows has never taken advantage of the right mouse button. The index finger has done all the work, clicking and double-clicking on the left button, while the middle finger rested, unused, on the right mouse button.

Windows 95 puts your middle finger to work by making the right button just as powerful as the left. The buttons don't do the same thing, though, so here's the rundown:

✔ Click *once* on something with your *left* mouse button to select it — to highlight an icon, for example.

✔ *Double-click* on something with your *left* mouse button to not only select it but to also kick-start it into action — to load a program, for example, or to open a folder.

✔ Click *once* on something with your *right* mouse button to bring up a menu that lists the things you can do with that item — adjust its settings, for example, or copy it to another location.

Figure 21-1 shows the menu that pops up when you use your right mouse button to click on a file in the My Computer window.

Figure 21-1:
Click on a
file's icon
with your
right mouse
button and
a menu
appears,
listing
things you
can do with
the file.

Open
Print
Quick View
Send To ▶
Cut
Copy
Create Shortcut
Delete
Rename
Properties...

When you're unsure of how to work with something on your desktop — a button, icon, or anything weird-looking — click on the confusing entity with your right mouse button. Often, a menu pops up that displays a list of stuff you can do to that confusing thing. By choosing from the options, you can often bluff your way to success.

The new Microsoft IntelliMouse has two buttons *and* a little wheel thingie poking out from between them. Spinning the wheel lets you do different things in different programs. The latest version of Microsoft Word lets you move your page up or down by spinning the wheel, for example. (Don't expect programmers to race out and add IntelliMouse support to their programs, though; they're waiting to see how many other programmers do it first.)

Peeking into Files Without Opening Them

When faced with a plethora of files, how can you tell which one you need? For example, all the icons for files created by the Paint drawing program look the same. How can you check to see if the file named Sea Food is that lobster picture you are searching for?

You can load the Sea Food file into Paint, but Quick View provides a faster way. Click on the file with your right mouse button and then click on Quick View from the menu that pops up.

A new window immediately appears, like the one in Figure 21-2, showing you the file's contents.

Figure 21-2:
Right-clicking on a file's icon and choosing Quick View causes a window to appear, showing the file's contents.

✔ Want to open the file for editing? Click on the little Paint icon in the upper-left corner. Windows 95 loads Paint, along with your file. The icon for the program responsible for creating the file is always in the upper-left corner.

✔ If the file on the screen isn't the one you're searching for, feel free to drag another file's icon into Quick View's open window. Windows 95 rapidly displays the contents of that file, too.

✔ Here's the bad news: The Quick View command only works on certain varieties of files. Only the most popular formats are displayed. You can "quick view" your WordPerfect and Microsoft Word files, for example, but you can't peek inside any files created in less-popular programs such as WordStar or XyWrite.

✔ You can find more information about Quick View in Chapter 8.

Much *L-o-n-g-e-r* Filenames

Somber industry analysts said it wouldn't happen in our lifetimes, but now people can name their files with descriptions longer than eight characters. Windows 95 even lets you use more than one word to name your files, and you can separate the words by a space!

Figure 21-3 shows a few filenames approved by Windows 95; as long as you keep the names under 255 characters, you're pretty much okay. (More detailed details on filenames are discussed in Chapter 12.)

Figure 21-3:
Windows 95
allows for
long
filenames.

Retrieving Deleted Files from the Recycle Bin

Earlier versions of Windows let you safely retrieve accidentally deleted files, so the concept of the Windows 95 Recycle Bin isn't new. The new part is how much easier the Recycle Bin makes it to salvage deleted files.

Whenever you delete a file, the sneaky Windows 95 doesn't *really* delete it. It just hides the file in the Recycle Bin — that green trash can sitting on the desktop. When you get that sinking feeling that you shouldn't have deleted that report on Coelacanth Tailfins, double-click on the Recycle Bin, and you can find your report inside, undamaged.

The Recycle Bin doesn't hold onto deleted files forever, though. It waits until you've filled up 10 percent of your hard drive's storage capacity. For example, if you have a 200MB hard disk, the Recycle Bin always holds onto 20MB of your most recently deleted files. When you fill up that 10 percent, Recycle Bin starts shredding the oldest files, and you can't retrieve them.

That 10 percent figure is adjustable; see Chapter 11 for details.

Selecting Bunches of Icons with a Lasso

This feature doesn't really seem like much, but you'll probably find yourself using it more than you think.

Windows has always allowed several ways to select files and icons. For example, hold down the Ctrl key and click on all the icons you want: Windows highlights all the icons you click on.

Or, when selecting items in a list, you can click on the first item, hold down the Shift key, and click on the last item in a list. Whoosh! Windows instantly highlights the first item, the last item, and every item in between.

Windows 95 can still highlight icons those ways, but it's added something easier. To select files or folders that are next to each other, you can drag a "lasso" around them. Point just above the first icon you want to grab and, while holding down the mouse button, point just below the last icon you want to grab. Windows 95 draws a rectangle around the icons, shown in Figure 21-4.

The lasso can only be rectangular, so all the files and folders have to be next to each other. But you can always lasso the big chunk and then hold down the Ctrl key to select the stragglers who are away from the main pack.

Figure 21-4:
Windows 95 can drag a rectangle around files and folders to select them easily.

Working with Windows 95 Wizards

Windows 95 tries hard to be personal, adding human touches whenever it can. Honestly, how many times have you wished for a computer wizard to materialize and automatically make your new modem or sound card work?

Well, Windows 95 comes with several Wizards, each customized for various bits of magic. For example, the Add New Hardware Wizard, shown in Figure 21-5, searches your computer for any new gadgets you've added. When the Wizard finds these accessories, it introduces them to Windows 95 so they can all start working together.

Figure 21-5:
The Windows 95 Wizards can help you install new parts to your computer.

The Wizards aren't magic by any means, but they can often work wonders when you need to set up Windows 95 to work with something new.

Jumping to the Right Place in Help

Windows has always come with a helpful Help program. However, the best Windows could do was tell you what part of Windows you needed to use to solve your problem.

Windows 95 goes one more step: It not only tells you where to go, it takes you there. Need to calibrate your joystick, for example? Type **joystick** into the Help program, and Windows 95 explains that you need to use the joystick calibration program. But the Help program also includes a little button; click on the button, shown in Figure 21-6, and the increasingly polite Windows 95 automatically takes you to the Joystick Calibration program you need.

Figure 21-6:
Click on the little buttons in the Help program, and Windows 95 takes you directly to the program that solves your problem.

Windows Help

Help Topics   Back   Options

To calibrate your joystick

1 Click here 🔲 to display Joystick properties.

2 In the Joystick Selection list, click the joystick you are using. If your joystick is not listed, click Custom.

3 Click Calibrate, and then follow the instructions on your screen.

Tips

- If your joystick has external rudder controls, make sure the Rudder box is checked.

- If you have not yet installed your joystick, click here 🔲 to start the Hardware Installation wizard.

Chapter 22

Ten Aggravating Things about Windows 95 (And How to Fix Them)

· ·

In This Chapter

▶ Bypassing the menus

▶ Keeping track of multiple windows

▶ Finding a missing taskbar

▶ Fixing the Print Screen key

▶ Installing a missing program

▶ Understanding why DOS programs run too slowly

▶ Lining up two windows on the screen

▶ Updating a floppy disk's contents in the Windows Explorer or My Computer program

· ·

*W*indows 95 would be great if only . . . (insert your pet peeve here). If you find yourself thinking (or saying) this frequently, this chapter is for you. This chapter not only lists the most aggravating things about Windows 95, but it also explains how to fix them.

Those Zillions of Mouse Menus Take Forever

Windows 95 has a zillion menus you can work through with the mouse, but you don't have to use them. If you want, you can use the keyboard to quickly select everything that you can click on in a menu.

Look closely at the words on the menu bar, along the top of each window. Somewhere in almost every word, you can spot a single underlined letter. Press and release the Alt key and then press one of the underlined letters you see in a word. Try pressing the F in File, for example. Presto! The File menu leaps into place. Look for underlined letters on the newly displayed File menu. For example, now press S for Save. Presto again! Windows 95 saves the current file, without a single mouse click.

To save a file in nearly any Windows 95 program, press and release Alt, press F, and then press S. It's that simple (after you memorize the combination, that is).

You find these underlined letters everywhere in Windows 95. In fact, you can see underlined letters in this book as well. They're the keys you can use to avoid rooting through all the menus with a mouse.

Note: A list of the most commonly used key combinations is included in the Cheat Sheet at the front of this book.

When maneuvering through the options listed in the Start menu, you only need to click once: Just click on the Start button to bring the Start menu to life. All the other menus contained in the Start menu pop up automatically as the mouse pointer hovers over them. When you spot the program or choice you're after, click on it, and the Start menu loads that program or choice.

✔ To move from box to box while filling out a form, press the Tab key. Each press of the key takes you to a new part of the form to fill out. Ecstasy!

✔ For some keys, you hold Alt while pressing a function key. For example, to close any Windows 95 program, hold down Alt and press F4 (Alt+F4).

✔ If you accidentally press Alt and are stuck in Menu Land, press Alt again. Alternatively, press Esc and bark loudly until it lets you out.

It's Too Hard to Keep Track of All Those Windows

You don't *have* to keep track of all those windows. Windows 95 does it for you with the taskbar. Hold Ctrl and press Esc, and the taskbar rises to the forefront. (If it doesn't, see the very next section.)

The taskbar, covered in Chapter 11, has a separate box listing the name of every window currently open. Click on the name of the window you want, and that window hops to the top of the pile.

Even better, shrink all the open windows into icons except for the window you're currently working on. Then click on the taskbar with your right mouse button and click on one of the two tile commands to line everything up neatly on the screen.

In Chapter 8, you find more soldiers to enlist in the battle against misplaced windows, files, and programs.

The Taskbar Keeps Disappearing!

The taskbar's a handy Windows 95 program that's always running — if you can just find it. Unfortunately, it sometimes vanishes from the screen. Here are a few ways to bring it back.

First, try holding down the Ctrl key and pressing Esc. Sometimes this effort makes the taskbar appear, but sometimes it only brings up the Start menu.

Still no taskbar? Try pointing at the very edge of your screen, stopping for a second or two at each of the four sides. If you point at the correct side, some specially configured taskbars stop goofing around and come back to the screen.

If you can only see a slim edge of the taskbar — the rest of it hangs off the edge of the screen, for example — point at the edge you *can* see. After the mouse pointer turns into a two-headed arrow, hold down your mouse button and move the mouse toward the screen's center to drag the taskbar back into view.

In Windows 3.1, double-clicking on the desktop brings up the Task List, which lists all the currently running programs. Double-clicking on the desktop in Windows 95 just makes two clicking noises in rapid succession. (The taskbar doesn't appear.)

- If your taskbar disappears whenever you're not specifically pointing at it, turn off its Auto hide feature: Click on a blank part of the taskbar with your right mouse button and choose Properties from the pop-up menu. When the taskbar Options menu appears, click in the Auto hide box until a little check mark disappears. (Or, to turn on the Auto hide feature, add the check mark.)

- While you're in the taskbar Options menu, make sure that a check mark appears in the Always on top box. That way the taskbar always rides visibly on the desktop, making it much easier to spot.

My Print Screen Key Doesn't Work

Windows 95 takes over the Print Screen key (labeled PrtSc, PrtScr, or something even more supernatural on some keyboards). Instead of sending the stuff on the screen to the printer, the Print Screen key sends it to the Windows 95 Clipboard, where it can be pasted into other windows.

> ✔ Some keyboards make you hold Shift while pressing Print Screen.
>
> ✔ If you hold Alt while pressing Print Screen, Windows 95 sends the current *window* — not the entire screen — to the Clipboard.
>
> ✔ If you *really* want a printout of the screen, hold Shift and press Print Screen to send a picture of the screen to the Clipboard. Paste the contents of the Clipboard into Paint and print from there. (Chapter 13 explains that process.)

Windows 95 Didn't Install All the Programs Listed on the Box

In an attempt to make friends with everybody, Windows 95 comes with gobs of programs — more than anybody would ever want. So, to keep from making enemies of everybody, Windows 95 doesn't fill up everybody's hard drive with every possible program.

For example, Windows 95 comes with sounds that make your computer sound like a robot or squawking bird. But it doesn't automatically install those sounds, nor does it tell you about them. If you want to add those sounds, you must go back and do it by hand.

Start by double-clicking on the Add/Remove Programs icon in the Control Panel and then click on the Windows Setup tab along the top. Windows 95 lists the programs it can install and offers to install them for you — a process described in Chapter 13.

(And if you want the robot sounds, double-click on the Control Panel's Sounds icon and choose Robotz Sound Scheme. The birds and frogs hang out in the Jungle Sound Scheme. Beware, however: Some employers may have already deleted these fun files from your computer.)

My DOS Programs Run Too Slowly (Or Not at All) Under Windows 95

DOS programs almost always run more slowly under Windows 95 than if they had the whole computer to themselves. And they run the slowest when they're in a window. And some DOS programs won't run at all.

Running DOS programs in a full screen speeds them up a little, as does beefing up the computer: adding more memory, upgrading to a faster 486 or Pentium computer, and buying a bigger hard drive.

What's the best solution? Well, Windows 95 is like a camper shell that is put on a pickup truck. Although the truck is more comfortable, it is slower and can't go underneath low bridges. To get back the speed and maneuverability, you simply have to remove the shell (or buy a more powerful engine).

That means don't run DOS programs under Windows 95. Click on the Shut down command from the Start menu and choose the Restart in MS-DOS Mode option.

Hint: When you're in DOS, type the word **exit** and press Enter to return to Windows 95.

It's Too Hard to Line Up Two Windows on the Screen

With all its cut-and-paste stuff, Windows 95 makes it easy for you to grab information from one program and slap it into another. With its drag-and-drop stuff, you can grab names of files in File Manager and drag them into Program Manager to install them as icons.

The hard part of Windows 95 is lining up two windows on the screen, side by side. That's where you need to call in the taskbar. First, put the two windows anywhere on the screen. Then turn all the other windows into icons by clicking on the button with the little line that lives in the top-right corners of those windows.

Now click on a blank area of the taskbar with your right mouse button and click on one of the two Tile commands listed on the menu. The two windows line up on the screen perfectly.

The My Computer and Windows Explorer Programs Show the Wrong Stuff on My Floppy Disk

The My Computer and Windows Explorer programs sometimes get confused and don't always list the files currently sitting on a disk drive. To prod the programs into taking a second look, choose the Window⇨Refresh command.

Chapter 23

Ten Expensive Things You Can Do to Make Windows 95 Better

• •

In This Chapter

▶ Buy more memory

▶ Shell out the bucks for a bigger hard drive

▶ Order a fast Pentium computer

▶ Put a graphics accelerator card on the credit card

▶ Beg for or borrow a bigger monitor

▶ Buy a faster CD-ROM drive

▶ Snap up a faster modem

• •

*G*ive a Ford Fairlane to the right teenage boy, and he'll get right to work: boring out the cylinders, putting in a high-lift cam, and adding a double-roller timing chain. And replacing the exhaust system with headers, if his cash holds out.

Computer nerds feel the same way about getting under the hood of their computers. They add a few new parts, flip a few switches, and tweak a few things here and there to make Windows 95 scream.

Even if you're not a computer nerd, you can still soup up Windows 95 a bit. Take the computer back to the store and have the *store's* computer nerd get under the hood.

This chapter talks about what parts to ask for so that you don't end up with high-lift cams rather than more memory.

Buy More Memory

If you bought a 386, 486, or Pentium computer, the salesperson probably tried to talk you into buying more memory, or RAM, for the computer. Windows 95 probably talks just as loudly about this issue as the salesperson.

See, Windows 95 can read and write information to RAM very quickly. The phrase *lightning quick* comes to mind. But when Windows 95 runs out of RAM, it starts using the hard drive for storage. Compared with RAM, hard drives are slow, mechanical dinosaurs. If you're short on memory, you can hear the hard drive grinding away as you switch between programs and Windows 95 frantically tries to make room for everything.

Windows 95 runs slowly on a computer with only 4MB of RAM. Twice that amount of RAM speeds things up more than twice as much. With 12MB or 16MB of RAM, Windows 95 can juggle programs even more quickly (and without dropping them as often).

If you're tired of waiting for Windows 95, toss the computer in the back seat, take it back to the computer store, and have the store people put some more RAM inside. (The price has dropped since the last time you looked.)

✔ After Jeff in the back room puts the memory chips inside the computer, he'll flip some switches on the computer's *motherboard* so that it knows that the new chips are there. People who plug in the chips themselves often don't flip the right switch and then wonder why their new chips don't work. (Some newer computers don't have a switch; they know automatically when they have more memory to play with.)

✔ Different computers can hold different amounts of RAM. Some older ones can't handle more than 8MB of RAM; others can be stuffed with 64MB or more. Before buying more memory, check with your dealer to make sure that your computer has room for it.

Shell Out the Bucks for a Bigger Hard Drive

Right on the box, Microsoft recommends that a computer have at least 45MB of free hard drive space in order to run Windows 95. That's *if* you want to run *Windows 95* and *no* other programs.

If you buy Microsoft Word for Windows, however, that program wants more than 20MB of hard drive space, too. Add a few other hoggy Windows programs, and you quickly run out of room.

Plus, you should leave part of the hard drive empty so that Windows 95 has room to shuffle information around.

The moral is to shop for the biggest hard drive you can afford. Then borrow some money and buy one that's slightly bigger.

Order a Fast Pentium Computer

Windows 95 works on a 486 computer, but just barely. The program is really designed for a fast Pentium computer.

As programs incorporate more and more sound and graphics, computers are becoming more and more burdened with computing chores. That's why you want a fast Pentium to keep the information flowing smoothly across the screen. Balance your need for speed with your checking account balance.

You can find this computer model/Pentium stuff thrashed out in Chapter 2.

Put a Graphics Accelerator Card on the Credit Card

When tossing boxes and bars around, Windows 95 puts a big strain on the computer's *graphics card,* the gizmo that tells the monitor what information to put on-screen.

Windows 95 also puts a strain on the computer's *microprocessor,* the gizmo that tells the graphics card what to tell the monitor.

A *graphics accelerator card* eases the burden on both parties. Simply put, a graphics accelerator is a hot-rodded graphics card. It replaces the VGA or Super VGA card and contains a special chip that handles the dirty work of filling the monitor with pretty pictures.

The result? Dialog boxes that zip on-screen almost instantly. You no longer have to wait for Windows 95 to repaint the screen when you move windows around. Everything just looks snappier.

> ✔ You probably don't need to upgrade the monitor when buying an accelerator card. A Super VGA accelerator card works just as well with a Super VGA monitor as the regular Super VGA card does.

✔ Upgrading the computer from a 386 to a 486 or Pentium also speeds up the graphics, even if you don't buy an accelerator card.

✔ Computers with special *PCI* slots can speed up graphics the fastest. These slots can accept the speedy PCI video cards. Anything else was obsolete a few months ago.

✔ If you'll be playing some fast-paced computer games or doing lots of computer graphics work — creating detailed computer representations of how the rose garden will look in Spring, for example — look into a "3D" PCI video card. The trendiest of new cards, the "3D video" ensures that your system will wait a few extra months before being obsolete.

Beg for or Borrow a Bigger Monitor

Part of the problem with the Windows 95 stack-of-windows approach to computing is the size of the screen. The Windows 95 desktop is the size of the monitor: a little larger than one square foot. That's why everything constantly covers up everything else.

To get a bigger desktop, buy a bigger monitor. The 17-inch monitors offer almost twice the elbowroom as the standard 14-inchers. You have more room to put windows side by side on the screen, as well as more room to spread icons along the bottom. The new 20-inchers give you an executive-sized desktop but at a mahogany price.

✔ Before buying, ask to make sure that the new monitor and video card can work together as a team. Not all cards work well with all monitors, although they're both catching up.

✔ If you have a stack of phone books holding up one side of your desk, buy a new desk when you buy the new monitor. Those big monitors can weigh 50 pounds or more.

Buy a Faster CD-ROM Drive

Software companies have just about given up on floppy disks. Their programs are simply too big to fit on one disk, and nobody wants to feed their computer handfuls of disks in order to install the program.

The solution? Package the program on a compact disc, which can hold the equivalent of hundreds of floppies.

But if your CD-ROM drive is a few years old, it's probably agonizingly slow. A 2X or double-speed CD-ROM drive used to be fast. Now it needs to be 8X to keep up with the crowd.

> ✔ The speed difference becomes most noticeable when the computer reads directly off the disc. If the disc doesn't spin fast enough, action sequences during games become jerky, as do videos.
>
> ✔ While you're shopping for a new CD-ROM drive, check into the ones that let you write to the disc as well as read from. By the time you read this, those writeable CD-ROM drives may be both speedy and inexpensive (making them a great way to back up your hard drive).

Snap Up a Faster Modem

Face it: The Internet isn't going to disappear, even after all the hullabaloo has died down. With the Internet's World Wide Web software, you won't have to leave the house to go to the library, read newspapers and magazines, meet people, research trips, and join Xena: Warrior Princess User Groups. You can even have food delivered to you while you tap the keyboard.

> ✔ If you find yourself using the Internet a lot, make sure that you're using a 28,000 bps or faster modem.
>
> ✔ If you find yourself using the Internet a *super* lot, call up your phone company and Internet Service Provider to see if they offer something called "ISDN service." ISDN can spew out the information a super lot faster — but at a higher price. (Especially because ISDN service requires special, ISDN modems — your old modem won't work.)

Chapter 24
Ten Atrocious Acronyms

In This Chapter

▶ Ten (and a bunch more) acronyms in alphabetical order

▶ Helpful pronunciation tips so that you won't just mumble them quietly

▶ What the acronyms mean to computer nerds

Computer geeks have a certain fascination for long, complicated strings of words. They've reduced these syllables into short grunts called *acronyms*.

This chapter lists, in alphabetical order, what the nerds are saying, what their grunts stand for, and what those grunts are supposed to mean.

ASCII

What it stands for: American Standard Code for Information Interchange

Pronunciation: ASK-ee

What they're talking about: A standard for saving information — usually words and numbers — so that most other programs can read it. Windows 95 Notepad, for example, saves text files in ASCII format.

BIOS

What it stands for: Basic Input/Output System

Pronunciation: BUY-ohss

What they're talking about: Information stored inside a computer that tells programs how the computer is designed. For example, if a program wants data to go to the printer, the program politely tells the BIOS, which subsequently sends the data to the printer. Windows 95 sometimes bypasses the BIOS and sends information directly to the computer's parts. This procedure is often faster but can sometimes confuse the rest of the computer. How do you fiddle with the BIOS? You have to pull out the computer's manual, unfortunately. Each computer comes with its own style of tweaks.

DDE

What it stands for: Dynamic Data Exchange

Pronunciation: Dee-dee-ee

What they're talking about: A way Windows programs can share information automatically in the background. Today, OLE is much more fashionable and powerful.

DLL

What it stands for: Dynamic Link Library

Pronunciation: Dee-ell-ell

What they're talking about: A file containing information for a program. You can find bunches of files ending with DLL on the hard drive. Don't think that they're trash and delete them, or you'll have some wide-eyed programs wandering around the system, searching for their DLLs.

DRV

What it stands for: Driver

Pronunciation: DRY-ver

What they're talking about: Drivers contain brand-specific information about a computer's parts: printers, mice, monitors, and other goodies. You see files ending in DRV scattered throughout the hard drive. Don't delete them, or Windows 95 won't be capable of talking to your computer's parts.

EMS

What it stands for: Expanded Memory Specification

Pronunciation: Ee-em-ess

What they're talking about: A special part of the computer's memory used by some DOS programs. When filling out a DOS program's settings in its Properties box, you may need to change this option.

FAQ

What it stands for: Frequently Asked Questions

Pronunciation: Fack

What they're talking about: A plain ol' text file containing answers to the most frequently asked questions. For example, the Peanut Butter Web Page may contain a Peanut Butter FAQ that explains why some peanut shells have three peanuts, and others have only two. *Hint:* When probing something unfamiliar, always look for the FAQ.

GPF

What it stands for: General Protection Fault

Pronunciation: Gee-pea-eff

What they're talking about: Windows 3.1 programs sometimes crash for no apparent reason. Before they zonk themselves into unconsciousness, they say that they have experienced a GPF. Windows 95 doesn't have as many GPF problems. Instead, the errors are labeled with a bunch of other terms, as described in Chapter 19.

IBM

What it stands for: International Business Machines

Pronunciation: Aye-bee-em

What they're talking about: A huge computer company that designed the first PC that's like the ones almost everybody uses today. Now, IBM's playing catch-up because all the other companies keep copying and improving upon its original design. Windows 95 requires an IBM-compatible computer. (Of course, one exception does exist. A new version of Windows 95, Windows CE, runs on little tiny handheld PCs, and they're covered in this book's Appendix.)

INI

What it stands for: Initialization

Pronunciation: IN-ee (as opposed to an OUT-ee)

What they're talking about: A file containing customized instructions for a program. Many Windows 3.1 programs look for their own INI file to make sure that they're working according to the user's whims. In Windows 3.1, a file called WIN.INI contains information about the way you like Windows: its colors, the settings you've made in the Control Panel, and other information.

Don't mess with the INI files unless you have a specific reason to do so. Changing them around can seriously affect how programs run in Windows.

Windows 95 now stores most of its customizing information in a more organized and much more complicated area called a *Registry*. Stay away from it.

IRQ

What it stands for: Interrupt Request Line

Pronunciation: Aye-are-cue

What they're talking about: The way parts of a computer can get the attention of the computer's main processor. For example, every time you move the mouse, the mouse sends a signal down its IRQ to the computer's processor, which stops what it's doing and displays the mouse's new position on-screen. Each device needs its own IRQ; if two computer toys try to share one IRQ, both work in a wacky way.

ISDN

What it stands for: Integrated Services Digital Network

Pronunciation: Aye-ess-dee-enn

What they're talking about: A speedy new way of connecting your computer to the Internet, ISDN requires a special ISDN modem, an Internet provider that supports the service, and a town that's big enough for its local phone company to offer an ISDN connection to your house. But boy, oh, boy, do those Web pages race across the screen!

ISP

What it stands for: Internet Service Provider

Pronunciation: Aye-ess-pea

What they're talking about: Just as you need to pay the gas and electric company to keep your house warm, you need to pay a company to provide you with access to the Internet. Your ISP gives you a phone number to dial, some software, and some special code numbers to make the whole thing work. (You can find more about the Internet and the World Wide Web in Chapter 15.)

JPEG

What it stands for: Joint Photographic Expert Group

Pronunciation: Jay-peg

What they're talking about: Yet another way to store pictures, the JPEG format packs files at their tightest. Because smaller files pass through the phone lines more quickly, the format is growing in favor on the World Wide Web.

MSN

What it stands for: The Microsoft Network

Pronunciation: Emm-ess-enn

What they're talking about: Microsoft's new online service — a way to grab information over the phone lines using a modem. The Microsoft Network is still in its infancy, but it's described in Chapter 13.

OLE

What it stands for: Object Linking and Embedding

Pronunciation: Oh-LAY

What they're talking about: A way to merge varieties of data into one file. For example, your boss can stick an icon into a letter file and give the file to your coworker; when your coworker double-clicks on the icon, he'll hear your boss's voice telling him that he's fired. Or you can add a chart icon to a word-processing file; when you double-click on the chart icon, a chart editor pops up, grabs the chart from your hard drive, and lets you change the figures around. When you save the chart and go back to your word-processing file, the OLE technology saves the *original* chart file, too, ready for somebody else to edit.

PCX

What it stands for: Nothing

Pronunciation: Pea-see-ex

What they're talking about: Some guy thought of a way to store graphics in computer files. He picked the letters PCX out of the blue. Today, PCX is one of the most widespread graphics standards. Windows 3.1 Paintbrush can read and write graphics as PCX files; so can most other graphics programs.

Paintbrush's Windows 95 replacement, Paint, can no longer write PCX files. Instead, Paint can only save files in Microsoft's own graphics file format, known as *bitmap* or BMP files.

PIF

What it stands for: Program Information File

Pronunciation: Piff (rhymes with sniff)

What they're talking about: A file containing the instructions Windows 95 needs to nurse along troublesome DOS programs. The PIF contains information about that program's memory needs, along with other data that helps DOS programs live pleasantly with Windows 95.

RAM

What it stands for: Random-Access Memory

Pronunciation: Ram (rhymes with cram)

What they're talking about: The memory Windows 95 reads and writes to when it makes stuff happen on-screen. When the power's turned off, RAM erases itself.

ROM

What it stands for: Read-Only Memory

Pronunciation: Rahm (rhymes with bomb)

What they're talking about: Memory that can't be written to — only read from. For example, a computer's BIOS is stored in ROM. Computerized microwave ovens and other fun consumer electronic goodies sometimes store their instructions on ROM chips as well. The latest technology, called Flash ROM, can be written to more than once, but only with special programs.

URL

What it stands for: Uniform Resource Locator

Pronunciation: You-are-ell (although some copy editors say it rhymes with *Girl*)

What they're talking about: An address that tells your Web browser which page to display. They almost always start with the wacky abbreviation `http://www`. Yes, it's `www.weird`. (See WWW, ISP, ISDN, and Chapter 15.)

WWW

What it stands for: World Wide Web

Pronunciation: Double-U, Double-U, Double-U (just like it looks)

What they're talking about: The Internet is a collection of computers linked together around the world. The World Wide Web is a collection of machines running software for sending graphics across the Internet, sort of like those informational kiosks you see in airports when you're checking to see if your hotel offers a free shuttle. To check the hotel's hospitality, you'd type in its *URL,* described earlier.

XMS

What it stands for: Extended Memory Specification

Pronunciation: Ex-em-ess

What they're talking about: The special type of memory that comes with 286, 386, 486, and Pentium computers. Windows 95 comes with a memory manager that can harness XMS memory and dole it out to DOS or Windows programs when they need it. The more memory your computer has, the happier you and your programs will be.

Chapter 25

Ten Windows 95 Icons and What They Do

● ●

*W*indows 95 uses different icons to stand for different types of files. That arrangement means that the program is packed with enough icons to befuddle the most experienced iconographer.

Table 25-1 shows pictures of the most common icons you'll come across in Windows 95 in the Windows Explorer and My Computer programs and what the icons are supposed to represent.

Table 25-1 Icons in Windows Explorer and My Computer Program

What It Looks Like	What It Stands For
📁	3½-inch floppy drive
📁	5¼-inch floppy drive
💾	Hard drive
💿	CD-ROM drive
📁	Folder or directory; a computerized storage area for files
▢	DOS program
📄	Word processor file, usually created by either WordPad or Microsoft Word
📄	Batch file; a collection of DOS commands for the computer to run automatically
🎬	Movie (usually stored in the Microsoft Audio Video Interleave — AVI — format)

(continued)

Table 25-1 *(continued)*

What It Looks Like	What It Stands For
	Sound; a recorded sound saved as a wave file
	Music; a MIDI file containing specially formatted instructions that tell synthesizers or sound cards what sounds to create
	System file; technical files for Windows 95 to use
	Old-style fonts that are stored in a certain size
	Newer, TrueType fonts that can be easily shrunk or enlarged
	Help file; contains instructions stored in a special format for the Windows 95 Help system
	Bitmap file; graphics usually created by Paint (in Windows 95) or Paintbrush (in Windows 3.1)
	A text file containing technical information, usually special settings for a program
	Text; usually created by Notepad
	A file Windows 95 doesn't think it recognizes

✔ Unfortunately, Windows 95 judges a book by its cover: It doesn't look *inside* a file to see what information it contains. Instead, Windows 95 merely looks at the file's name, particularly the last three letters of the file's name. If Windows 95 recognizes those three letters, it assumes that it recognizes the file. The result? Sometimes Windows 95 uses a familiar icon to represent a file but refuses to open the file when you double-click on the icon.

✔ For example, Windows 95 uses the word processor file icon for files containing Word for Windows 2.0 documents. But if you don't have a copy of Word for Windows 2.0 installed when you double-click on the icon, Windows 95 stops, saying that WordPad can't open Word for Windows 2.0 documents. The solution? Buy a file conversion program that lets you tweak files so other programs can read them. (Or upgrade to the latest version of Word for Windows, which can read its predecessor's files.)

Appendix

Are Those Windows Handheld Computers Any Good?

• •

In This Chapter

▶ What is a *palmtop* or *handheld* computer?

▶ What is Windows CE?

▶ What's good about Windows CE?

▶ What's bad about Windows CE?

▶ How do I buy the right handheld computer?

• •

*1*f you've seen an old science fiction movie, you know that computers are shrinking. What once consumed the entire floor of a research lab now fits into a wristwatch — even a lady's model.

Microsoft began smelling mega-cash and recently teamed up with wristwatch king Timex. The computerized result? *Data Link* wristwatches that include an alarm clock and storage for up to 50 phone numbers or appointments. The latest models can time events like a stopwatch, convert foreign currency, monitor their user's pulse rate, and track the score of a golf game.

But these high-tech devices pose a computing problem: Dumping information into them while on the road is too hard. The solution, according to the computer industry, is to replace them with a *handheld PC:* a tiny new type of PC that slips in your shirt pocket.

Smelling even more cash, Microsoft released a special new operating system to boss around these new little PCs. Dubbed Windows CE, the new operating system looks and acts like an abbreviated Windows 95.

This appendix examines the handheld PCs flooding the market, as well as the operating system Microsoft created to run on them.

What Types of Palmtops Exist?

Although Microsoft Windows CE machines currently get all the attention, palmtops and their relatives have been around for years. Here's a quick rundown on these small machines so you know what's waiting at many computer and office-supply stores.

Calculators (Free on keychains to $200)

Nothing new here in the past few years. Pocket calculators started out as simple addition, subtraction, multiplication, and division gadgets. Today, the fancier ones come with larger screens for doing simple graphs. (A few engineering models even let you play games — if you feed the programs into the calculator the right way.) They're fantastic for assaulting numbers, and some let you type in your own programs, but that's it. Forget about tracking appointments and phone numbers or doing other tasks like word processing.

The best ones: Hewlett-Packard seems to have this category sewn up.

Organizers or databanks ($50 to $800)

When people learned that they could organize their financial lives on calculators, they began clamoring for a way to organize their social lives, as well. So the gadget manufacturers began releasing *pocket organizers* or *databanks*. Today, a wide variety of these machines fill the market, and they let you store names, addresses, phone numbers, appointments, and databases of favorite wines for referencing in restaurants.

Most organizers come with a little plastic wand called a *stylus*. By tapping the stylus on various areas of the screen, you make the organizer perform various chores.

The best organizers can use modems for checking electronic mail; these organizers also allow information to be sent back and forth to a desktop computer. The simplest and cheapest ones simply track phone numbers.

The best ones: The Sharp Zaurus 5800 currently leads the pack in balancing utility, size, and price. Some people prefer the smaller, but more limited, US Robotics Pilot. Still others prefer models from Psion or Casio, which have more software available.

One final caution: Organizers don't run Microsoft Windows; they all use their own special methods for processing information. This means that you have to fiddle with them for a while before figuring out how they work.

Palmtops ($400 to $500)

Although the word *palmtop* can mean a lot of things, it's beginning to refer to last year's generation of pocket computers — the versions that ran MS-DOS. The Atari Portfolio and the Hewlett-Packard HP200XL both aimed at the DOS market are examples.

The best ones: Atari folded, leaving the Hewlett-Packard HP200XL almost alone in the market. (And the 200XL might be feeling a little gray-haired when compared to this year's new handheld PCs, described next.)

Handheld PCs ($500)

Today, the computer industry is vibrating with excitement over the new *handheld PCs*. Because Microsoft wants to place Windows on every mechanical device, the company came up with a miniature version of Windows 95 suitable for tiny computers. Called Windows CE, the operating system looks sort of like Windows 95 running on a postcard.

Casio, Compaq, Hewlett-Packard, Hitachi Ltd., LG Electronics, Inc., NEC Corp., and Philips Electronics all have their eyes on Windows CE-based handheld PCs. In addition, more than 90 companies are murmuring about creating Windows CE-based gadgets to run on the little computers.

The best ones: The screen's clarity of display is one of the most determining factors for quality among handheld PCs. While in the store, pay special attention to a program's visibility on-screen under different lighting conditions. The Casio Cassiopeia handheld PC hit the market first; if its screen had been legible, it might have wiped the competition off the market.

✔ Organizers, palmtops, and handheld PCs are often called *Personal Digital Assistants,* or *PDAs.*

✔ Some tiny computers let you write directly on the screen with a little plastic stylus; the computer then understands what you're writing and translates the letters into neatly typed words. Other palmtops come with keyboards for people who prefer to touch-type. Handheld PCs running Windows CE use a keyboard for inputting information; third-party software can translate handwriting into type if you desire.

- Each of the four categories of handheld devices fills a different purpose; you won't find one that does everything. Some people want to write on a word processor, for instance, so they want a keyboard. Others want a smaller-sized gadget, so they scrap the keyboard and buy a unit that uses the handwriting approach for input.

- The Casio Cassiopeia and the Compaq PC Companion look identical because they *are* identical. Casio is making them for Compaq, and Compaq is slapping its own label on it.

- The Microsoft and Timex joint venture, Data Link wristwatches, can absorb information from your PC. Just hold the watch in front of your PC's monitor, push a button, and watch the screen blink. The watch translates the screen's flashes into important "watch information," like phone numbers for pizza parlors and times of important TV shows.

What Is Windows CE?

As calculators grew into organizers, which grew into palmtops and handheld PCs, corporations began enthusiastically entering the small-machine market. However, every machine worked differently. Because buyers didn't want to learn a new computer's operating system, Microsoft jumped in. Microsoft created Windows CE specifically for the new breed of handheld PCs, such as the one shown in Figure A-1.

Figure A-1: Microsoft Windows CE is an abbreviated version of Windows 95 that runs on special handheld PCs.

Windows CE *looks* a lot like Windows 95, if Windows 95 had been stuffed on a computer with an itty-bitty screen. And it acts like Windows 95, too. The Start button and Start menu haven't strayed, as you can see in Figure A-2, and the familiar folders and files still await your touch. You can still play with the wallpaper, and the Control Panel still lets you assign different sounds to different actions.

Figure A-2:
Microsoft
Windows
CE looks
just like
Windows
95, only
smaller.

But beneath the surface, Windows CE is very different from its parent. Because Windows CE is only a tiny subset of Windows 95, it can't run regular Windows 95 programs or DOS programs. In fact, you can't even copy your data files from your desktop PC to the handheld PC without first running the files through a special conversion program.

- Microsoft tossed in some extra goodies with Windows CE. It includes abbreviated copies of Microsoft Word (the word processor) and Excel (the spreadsheet), as well as brief programs for tracking appointments and contacts.

- Unfortunately, all those programs are abbreviated versions. The "Pocket Word" can read a Word file, for example, but can't handle some of the formatting or spell-checking. "Pocket Excel" doesn't have the ability to use macros, and it lacks other number-handling capacities.

- Windows CE is often called Win CE. Frustrated programmers call it WinCE.

- Microsoft made Windows CE and also created a program for transferring information back and forth between your desktop computer and your Windows CE handheld PC. Simply connect a cable (included) to an available serial port on your desktop computer. The handheld PC also includes an infrared port for shooting information to suitably equipped computers and printers.

What do I need to run Windows CE?

First, you'll need a handheld PC that's designed to run the Windows CE operating system; at least six companies have their foot in the door, giving you plenty to choose from.

When you open the handheld PC's box, you find a CD-ROM with software for transfer-

ring data between the handheld PC and desktop PCs.

But before you can transfer the information back and forth, here's what Microsoft expects from your *desktop* computer:

The Windows CE Desktop PC Transfer Requirements

Microsoft Requirements	*Notes*
A 486/33 DX or faster processor	Pentium 90 recommended
Windows 95 or later	Windows CE transfer programs won't run on earlier versions of Windows or Windows NT
8MB of RAM	12MB recommended
10 to 20MB of hard disk space	Varies according to chosen features
Available serial port	Adapter required for 25-pin port
CD-ROM drive	3.5" disks available on request
VGA or better card and monitor	SVGA and 256 colors or better recommended
Mouse	
Audio card and speakers	Optional

What's Good about Windows CE?

Windows CE has a *lot* of things going for it besides Bill Gates' multimillion-dollar promotional campaign.

First, Windows CE looks and acts just like ol' Windows 95. If you already know how to point and click your way through Windows 95 windows, menus, and scroll bars, you can easily adapt to "poking" the handheld PC's screen with a stylus to get things rolling.

Have you ever kept track of your contacts or appointments on an organizer or handheld PC? Windows CE provides a great way to keep track of Christmas card lists as well as appointments: You'll never forget when to put the water bottles out, or when you scheduled that lunch appointment with Suzi at Mr. Chows.

By including a cable and software, Microsoft made dumping information back and forth between a desktop PC and a handheld PC easy. An HPC Explorer window appears on your desktop PC's screen — the program looks and acts like the normal Windows Explorer program. Drag and drop the icons of the files you want to move from one version of Windows Explorer to the other, and the program automatically converts the data and moves it in the right direction.

Some of the new programs sound fun, too. bFAX Express (costing around $29.95), shown in Figure A-3, can send faxes quickly with a PC Card fax/modem and a phone line. It automatically generates a cover page for every fax you send, letting you type a quick note or attach a document to the fax.

Figure A-3:
bFAX
Express lets
your
Windows
CE
handheld
PC send
faxes
through a
PC Card
fax/modem
and phone
line.

✔ Most handheld PCs have infrared ports for transferring information without cables. Need to swap business cards? Just hold your PC up to the new contact's PC and push the appropriate Send/Receive buttons.

Figure A-4:
bFax
Professional
expands the
features of
bFAX,
letting you
receive
faxes and
send
recurring
faxes to
multiple
destinations.

✔ Windows CE and the handheld PCs can handle PC Cards (once known as *PCMCIA cards*). You can store information on a PC Card, or you can use a fax/modem card for sending and receiving information over the phone lines.

✔ With a modem, you can check your e-mail while you're on the road. Plus, you can add an Internet Explorer program for Web surfing.

What's Bad about Them

Windows CE comes with lots of goodies, but it left out just as many. For example, most Windows CE handheld PCs can't dial a modem unless the PCs are plugged into the wall via an AC adapter. And, of course, most units don't come with an AC adapter. (And when you bought the unit, did you think about how you'd have to carry your adapter around in order to get e-mail at the airport?)

Here's another problem: Windows CE *won't* run Windows 95 programs. You can't take a favorite program from your desktop PC and install it onto the Windows CE program. Windows CE includes a pocket version of Word and Excel, but it doesn't come with a database — unlike many of the competing organizers that don't use Windows CE.

And here's a wacky one: Most of the little PCs can't hook up to a printer. To print, you have to dump information to a PC and print from that source.

✔ The biggest problem? Many people are claiming they simply can't read the tiny screens. Some screens are lit up; others rely on light in the room.

✔ Windows CE tries to mimic Windows 95, so it doesn't include very sophisticated programs for organizing appointments and contacts.

✔ If you don't have Windows 95 running on your desktop PC, you won't find Windows CE to be of much use. The transfer software won't work.

✔ Did you buy the Casio Cassiopeia? Then be sure to push those little battery compartment knobs back together toward the left — the PC Card's side — or the computer refuses to turn on.

How Do I Buy the Right One?

Buying a handheld PC or pocket organizer should be a simple, three-step process — just like buying a desktop PC. It works like this:

1. Carefully decide what you want the handheld computer to do.

Think carefully about why you're buying the little machine. Do you need a modem? Will you be typing? Or will you be accessing databases? Do you need to print? Will a keyboard make the computer too large for your pocket? Do you even need a keyboard? How much will the gadget *really* cost, once you've bought the AC adapter, modem, software, cigarette lighter adapter, RAM storage cards, and cables for swapping data with the desktop PC?

2. Find the computer that meets those needs.

Spend some time in the store playing with the handheld PC's stylus and built-in programs. Are they easy use? Can you read the screen? Does the case have a sturdy feel to it? Or will it die when you leave it in your back pocket and sit down at the bar? Are you buying a computer when you *really* just need something to keep track of your appointments and phone numbers? Or are you buying a business-card holder when you need a way to grab your e-mail?

3. Buy that computer and keep track of the new toys that come out for it.

Found the right computer? Then make sure you can take it back if you don't like it within at least a week. You need to check how the lighting affects the screen display under a wide variety of conditions.

✔ Ask the salesperson to toss in a few 8-packs of AA batteries. You'll start going through them pretty quickly.

✔ Make sure the cable is long enough to connect to your computer's serial port and still reach your desk. You might need an extension.

✔ More than one computer manufacturer makes Windows CE handheld PCs, and the models vary widely. The Philips version comes with a built-in sound recorder, for example. Be sure to check them all out before choosing one.

✔ Or, blow off Windows CE completely. For example, the Sharp Zaurus handheld computer can do as much or more. Call Rupp Technology at 602-941-4789 for a catalog of Zaurus organizers and wares, or drop by their web site at http://www.rupp.com.

Table A-1 provides you with a handy quick reference for using Windows CE.

Table A-1	Windows CE Cheat Sheet
To Do This	*Press This*
Open the Windows CE Task Manager	Alt+Tab
Access the desktop	Windows Key+Tab
View a list of Windows key functions	Windows Key+Space
Recalibrate the touch screen	Ctrl+Alt+= (equal sign)
Open the property sheet of the selected item	Alt+Enter
Activate the next program on the taskbar	Alt+Esc
View the desktop in Folder view	Windows Key+E and then Backspace
Get Help in most programs and dialog boxes	Alt+H
Copy, Cut, or Paste text from almost any program to any other program	Ctrl+C, Ctrl+X, Ctrl+V (respectively)
Open the Start menu	Ctrl+Esc or Windows Key+Enter

Glossary

*W*indows 95 no longer comes with a separate Glossary program; it's built in. If you spot an unfamiliar word in the Help program — and it's underlined — click on the word, and Windows 95 defines it for you. But if Windows 95 refuses to give you a helping hand, here's a list of some of the more common Windows 95 words you may encounter.

32-bit: Computers push their information through *pipes*. The first IBM PC used eight pipes. The next version, the 286, used 16 pipes. A 386 computer can use 32 pipes, but most programs just shoot their stuff through 16 pipes. For extra speed and power, Windows 95 uses all 32 pipes at the same time.

active window: The last window you clicked on — the one that's currently highlighted — is considered active. Any keys you press affect this window.

Apply: Click on this button, and Windows 95 immediately applies and saves any changes you've made from the current list of options.

AUTOEXEC.BAT: A file that old-school MS-DOS computers read when first turned on. The file contains instructions that affect any subsequently running DOS programs — and older Windows programs, as well. Windows 95 no longer needs an AUTOEXEC.BAT file, but it keeps one around in case older programs may need to use it.

bitmap: A graphic consisting of bunches of little dots on-screen. They're saved as bitmap files, which end with the letters BMP. The Windows 95 program called Paint can create and edit BMP files.

border: The edges of a window; you can move the border in or out to change the window's size.

case-sensitive: A program that knows the difference between upper- and lowercase letters. For example, a case-sensitive program considers *Pickle* and *pickle* to be two different things.

click: To push and release a button on the mouse.

Clipboard: A part of Windows 95 that keeps track of information you've cut or copied from a program or file. It stores that information so that you can paste it into other programs.

command prompt: The little symbol that looks like C:\ or [C:\] or A:\ or something similar. It's the place where you can type instructions — *commands* — for DOS to carry out.

CONFIG.SYS: A file that your computer reads every time it boots up. The file contains information about how the computer is set up and what it's attached to. Both DOS and Windows programs rely on information contained in the CONFIG.SYS file. Windows 95 no longer needs a CONFIG.SYS file, but it keeps one around in case other programs need one to run.

cursor: The little blinking line that shows where the next letter will appear when you start typing.

default: Choosing the default option enables you to avoid making a decision. The *default option* is the one the computer chooses for you when you give up and just press Enter.

desktop: The area on your screen where you move windows and icons around. Most people cover the desktop with *wallpaper* — a pretty picture.

directory: A separate *folder* on a hard disk for storing files. Storing related files in a directory makes them easier to find. Windows 95 no longer uses the word directory and prefers the word *folder,* instead.

document: A file containing information like text, sound, or graphics. Documents are created or changed from within programs. See *program*.

DOS: Short for Disk Operating System, it's an older operating system for running programs. Windows 95 can run programs designed for DOS as well as programs designed for Windows.

double-click: Pushing and releasing the left mouse button twice in rapid succession. (Double-clicking the *right* mouse button doesn't do anything special.)

drag: A four-step mouse process that moves an object across your desktop. First, point at the object — an icon, a highlighted paragraph, or something similar. Second, press and hold your left mouse button. Third, point at the location to which you want to move that object. Fourth, release the mouse button. The object is dragged to its new location.

drop: Step four of the *drag* technique, described in the preceding entry. *Dropping* is merely letting go of the mouse button and letting your object fall onto something else, be it a new window, directory, or area on your desktop.

DRV: A file ending in DRV usually lets Windows talk to computer gizmos such as video cards, sound cards, CD-ROM drives, and other stuff. (DRV is short for *driver.*)

FAQ: Short for Frequently Asked Questions, these text files are usually found on online services. Designed to save everybody some time, the files answer questions most frequently asked by new users. The Scanners FAQ explains all about Scanners, for example; the Xena FAQ would trace Xena's history, starting with Hercules.

file: A collection of information in a format designed for computer use.

folder: An area for storing files to keep them organized (formerly called a directory). Folders can contain other folders for further organization. (See *subdirectory.*)

format: The process of preparing a disk to have files written on it. The disk needs to have "electronic shelves" tacked onto it so that Windows 95 can store information on it. Formatting a disk wipes it clean of all information.

highlighted: A selected item. Different colors usually appear over a highlighted object to show that it's been singled out for further action.

icon: The little picture that represents an object — a program, file, or command — making it easier to figure out that object's function.

INI: Short for _initialization,_ INI usually hangs on the end of files that contain special system settings. They're for the computer to mess with, not users.

Internet: A huge collection of computers linked around the world. The _World Wide Web_ rides atop the Internet along with other computer transactions. You can connect to the Internet's World Wide Web by paying a fee to an Internet Service Provider — much like paying a monthly phone bill.

maximize: The act of making a window fill the entire screen. You can maximize a window by double-clicking on its title bar — that long strip across its very top. Or you can click on its maximize button — that button with the big square inside, located near the window's upper-right corner.

memory: The stuff computers use to store on-the-fly calculations while running.

minimize: The act of shrinking a window down to a tiny icon to temporarily get it out of the way. To minimize a window, click on the minimize button — that button with the little horizontal bar on it, located near the window's upper-right corner.

multitasking: Running several different programs simultaneously.

network: Connecting computers with cables so that people can share information without getting up.

operating system: Software that controls how a computer does its most basic stuff: stores files, talks to printers, and performs other gut-level operations. Windows 95 is an operating system.

path: A sentence of computerese that tells a computer the precise name and location of a file.

program: Something that lets you work on the computer. Spreadsheets, word processors, and games are _programs_. See _document_.

RAM: Random-Access Memory. See _memory_.

scrap: When you highlight some text or graphics from a program, drag the chunk to the desktop, and drop it, you've created an official Windows 95 _scrap_ — a file containing a copy of that information. The scrap can be saved or dragged into other programs.

Shortcut: A Windows 95 icon that serves as a push button for doing something — loading a file, starting a program, or playing a sound, for example. Shortcuts have little arrows in their bottom corner so that you can tell them apart from the icons that _really_ stand for files and programs.

shortcut button: A button in a Help menu that takes you directly to the area you need to fiddle with.

shortcut key: As opposed to a Shortcut, a shortcut key is an underlined letter in a program's menu that lets you work with the keyboard instead of the mouse. For example, if you see the word Help in a menu, the underlined H means that you can get help by pressing Alt+H.

Shut Down: The process of telling Windows 95 to save all its settings and files so that you can turn off your computer. You must click the Shut Down option, found on the Start menu, before turning off your computer.

Start button: A button in the corner of your screen where you can begin working. Clicking the Start button brings up the Start menu.

Start menu: A menu of options that appears when the Start button is clicked. From the Start menu, you can load programs, load files, change settings, find programs, find help, or shut down your computer so that you can turn it off.

subdirectory: A directory within a directory, used to further organize files. For example, a JUNKFOOD directory may contain subdirectories for CHIPS, PEANUTS, and PRETZELS. (A CELERY subdirectory would be empty.) In Windows 95, a subdirectory is a folder that's inside another folder.

taskbar: The bar in Windows 95 that lists all currently running programs and open folders. The Start button lives on one end of the taskbar.

VGA: A popular standard for displaying information on monitors in certain colors and resolutions. It's now being replaced by SVGA — Super VGA — which can display even more colors and even finer resolution.

virtual: A trendy word to describe computer simulations. It's commonly used to describe things that *look* real but aren't really there. For example, when Windows 95 uses *virtual memory,* it's using part of the hard disk for memory, not the actual memory chips.

wallpaper: Graphics spread across the background of your computer screen. The Windows 95 Control Panel lets you choose among different wallpaper files.

Web browser: Software for maneuvering through the World Wide Web, visiting Web pages and examining the wares. The Microsoft Web browser, Internet Explorer, comes free with the latest version of Windows 95 or can be downloaded for free from the Microsoft Web page at www.microsoft.com. (Other people may have bought Internet Explorer in the Microsoft Plus add-on package for Windows 95.) A Microsoft competitor owns the most popular Web browser, Netscape, and Netscape currently enjoys much more industry support.

Web page: Just as televisions can show bunches of different channels, the World Wide Web can show gazillions of different *Web pages*. These screenfuls of information can be set up by anyone: The government can display county meeting schedules; corporations can project flashy marketing propaganda; publications can display online versions of their works. (Or, the Cushmans can put up a Family Page with pictures of the baby at Disneyland.)

window: An on-screen box that contains information for you to look at or work with. Programs run in *windows* on your screen.

World Wide Web: Riding atop the Internet's motley collection of cables, the flashy World Wide Web works as a sort of computerized television, letting you jump from channel to channel by pointing and clicking at the pages. Also known simply as "The Web," it sorta looks like the informational kiosks found in the best airports, where you can find out which place serves the best penne with sausage.

Index

IDG BOOKS WORLDWIDE REGISTRATION CARD

RETURN THIS REGISTRATION CARD FOR FREE CATALOG

Title of this book: Windows®95 For Dummies,®2E

My overall rating of this book: ❑ Very good [1] ❑ Good [2] ❑ Satisfactory [3] ❑ Fair [4] ❑ Poor [5]

How I first heard about this book:

❑ Found in bookstore; name: [6]

❑ Advertisement: [8]

❑ Word of mouth; heard about book from friend, co-worker, etc.: [10]

❑ Book review: [7]

❑ Catalog: [9]

❑ Other: [11]

What I liked most about this book:

What I would change, add, delete, etc., in future editions of this book:

Other comments:

Number of computer books I purchase in a year: ❑ 1 [12] ❑ 2-5 [13] ❑ 6-10 [14] ❑ More than 10 [15]

I would characterize my computer skills as: ❑ Beginner [16] ❑ Intermediate [17] ❑ Advanced [18] ❑ Professional [19]

I use ❑ DOS [20] ❑ Windows [21] ❑ OS/2 [22] ❑ Unix [23] ❑ Macintosh [24] ❑ Other: [25]_____
(please specify)

I would be interested in new books on the following subjects:
(please check all that apply, and use the spaces provided to identify specific software)

❑ Word processing: [26]

❑ Data bases: [28]

❑ File Utilities: [30]

❑ Networking: [32]

❑ Other: [34]

❑ Spreadsheets: [27]

❑ Desktop publishing: [29]

❑ Money management: [31]

❑ Programming languages: [33]

I use a PC at (please check all that apply): ❑ home [35] ❑ work [36] ❑ school [37] ❑ other: [38] _____

The disks I prefer to use are ❑ 5.25 [39] ❑ 3.5 [40] ❑ other: [41]_____

I have a CD ROM: ❑ yes [42] ❑ no [43]

I plan to buy or upgrade computer hardware this year: ❑ yes [44] ❑ no [45]

I plan to buy or upgrade computer software this year: ❑ yes [46] ❑ no [47]

Name: _____ Business title: [48] _____ Type of Business: [49] _____

Address (❑ home [50] ❑ work [51]/Company name: _____)

Street/Suite# _____

City [52]/State [53]/Zipcode [54]: _____ Country [55] _____

❑ **I liked this book!** You may quote me by name in future
IDG Books Worldwide promotional materials.

My daytime phone number is _____

IDG BOOKS

THE WORLD OF
COMPUTER
KNOWLEDGE

❏ YES!

Please keep me informed about IDG's World of Computer Knowledge.
Send me the latest IDG Books catalog.

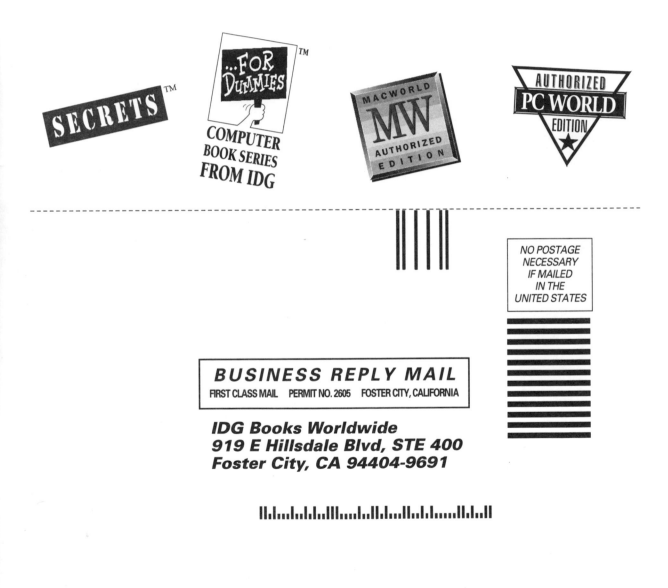